Praise for *Fish*

"Prose of the highest calibre: every detail resonates with absolute authenticity, you can feel and hear the heroine's every breath."

— Maya Kucherskaya

"An engrossing portrait of the narrator 'Fish' and of Soviet and post-Soviet life, combining rich detail with a shimmer of mystery... A wonderful discovery!"

Sibelan Forrester, Swarthmore College

"The writing in *Fish* is excellent, it is an easy read in one sitting. You simply can't tear yourself away from this novel, you just want to turn the page to see what new plot twist awaits."

— Sergei Belyakov, *Zhurnalny Zal*

"Aleshkovsky is one of our finest prose writers... The novel *Fish: A History of One Migration*, was the literary event of recent years."

— *First of September*

"For 15 years, I have been avidly following Peter Aleshkovsky's work. This is a writer with an unusual gift for description. He writes deliciously, exactly, specifically... Aleshkovsky's new novel is written from the viewpoint of a woman. And again the effect of reliability, the 'effect of presence' is exceptional... It should be read by all lovers of classical realism, those who want a taste of this unfading Russian style."

— Pavel Basinsky, *Rossiyskaya Gazeta*

"The attention to detail, the smell of the era (the action takes place in the 1970s and 1980s, the fall of the Soviet Union, the restless 1990s, and the present), the depth of understanding for human nature is all combined with the author's affectionate sympathy for all that touches his pen."

— Polit.ru

Fish

A History of One Migration

Fish

A History of One Migration

Peter Aleshkovsky

Translated by Nina Shevchuk-Murray

Russian Life
BOOKS

PRINTED ON RECYCLED, FSC PAPER

Russian Life BOOKS
PO Box 567
Montpelier, VT 05601
orders@russianlife.com
www.russianlife.com

Fish: A History of One Migration
(*Рыба: История одной миграции*)
by Peter Aleshkovsky
© 2006 Peter Aleshkovsky
English translation © 2010, Nina Shevchuk-Murray
Cover image © 2010, Alexander Bityutskikh
Layout and design © 2010, Russian Information Services, Inc.

Manufactured in the United States of America.

Library of Congress Control Number: 2010931604

ISBN: 978-1-880100-62-2

A RUSSIAN RIDDLE

"Thieves came and stole the owners,
and the house left through the windows."[1]

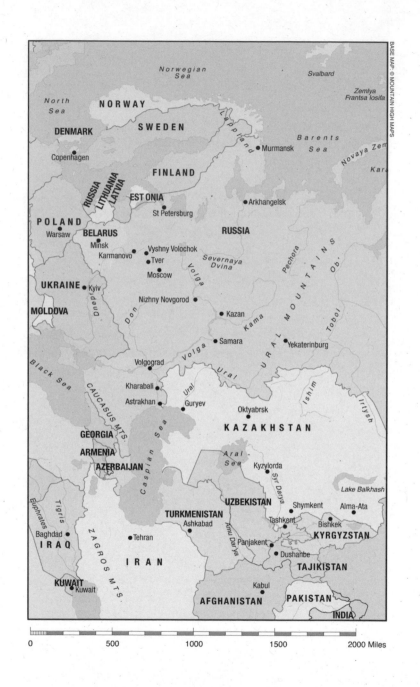

Norwegian Sea

Svalbard

Zemlya Frantsa Iosifa

North Sea

NORWAY

DENMARK

SWEDEN

Lapland

Barents Sea

Murmansk

Novaya Zeml

Kar

Copenhagen

FINLAND

Arkhangelsk

RUSSIA
LITHUANIA
LATVIA

ESTONIA

St Petersburg

POLAND

RUSSIA

Warsaw

BELARUS

Minsk

Vyshny Volochok

Severnaya Dvina

Pechora

Ob

Karmanovo

Tver

U R A L   M O U N T A I N S

UKRAINE

Kyiv

Volga

Moscow

Don

Nizhny Novgorod

Kama

Kazan

MOLDOVA

Dnepr

Tobol

Samara

Yekaterinburg

Volga

Volgograd

Ural

Black Sea

Ural

Kharabali

CAUCASUS MTS.

Astrakhan

Guryev

Oktyabrsk

Ishim

Irtysh

GEORGIA

Caspian Sea

K A Z A K H S T A N

ARMENIA

Aral Sea

AZERBAIJAN

Kyzylorda

Lake Balkhash

Syr Darya

UZBEKISTAN

Shymkent

Alma-Ata

TURKMENISTAN

Tashkent

Euphrates

Tigris

Ashkabad

Bishkek

KYRGYZSTAN

Baghdad

Tehran

Amu Dar'ya

Panjakent

IRAQ

ZAGROS MTS.

I R A N

Dushanbe

TAJIKISTAN

KUWAIT

Kabul

PAKISTAN

Kuwait

AFGHANISTAN

INDIA

0   500   1000   1500   2000 Miles

one

. 1 .

MOM AND DAD were both geologists. Life had tossed them all over the country before they landed in Tajikistan, in the town of Panjakent. We lived on the Russian-Tatar street named after Zoya Kosmodemyanskaya.[2] Tajiks didn't care for this street, and, I see now, with good reason. Here, people drank port, prohibited by the Quran, and did not hoard every penny for a raucous *tui-pisar*, one of life's biggest celebrations—a son's circumcision, when custom prescribed that one must treat several hundred guests to *plov*.[3]

In three days, they would burn through all the wealth long accumulated for the celebration of a *tui-pisar*. Consumed like light kindling in a wood stove. Poof-poof-poof, and the fires expired under the huge cast-iron pots, the women wiped the sweat from their brows and set about cleaning their pots of the congealed fat that clings to the dark metal like spring ice to cliffs. I saw ice like that in the Dashtiurdakon Pass, when we went camping with our troop of Young Pioneers.

Mom was often hired to clean up after such feasts; after Dad's death, money was always short. Helping out at the feasts came with a bonus: the hosts gave us leftovers, and we would eat nothing but *plov* for a whole week. To this day, I can't stand rice fried in cotton oil; just thinking about it gives me heartburn. Tajiks regarded our street's ragtag gang of Soviet geologists the same way they did the sand swept in by the wind or the tangles of tumbleweed that were always ready to break loose. They tolerated us as one tolerates bad weather. The Russians responded with mutual disdain. To us the Tajiks were rich and lazy *bais*: they owned their own land.

Now I understand that, in fact, there was no wealth whatsoever. The truly lavish *tui-pisars*—put on by the big bosses—were hidden from us; behind the mud *duval* walls of the old neighborhood they lived a completely different life. Only some of it was on display: big-bellied men, brimming with good spirits, sat out their days in teahouses, like moscato grapes in the sun. Their secrets were hidden behind oily eyes; their narrowed pupils were chilly and small, like pebbles in the glacial Zaravshan River; a hideous light glowed from the cleanly washed skin of their faces—faces that scared me, a girl, more than the *pichak* knives the men wore at their waists. They said the knives were so sharp, that, with a just few swipes of the blade across their belts, they could use them to shave their heads as their Mohammed had commanded them.

We, the residents of Kosmodemyanskaya, were always moving, always swinging our arms, always gesticulating, eager to prove something, and did not shy from cursing in public. Our girls braided their hair into two braids; theirs—into more than you could count. We played *lapta*,[4] volleyball and "shtander-stop,"[5] but not the lamb-bone game "*oshichki*," and we didn't gleefully squeal "Horse!" or "Bull!"—to be heard clear across the school yard—when the tiny polished fragments fell just so. We were swallows at the face of a cliff on the river, and they were not even the eagles in the clouds, but those barely visible shadows of heated air, trembling and taut, that support the eagles' wings high in the sky.

The Kosmodemyanskayas would drink any kind of alcohol, but also smoked weed, which made them giggle and whoop and crawl around on all fours—"mule" as they called it, strutting their stuff, exorcising the demons of their souls, prancing and blabbering. The desperate "me, me, me" of the mob, kept in check for so long, would spill onto our street like guts from a slashed sheep's stomach; it would writhe, extending its neck and straining its shoulders; it would stomp, desperately slapping its hands on its thighs like a goose that flaps his wings to get the gaggle's attention. Base couplets and the whiny suffering of an accordion were braided into a single rope, tossed into a single pot, gobbled up by the same crew. All this debauchery always ended in a mindless fight, which both affirmed the profane "me" and abused it with profanities; punch someone in the face or be punched in the face—it was all the same. Afterward, shiners were displayed like medals, knocked out teeth signaled a new, higher rank, cracked skulls were healed with port, and bones grew back together like grafts on an apple tree, with bulging, scabby scars.

The fat Tajiks, the Uzbeks wearing embroidered Shahristani skull-caps,[6] the tribal people from the Pamir Mountains who came—sinewy, dirt-poor, and proud—to the market, and even the savage Turkmen who hid their beautiful daughters under *paranjas*, none of them ever brawled or drank the stupefying wine. They did not push at the seams of time with their elbows, but rather stepped out of it. They would put a pinch of *nasvai* behind a cheek and transform themselves into a pile of compressed, sun-dried *pahsa*, that special mixture of dirt and goat droppings from which they built their homes, mosques, *duval* walls, and the fortresses and towers of ancient Panjakent. With time, *pahsa* crumbles to dust, becomes raw material for a new mixture or seeps underground, where it settles imperceptibly into a new cultural stratum.

The ancient fortress settlement—the main attraction in our regional center—had long been abandoned, and was now being excavated by archaeologists. Some of their digs went deeper than fifteen or twenty feet: large dry wells reaching into the depths of the earth, through layer after layer of departed lives, cut through with pickaxes, shovels and hoes; they were lives of people whose descendants so frightened me when I passed the teahouse on Abulkasym Lahuti Street on my way for a flatbread or cold milk from the store.

Later, after the geological exploration party had fallen apart, after Father had started drinking and perished stupidly down a deep prospect-hole, and Mom had gone to work as a nurse's assistant at the city's maternity hospital, I met and came to love Aunt Gulsuhor and Aunt Leila,[7] Aunt Fatima and Uncle Davron—the young doctor who brought me little gifts of candy. Silly me, only later did I realize that they were all hardworking, honest people, and that even those who sat like totem poles in the teahouse had once worked somewhere to earn their rest. I, a girl from Zoya Kosmodemyanskaya Street with two measly braids was nothing to them; I was dust, both because I was a girl and because I lived on the wrong street, where every night a police car was parked on duty. In that car (at the wheel) sat Uncle Said and (at the radio) Kolya Pervukhin, a sergeant. Kolya was always smoking a cigarette. He watched the poorly-lit street like a guard dog perched in his doghouse, always ready to fly, gun in hand, after the first suspicious shadow, to do whatever it took to catch, throw to the ground, and stomp out the evil that kept the newcomers—tight in their beds like flies wintering under the wallpaper—from sleeping soundly in the two-floor shanties that lined the street.

It's been a long time since I lived on Zoya Kosmodemyanskaya Street in Panjakent. For twenty-seven years I have not woken up to the rooster's crow and the bleating of the neighbors' black goat; I have not peered out my window at the nightly gathering of a terrifying dog pack under the streetlamp. Less and less often do I recall the Zaravshan mountain range, bluish-green in the pre-dawn mist, and the dark ribbon of the river below. By eleven o'clock the mountains would fade in the oily smoke of heat, and only their shadow would remain, a mere outline, a hint. They would appear again, dim and purple, before the sunset, after the heat of the day had passed. Then Mom would come home from her shift at the hospital and take a watermelon for the two of us from the *haús*—a shallow pond in the garden. We'd sit down to dinner, and I would bite into the cold, sugary watermelon flesh, then afterwards count the black seeds on my plate and ecstatically slap my watermelon-stuffed belly with my sticky hand. All this, and much more, rarely surfaces in my memory, but sometimes, when I am falling asleep, the faces of the old people and the men in the teahouse pass through my mind. They gaze toward the vanishing mountains, deep in thoughts not given to a girl's understanding or feeling. Their faces are like the faces of huge fish suspended in a canal: heavy, silvery carp with tightened cheeks, their lips moving as if lazily repeating a prayer, their tiny eyes looking straight through you, unblinking, eerie and cold like sleeping water.

Probably this all comes back because I so often stare at the face of Grandma Lisichanskaya, the old lady with whom I have been living as a nurse for the past two and a half years. She only has the use of one arm—her left, has almost completely lost her speech, and recognizes only me. She cannot say my name—Vera—but has learned to repeat words after me. And thank God for that.

In the mornings I enter her room and look into her dry, upturned face. If her eyes gleam, I say, "Good morning!" Then her mouth opens, a shadow crosses her face, she wrinkles her forehead as if trying to trap the word that has reached her consciousness. In a small voice, she repeats, "Morning." It is difficult for her to utter two words, but sometimes she does send another one chasing after the first, and it comes out as, "Morning. Morning." This means that we're truly having a good morning. We set about our routine. She is weightless, like a small girl, and it is easy to move her around.

If, however, her gaze is frozen and still, and her eyes look cloudy and vacant, it is pointless to greet her. I immediately come to the bed, change her Pampers, give her a sponge bath, treat her bedsores with buckthorn oil, and begin to rub her back and legs to bring back the blood and warmth.

If her eyes are closed and her hand lies on top of the blanket like a lash, that's very bad news: we're dying again. Her blood pressure can jump from 90 over 60 to 220 over 140; the blood vessels in her head are worn to shreds. Of course, feeding her is out of the question, and on days like these I suckle her on a bottle, like a baby. Reflexively, she moves her lips, and I am happy if she at least manages to get down some juice. I once tried giving her soup that way, but she shut her lips like subway doors and that was it, they were not opening until the next stop.

I put an oxygen mask on her to help her breathe, and if she starts sweating I run a warm sponge over her almost lifeless body, knowing that my grandma is far, far away, and all I can do is wait and pray. Since I don't know how to pray properly, I just mumble quickly, "Father-God, do with me what you will, but help Grandma Lisichanskaya today." After these words, I always cross my forehead and add, "Amen of the Holy Spirit!" Then I put my hand on her head, my warm hand onto her cold little skull (even marble statues are warmer), and hold it steady. Each time it is very different; sometimes it takes a full thirty minutes before I can finally sense a weak pulse. Once I enter its rhythm, I can begin to pick out despair, deathly exhaustion, disappointment, pity, pain. From a medical point of view, there is nothing left inside her to feel pain, yet sometimes this pain overwhelms everything else and is the only thing I hear—it is like the chirr of cicadas overpowering all the other small nocturnal noises. I long ago stopped looking for an explanation; I just hold my hand there as it grows heavy as lead, and, as a distraction, I open a book and silently read. I have learned to turn pages with one hand. At times like these she cannot hear me anyway.

Grandma is swaddled in her emotions like a cabbage in its leaves. They cover her core, and, in order to reach her, one must free her from everything external and overgrown. While my one hand mechanically leafs through a book, the other seems to be freeing, purifying something deeply hidden. Nothing is happening on the surface, in this room—there is just a mute old woman and a mute hand. I am reading. But we are hard at work, we are inching towards each other, I aim to free her—she aims to be set free. Sometimes she can lie like this for several hours and God knows when she will fall asleep. Gradually, the hellish pain subsides, the helplessness, the hurt, the anger fade along with the distrust, despair, regret, fear, shyness, suspiciousness and endless sorrow, and then there is a moment when I'm suddenly jolted, as if by electricity, and I jerk my hand away. The hand goes numb and turns ice-cold. Grandma's forehead is warmer, which means everything is well. She has fallen asleep. I go to the bathroom and run hot water over my hand, gradually bring it back to life.

. 2 .

WE SLEEP POORLY. It is a gift if we have two or three quiet nights a week. Time has abandoned my grandma, has fluttered away and tangled up, like clumpy, freshly-shorn wool before it is made into felt. At night, grandma stares at a point on the ceiling. Mark Grigoriyevich, her son, sent us a nice Italian nightlight that casts a warm orange glow. Its light does not penetrate the darkness at the ceiling or in the corners, but warms the bed and my armchair alongside it. And it reaches the door, on which hangs a picture of a Japanese horse. I like looking at that picture: you can't tell if the horse is galloping or rearing up. It's painted with upward brushstrokes. At the bottom the ink is thick and black, but at the edges the lines are grey, and it looks like the animal has light, smoothly brushed hair that gleams in the sun—the model must have been a well-cared-for horse. In Panjakent we had all kinds of horses, and, of course, many donkeys, but only once did I see a horse that was this fast and well-groomed. It would have been better if I hadn't. For some reason, horses, unlike donkeys, inspired in me a special kind of love, one made of equal parts pity and adoration. At the sight of a horse, a warm feeling bloomed in my chest; my eyes seemed to open wider and follow the animal. Even when it was just the nag pulling the trash barrel, I gazed longingly after it and could not turn away. When I was in the first or second grade, I had a bet with my friend Ninka Surkova that I would dare kiss the face of the first horse we met.

At stake was an Alyonka chocolate bar. To seal the deal, at Ninka's insistence, I swore a terrible oath, spinning on my heel, pressing my hand to my forehead and heart, and invoking the promise of sure death to my family, should I break my word. I never swore like that again, and it left me no choice but to kiss a horse, since I had no money to buy a chocolate bar. I wasn't scared, because I knew I really would kiss any horse out there;

I just tried not to dwell on the fact that sometimes they bite you.

Ninka must have known what she was doing. She led me down a route only she knew, then pretended that we were playing a game in which we were fleeing from someone down backyard alleys, even though the only thing chasing us was the barking of guard dogs. We crept low through the wet morning grass and slipped around the trunks of fruit trees; white and pink petals showered us, and wild barberry scratched us with its long, strong thorns. It was April, the time when everything is blooming and fragrant. I remember a snake slipping into its lair just below our feet; it must have been a harmless rat snake, but Ninka shrieked, "Viper!" and, infected with each other's madness, we took off running. Low-hanging branches of dry, thorny bushes slammed shut behind us, yet surprisingly we got only a few scratches. We climbed shapeless clay walls like Red *partizans*, crawled on our bellies across strangers' orchards, and soon found ourselves in the old city, in the Tajik neighborhoods.

In a corner, leaning against a mud wall amid thick cherry-plums, stood a shed with a holey roof. The roof was all but stripped of its straw cover, and the thin beams stuck out like the ribs of a cow carcass baked by the sun. Ninka dove into the lopsided doorway; there must have been a gate there once. I followed her into the foul-smelling darkness. Somewhere close a dog barked loudly, but we did not care. In the darkest corner, a horse stood on what was left of the rotten straw. When young, he must have been reddish brown. Now he was completely grey; his tail was tangled and studded with burrs. When we came in, the horse startled, slashed the air with his tail, swept it across his hind legs and fell still again. The tail hung limply; only the ears stood up straight and took aim at us, even though the horse did not turn his head. It was quiet; the flies buzzed angrily.

"Kiss him!" Ninka ordered.

I circled the horse on the left, put my hand on his skinny back and ran it along his spine. It left a trace on his coat. The horse was dirty; dust and tiny hairs stuck to my hand. A vein shuddered in his neck, his hind leg jerked, and a hoof thumped on the ground. I did not shy away; instead, I patted his bony back, moved my hand to his neck and rubbed it several times, making a curry-comb with my fingers. I had seen men soothe their horses this way.

The horse was bridled and tied to the trough. Finally, his head turned towards me. A large, weary eye regarded me; the eyelid twitched. Puss ran in a stream from the corner of his eye down his nose; a thinner stream dripped from the other eye. A clump of flies rose angrily from the horse's head; a few got trapped in my hair. I did not take my hand back and did not shriek, but my whole body suddenly went stiff. I felt my cheeks ice over. I took the lifeless head in my hands, pulled it towards me, and kissed it, not even closing my eyes. Then I left the shed, picked up a can, and drew water from the irrigation ditch. I found a threadbare rag in the same ditch and washed the horse's face as best I could. He stood there, all wooden and stiff, his slightly flaring nostrils the only sign of life. I rubbed and rubbed, and tried not to think about the smell and the sticky puss. I kept staring at the dark-red coat that began to shine magically under my wet rag. I must have given orders, too, because twice Ninka ran to refill the can with fresh water, I don't remember.

I only remember that a shape suddenly appeared in the doorway, blocking the light. The owner of the place stood there, a hoe in his hand: he had armed himself against horse thieves. He shouted something in Tajik. I kept doing my job. Suddenly, the man calmed down and crouched in the corner. When I was done, I kissed the indifferent horse again straight on a dry nostril. The owner stood up, gathered me in a fatherly hug and mumbled, "Thank, thank, good girl, horse old, Nureddin very old, it's a pity."

He took us to the house, to the open porch-*aivan*, and treated us to tea with quince jelly and tasty flatbreads. The old man lived alone; his wife had died a long time ago. The teacups were dirty, with chipped rims. He hushed at the dog, saw us off to the street, and stood at the gate waving as we walked away. He glowed like a light bulb in a dark closet. I walked down the street and did not hear anything of what Ninka was saying. I surreptitiously felt my cheeks: the ice melted, but inside I was still cold and felt good, because the chilly weariness was fading away and something else was seeping in, something I cannot describe to this day.

Later, when I worked in Dushanbe General Hospital, I saw and treated many pus-filled wounds. I did my job just as I am doing it now with Grandma Lisichanskaya. Two and a half years ago, when she had her stroke, they said she had a week to live, two weeks at the most. But the old woman proved strong. She is eighty-nine. In 1944, when she was thirty, she smuggled her two children out of besieged Leningrad, where she had just begun her doctoral studies, but got trapped in the city herself and survived the terrible 900 days before hitchhiking to Moscow when the siege was over. She waited for her husband to return from the front, then survived his arrest and ten-year labor camp sentence. She wrote to Stalin asking him to protect her from the illegal claims of a greedy NKVD officer who wanted to add one of her rooms to his apartment, and she succeeded in keeping the flat intact until her husband returned from Vorkuta. He was diabetic and had had a leg amputated; she nursed him for another ten years. She put her children through college. She gave Mark Grigoriyevich—her beloved oldest son—her blessing to emigrate when an impresario friend of his invited him to Italy. She stayed behind, surrounded by her well-worn books, at the helm of a vast family clan which she ruled with a firm hand for as long as she had the strength. All her life she turned away any help. And now, unconscious, halfway between heaven and earth, with her mind gone, she recognizes only me, an unknown stranger among all those she had loved and raised to survive in the world.

That's what Mark Grigoriyevich told me. Of all the family members, he alone insisted on caring for his mother and paid all the expenses. He calls constantly to ask how she is feeling; he sends money readily but always remembers to note, "Verochka, not a word to my wife." Of course, I am mute as a fish.

When grandma is not dying and not sleeping at night, I sit in the armchair and read aloud. I think she listens with interest. We have already read *Dead Souls*, made our way through Dickens, Mark Twain, Jules Verne, *Arabian Nights*, and now I am reading Jack London's *Smoke Bellew* to her. My Pavlik loved this book. I love it too; we used to have all these books: I bought them for the kids. But Valerka did not like reading; I think that from the day he was born he simply preferred building things. And he is still doing it, fixing cars. His skills feed him, his wife Svetlana, and their girl—my granddaughter, born two months ago. That's when I became a grandma myself.

My grandma here is listening; occasionally she lifts her good hand, and flexes and unfolds her long, dry fingers, which means she is feeling well. Slowly, she falls asleep. Then I go to bed myself. Long ago she was a decent piano player.

· 3 ·

I DID NOT LISTEN to much music when I was a child, only what we sang in school or heard on the radio. Sometimes, on holidays, a folk-instrument band played at the Culture Center. At first, its sound was pleasing, like a coyly sweet voice floating through the night air. It seemed to weep and laugh at the same time, emphasizing the foreign words; it wove its tune around you like a vine winding its way about the post of a gazebo. My Tajik classmates' faces would assume a dreamy look that reminded me of prairie dogs in the midday sun, standing next to their holes on their hind legs. It did no good to ask what the song was about, the answer was always the same: shaken out of her sweet trance by my stupid question, a girlfriend would wave dismissively and spit through disdainfully curved lips, "You wouldn't understand anyway, it's about love!" Once uttered, the magic word would return the girl to the land of her dreams, and her face would melt into the kind of smile that the poets of the East customarily compare to a rose in bloom. And the voice continued singing about a love that could not be translated into Russian, about roses, and about the moon floating in a bottomless, starry ocean, so unlike the northern skies overtaken by clouds. And the listener laughs and cries at the singer's words, which have turned into a monotonous chant. All of a sudden, you cannot bear listening anymore. The chant clings to your body like the juice of an overripe peach; you want to wash it off, rinse your face and ears, chase away the obnoxious whiner, chase him off the stage where he is begging—his right hand over his heart, his left reaching out, as if asking for small change.

Now, when I get around to ironing, I sometimes turn on the TV. But the words of the songs they play might as well be translated from Tajik. I spit onto the iron and it sputters back, expressing our shared disgust with trite rhymes and talentless music. I switch channels or iron in silence, which is even better: I am soothed by the iron's weight, the warm smell of clean steam, the arrow of the fold and the sheet's melting wrinkles.

Having had my fill of Eastern singing, I would run as far as I could from the Culture Center, climb a clay wall across the street from our house and gaze at the Milky Way, at the myriad stars and the still moon to whom I entrusted various silly thoughts.

Not far from our street, on the Samarkand highway at the edge of town, in the middle of a large, lush garden, was a museum. It was where they kept the things the archaeologists found in their digs: enormous clay barrels (*humas*); copper vats with copper, round-horned mountain goats perched on their patina-covered handles as if they were on the edge of a cliff; soot-covered pots and thick-walled clay frying pans; jewelry, green with age; and similarly frog-colored knives and darts, axes and hammers, along with the clay molds in which they had been shaped.

In summer, we went to the dig site for archaeological practicums. Our school did such a good job that the city's Party Council issued a special decree not to send us cotton-picking in September, instead leaving us to help the archaeologists. This was doubly good, because the expedition paid a bit of money, and for Mom and me the extra cash was very welcome. I was extremely proud of the fact that I was bringing home honest earnings at the young age of fourteen. But, most importantly, it was interesting.

The head of the expedition, Boris Donatovich—or, as he was called in respectful Tajik style, *akó* Boria—was a short, chubby man who always wore an old, patched-up padded overcoat and an even older canvas military hat that was said to be his good-luck charm. He had heady eyes and a strange habit of constantly chewing the insides of his cheeks. After work, *akó* Boria would gather us around him on the *aivan*, pour us tea and begin to tell stories.

He told us about the Prophet Mohammed: how he fled from his tribesmen to the mountains, fell into a trance, and saw the surahs of the Quran in a poetic fit. Mohammed was weak of body, like Boris Donatovich, but mighty of spirit and possessed the gift of words, which Muslims believe can move mountains.

When Boris Donatovich spoke, he was transformed. He could be soft, or hard, depending on what the story required. His energy and power gave us goose bumps, a feeling that was joyful and unsettling all at once. His voice rang confidently in the electrified silence, and his precise words, so perfectly stacked one onto the other, fell into our mute admiration. It was unthinkable to interrupt the wizardly music of his words; I was too ashamed even to run to the bathroom.

The *Arabian Nights* tales were beloved by all in Panjakent. We even staged some scenes from the tales in our school drama group: threw ourselves at the feet of the boy who played the Shah, wringing our hands and pleading for our lives in flowery and elaborate language that none of us ever used in real life. Still, the tales' true beauty was revealed to me only when I heard them in Boris Donatovich's narration. He would begin the story on the *aivan* under the starry sky, and we could almost see a disgusting, humpbacked dwarf in front of us—the dwarf who rode about on Sinbad's shoulders, spit and sizzled with venom, and ordered the sailor around. Suddenly, I'd feel him on my own shoulders: there he was, weighing me down, choking me. There was no relief from this burden; I'd have to carry this monster around until I died, like a terrible disease for which there's no vaccine.

Or I would see a rich, eastern bazaar: Ali, the Prophet's closest relative, rides wherever he pleases on a fiery steed, not at all concerned about where the horse treads. He is a dandy and a spendthrift, and has ordered the smith to make a beautiful, mysterious, battle-worthless double-bladed sword, Zulfikar. After Ali's death, rumor had it that this trinket—a rich man's toy—was sheathed in pure magic.

Or Iskander the Double-Horned, the great Alexander, young and beautiful, would appear on our *aivan* surrounded by his generals. Warriors by birth, they had marched across half the world undefeated, but quickly lost their zeal for battle when they came up against Eastern luxury and languor. Charmed with the gold and the moon-faced dancers, they lost the miraculous strength they had when they were just a rogue troop of poor Macedonians, hungry for the world.

We heard tales of Ulysses and his travels, of the siege of Troy and the archeologists who uncovered the city from the depths of the earth, centuries after the ancient battles. We heard tales that were depicted on the walls of old Panjakent houses. This city once stood on the Silk Road, amid the flow of goods and tales that connected the civilized world; they were carried here by peoples who spoke many different languages. The Silk Road—that great trading artery—traversed the world, flowing over borders; customs officers welcomed traveling merchants and did not oppress them; the earth was flat and endless. The roaming tribes spread their tales and knowledge (the same thing in those days) about the world. Knowledge and beautiful stories were prized like gold, and travelers valued life because they understood that love and freedom, daring and betrayal were the same everywhere, just as heat and cold, the sun and the mysterious moon, sand and clay were the same. The celestial bodies may rise at different angles in different corners of the earth, the sand may glimmer in different colors, the clay may crumble differently, and different languages may have different names for these basic elements, but their essence remained the same. Everywhere clay and sand made walls for homes; in the beginning of time, God made man himself from clay and sand, breathed divine life into him, and taught him to love, to suffer and to hate, to greet the sun and to sing to the moon. Men were doomed to eternal wandering. When they migrated peacefully, their movements went unnoticed and unremarked. But when uprooted hordes hacked their paths with swords and paved them with corpses, the ancient chronicles took note. Life in peacetime, at best, turns into fairy tales; historical memory clings to troubles, bad years, storms, births and deaths of kings under whose gaze the simple and happy life crumbled to dust and faded. In Panjakent, tucked cozily away between the mountains, tribes mixed like clay in a potter's drum; the local merchants and the tax-fattened rulers preferred peace, culture, and order. Warm sun nurtured rich harvests and contemplative moods; the Silk Road brought world news and tales; life, when one rose above its routine aggravations, could seem like a well-told dream of life. Cool dining rooms in rich homes were painted with scenes from didactic tales, so that one would not be bored at mealtime—sort of like was done in Soviet restaurants.

Later, when I read the same stories in books, I always recalled them as they were told at the *aivan,* those cool evenings, the hot tea with flatbread and apricot jam. Layla and Majnun, Romeo and Juliet—everyone was against their love, but they loved so much that they died for each other and were buried in the same tomb. Our expedition had its own Layla and Majnun, or Juliet and Romeo. Everyone knew and pretended not to notice that the driver *akó* Ahror and Lidiya Grigoriyevna, a conservationist from Leningrad, were in love.

I had known *akó* Ahror for a long time: he had driven the coffin with my father's body to the cemetery. Mom had invited him to the wake, but he politely declined. Ahror, being a Muslim, did not drink vodka, shaved his head, and observed *ruza,* a long fast when it is prohibited to taste food from early morning until the first star appears. On the hottest days, Ahror, a true *ruzador,* would rinse his mouth with water and spit it out, not letting a single drop trickle inside him.

He had a small truck which he loved and cherished. The car was ancient, with lettering on its hood that said "Molotov Plant,"[8] and I had heard men marvel at the fact that it was still running. Ahror always responded by saying that he would never have another car. He was constantly checking the engine or polishing the truck's metal body, greenish with time like the axes in the museum, but still strong, as if tempered for a long life with its owner.

Ahror was married. No one had ever seen his wife or children, because they lived on the other end of the city. We only knew that Mukhibá, his wife, had been very ill for quite a while and could barely move around the house. The children helped her, and the husband was the breadwinner: he spent the summer with the archaeologists, and when the expedition left, hired himself out in the market to deliver small loads. He never pushed the truck beyond its limits.

His love for Lidiya Grigoriyevna was the same: tender and solicitous. She worked in the conservation lab at the base camp. On the rare occasions when it was necessary to treat a fresco on-site or to transfer it from a wall, she went to the dig. Sometimes we found the frescoes already crumbled, and Lidiya Grigoriyevna had to piece them together from the fragments, which she laid out in large cardboard trays. She used a common clyster to blow dust off them and then wiped them with rags soaked in her various solutions until the colors returned. Then she began to assemble the picture, just as kids now put puzzles together, except that she did not have the finished photo to match and had to guess where to place each little piece so that they would come together, months later, into a glued and preserved ancient painting.

I remember how long it was taking Lidiya Grigoriyevna to put together a giant fish: she might as well have been putting it together scale by scale. *Akó* Ahror, as usual, was sitting out of her way on his stool by the window and watching adoringly as her long fingers picked over the specks of color. I kept stopping by the lab to see how things were going and also stood there silently, watching her work. I was looking at the half-assembled body—she already had three fins on the table, two on the fish's back and one behind the gills—and the waves that looked like funny little worms as if drawn by a child. Then I glanced at the pile of unmatched fragments and suddenly clearly saw the fish's eye and what looked like the curve of a gill.

"Here's the eye," I said, having summoned my courage.

Lidiya Grigoriyevna took the fragment, turned it around in her hand, then smiled glowingly and added it to the fish's body. The fragment fit.

"That's the eye alright! Great job, Vera!"

Her words gave me confidence. No longer afraid of being wrong, I said, "And here is the gill."

The gill fit, and now the head was complete.

Lidiya Grigoriyevna hugged me and kissed me on both cheeks. The eye made the fish come alive, and the rest of the picture came together quickly.

After that I was transferred from the field to the lab. I washed fresco fragments, sometimes finding bits of a picture. One time I found a tip of a camel's tail and his hind leg, and Lidiya Grigoriyevna figured it out and pieced together an island with a big tree and the camel resting in its shade, and even the pattern around the picture made out of those endless curlicues that sometimes were found on clay pots. This pattern was called meander, I remembered the word.

When the eye of the fish was found, Lidiya Grigoriyevna stopped, went to the piano that was standing in the corner, and played for a long time, for me and *akó* Ahror, both. She played Beethoven. I looked at the fish swimming in the sea, and *akó* Ahror sat with his hands clasped around his knee and studied the floor as if it were a mirror that could reflect Lidiya Grigoriyevna at the piano, her fingers flying across the keys, her proud foot forcefully stomping on the pedal and her eyes shining with unknown delight.

Lidiya Grigoriyevna often played after work. It was her way of resting and, it also seemed to me, of talking to *akó* Ahror. In public, they said little to each other and, of course, kept pretending that there was nothing between them. Their eyes always betrayed them.

One day I took my lunch (a flatbread and a slice of cantaloupe) to the orchard, lay down under a peach tree and stayed there, in silence, for a while, chewing and staring into the sky. Water gurgled in the *aryk*,[9] I was cool in the shade; burst peaches that littered the ground gave off an intoxicating smell. Drunken wasps crawled in and out of the tunnels they had gnawed in the over-ripened fruit. My face, hands, and even my neck became sticky with cantaloupe juice. I unbuttoned my dress and bathed quickly in the cool water of the irrigation canal, pressed my fingers on my hardened nipples. I wrapped my dress around me and fell on my stomach into the soft grass. Suddenly I flushed as if I hadn't refreshed at all. Somewhere close by a twig cracked on the ground and the grass rustled under someone's feet. Carefully, I peeked from around a tree.

In the shade of an old walnut tree stood *akó* Ahror and Lidiya Grigoriyevna. Ahror offered her a yellow flower. Lidiya took the flower and brushed it around his face, barely touching, as if setting down a vague outline of a portrait. Ahror, his eyes closed, stood there for a long time, blind and happy. Then he held her head tenderly in his hands and kissed her forehead, not opening his eyes. Very lightly, he touched her hair with his lips, inhaled its aroma, and pulled her closer.

They fell into the grass together. When they laughed, it sounded forced to me, but the laughing was quickly replaced with garbled sounds of speech from which I could only sometimes pick out the words "Ahror" and "Lida." Their quick, heavy breathing muddled the rest of the words as if they were speaking a special language whose speed made blood thump in my temples and filled my cheeks, face and neck with the color of a fired-up bread-oven. A butterfly darting around a night light could not hope to match the haphazard trajectories of their hands. It looked like a strange game in which it was important not to let the other player into your space. Sparks flew whenever their hands touched; I was afraid they would set the grass on fire.

Ahror won. He was already undoing the small buttons of Lidiya Grigoriyevna's dress, and she was yanking off the thick, home-made shirt over his head. Electricity spread from their hands across the orchard. Every leaf on every tree froze in an unnatural tension. Sparks rolled off their bodies with unmistakable crackling; if they fell on their skin, they nipped and bit the flesh in throbbing ecstasy. Insects fell silent as if before an earthquake. The sun forced its heat through the tree-canopy with the same abandon, but it could not be felt in the shade of the orchard. Lidiya Grigoriyevna's sandals and Ahror's loafers flew aside like shards of an exploded light bulb; his powerful tanned back glistened above the green grass, and from the darkness under his arm her white breast gleamed, with its almond-hard nipple. Ahror kissed her neck, then found her nipple and sucked from it, like an infant, the milk of love that a woman gives at such moments (as Aunt Gulsuhor later explained men's yearning for our breasts).

The hair crackled on my head. I could not look away from their duel. My body felt like a chunk of iron glued to the magnetic earth. Right before the climax I came back to my senses, and realized I had to flee. I must have started from the ground too clumsily and suddenly, and a branch snapped loudly beneath me. Lidiya Grigoriyevna turned her head. Our eyes met; hers shone with triumph. *Akó* Ahror did not hear anything; his fingertips were dancing on his belt. I crawled backwards awkwardly, almost not hiding any more, then jumped up and ran to the expedition camp, to the *haús* filled with watermelons that were cooling it for dinner. I fell into the water dressed as I was, and the living water instantly returned me to the real world.

Later I sat drying in the sun—the normal sun that burned straight to the bone—turning this way and that. Finally, with my mottled, wet hair, I snuck into the lab, went to my table and busied myself with my sponge and the fresco fragments.

They came in. I was shaken: happy for them, and envious of Lidiya Grigoriyevna. Ahror went for the teakettle, filled it with water, put it on. Lidiya Grigoriyevna sat at her table. I could not work; everything fell through my fingers, the fragments were blurry in my eyes. Lidiya Grigoriyevna noticed this and sent me home early, saying that I must have spent too much time in the sun.

The next day I asked to return to the dig. Lidiya Grigoriyevna agreed readily, and I began going to the old fortress again. Often, instead of *akó* Boria's lectures, Lidiya Grigoriyevna played improvised concerts for us. We listened, and it was great, but not the same as when she played for her Ahror and for me, who had accidentally strayed into the orbit of their love.

· 4 ·

IT IS STRANGE that so many years have passed and I still do not want to say the girl's name, which must mean I have still not forgiven her. To be honest, the mere thought of her makes me feel queasy; I just glanced in the mirror, and my cheeks are aflame, but that could also be because it is stuffy in here. I got up, cracked the window open, tucked the blanket in around my sleeping grandma, and came back to the table.

The girl was from Leningrad, a first-year student, a daughter of some high-ranking parent. She had a very high opinion of herself, but she was smart, and at first I sought her attention. Could it be that to this day I am ashamed I was so wrong about her?

I remember the scene as if it were yesterday. We were sitting on the *aivan* with our morning tea. There were only a few of us left, five or six people. Normally only archaeologists went from the base-camp to the dig; this privilege was extended to me after my work in the conservation lab and because I lived four fences over from the camp. We were finishing our flatbreads with jam, washing them down with hot black tea. Ahror, as always in the morning, stood by his truck waiting for us to load up. He was wearing the same shirt he always wore, albeit washed and ironed daily, a pair of light, loose trousers, warm felt loafers, and no socks. He had a rag in his hand: he had just finished his periodic ritual of dusting off the truck's windows, mirrors and lights, and then wiping down the hood. Now he fumbled with his rag, not knowing how to occupy himself, gazing toward the orchard and the old walnut tree. His cheekbones and his sharp, thin nose looked as if they were carved out of stone.

"I hate him," said that girl, her eyes narrowed. "He puts up this whole Muslim thing, and he fucks Lidka."

I don't know if *akó* Ahror heard her—he was a good hundred feet from the *aivan*, and nothing changed in his face—but I, idiot, could not take it, splashed my hot tea at her, stomped my foot and said loudly, "How dare you say that, you hen!"

The tea did not really burn her, but it did give her a good fright: she started, screamed, flailed at the drops on her dress as if trying to get rid of a nasty bug. I was about to grab a fistful of her hair, but two guys caught me and held me back; they were the draftsmen from Repin College, Vova and Andrei. Somehow, they pulled us apart and made us calm down. Thank God it didn't occur to anyone to try to get us to make up.

The girl stayed at the base (it was her turn for kitchen duty), and I went to the dig. It was very early, around four-thirty, the dusk was just slipping towards the mountains, and the sun had not yet risen: we started work early, stopped to wait out the heat of the day, and finished from four to six, when the heat let up.

Ahror and *akó* Boria rode in the cab, and the rest of us huddled in the bed in our padded overcoats: the wind still held the night's bone-chilling air. The climate in Asia is extreme, and even in summer one can perish overnight if caught without a fire and a blanket.

The truck, slowly grinding through its gears, climbed the fortress hill. Leaving behind the vineyards, it rolled in a cloud of dust along the road at the bottom of the gorge between the *shahristan*—the ancient settlement— and the *kuhendiz*—the citadel that had been the king's palace. *Akó* Boria had told us that in the old days the fortress was considered unassailable,

since the only way to access it was by a bridge over the gorge. The settlement itself had been circled with walls topped with tall, round towers.
These were spaced evenly around the town, and each had a street running
toward it. The residents of that street were responsible for manning and
maintaining the tower, and in exchange received a tax from everyone who
entered the town through its gates.

Seen from a distance, the settlement—now a large hill of *pahsa* and
sand covered in sun-burnt grass, burrs, and scraggly wild rose bushes—resembled a Muslim's skull. The dominant color was the gray-white of a
shaven head, since the sun burned everything to dust, until the gray grass
mixed with the dry packed *pahsa* and the dusty sand. In the bright light,
the bumps and cracks, flushed by the spring rains, would disappear. The
hill looked naked, adorned only with goat paths twisting across its slopes,
like veins on the temples of a giant head.

In the mornings, in the receding twilight, the light and shadows sometimes fell just right, creating a miraculous vision: the crumbled shapes
of walls and towers appeared suddenly from around the hill. This would
only last a moment, as the ancient city, as if caught on photo paper,
revealed its lines. The lines were vague, yet still visible from the slowly
moving truck; the city emerged, showed itself, and instantly began to melt
back into the mud slides that had buried it. Somewhere in the depths
of the earth, the sun was being born; its light was not yet visible, but its
unseen messengers had been sent ahead to change the angle of light in
the air, to hide the secret. We were still driving along the foot of the hill,
but the towers and walls were no longer visible. *Akó* Boria once explained
this phenomenon to us. I did not remember the difficult words; it was
something about the laws of optics. It all remained a mystery for me, like
the wonder of a fading rainbow: now it's here, half-a-world tall, with all
its colors, and now it is fading and is already gone, and only the joy of
communion remains.

When the walls emerged from the hillside, we shouted, "Open, Sesame!" from the truck bed. We were convinced that one day the hill would
open wide and we would see the blooming, clean-swept streets, lined with
rich houses, running toward the market square. And the square would be
thick with stores, filled with Chinese silks and Syrian seeing-eye beads,
pure Arab silver, Indian spices and incense, and the local blue-black steel.
In the center, there would be vats of rich *plov*. There would be rows of
barrels filled with millet and sorghum, and flocks of insatiable sparrows

would flit about stealing the grain. Old men, hired specifically for the task, would lazily shoo them with twisted sticks. The main *haús*, the water source in case of a siege, set apart from the residential streets and the two main temples, would be hidden in the green shade of trees. Their branches would bend towards the water like the courtesans who dance at the feast in the king's palace. Captives from faraway lands, they bow to the floor, touching it with their hands as they begin their dance, to show respect for their master and his rich, distinguished guests.

Akó Boria told us about that world, long gone. I could see it then just as I can see it now as I keep my bedside watch over the dying grandma Lisichanskaya, half-dreaming, half-awake in my armchair. When I am not reading, I remember things and indulge my visions. I am forty-two, and it will be a long time before I can rest in retirement. If ever.

The truck climbed the last steep slope and we arrived at the dig. Tents were pitched in a row: one for the preservation crew, another for the architectural draftsmen, and the large communal one for breaks, where it was always stuffy and smelled of sweat. Actually, we rarely took breaks there, since everyone preferred to rest in the shade of the tall earthen wall surrounding the dig, sitting on a padded coat tossed on the ground. The shade is treacherous: when you are overheated, you can catch an inflammation of the kidneys or testicular ducts[10] just from sitting on the cool ground.

The guys jumped off the truck before it stopped—show-offs, it was a game for them. Ahror drove around the settlement slowly anyway, as if he did not want to make even a tiny impression in the road, already worn smooth by years of expeditions.

I remember that I got off next to the architects' tent, and went in to get the folding two-meter ruler, since I was going to hold it upright while Andrei, looking through a level, measured certain points on the strata and shouted the numbers to Vova, who wrote them on the map. For a moment, I was alone in the tent. The flap swung back, and *akó* Ahror entered. He came up to me and held me by the shoulders; his hands were strong, and I tensed up unconsciously, as if clenched in a trap; my heart sank. He turned me towards him, looked straight into my eyes, and said, "I love her, Vera, love her more than life. Thank you."

My face felt as if it had been burned with boiling tea, but I did not look away. I simply answered, "I know."

And burst into such hopeless tears that I had to break away from him and run out, run not knowing where.

I rushed out, almost knocked over *akó* Boria, ran up the mound of dug-up dirt, kicked up a cloud of dust and tumbled down, down the slope like a rubber ball, not thinking that I could get hurt, that burrs would shred my legs and dress, hitting my elbows and sides against the hard stale crust of the ancient shaved skull.

Somehow I brought myself to a stop. I hid my face in my hands and wept out loud. I knew that I was alone, that no one could see or hear me, and I howled like a dog, I screeched and clawed at the ground. Then I pressed against the still cool dirt, hoping that it would draw the heat from my chest and stomach. It did. Gradually, I came back to my senses—dirty, disheveled, in a torn dress, and with an intolerable need to pee. I peed, walked away a bit, crouched down on a little bump, picked up a dry grass stalk and sucked on it hungrily. I remember my head was spinning; my eyes, already dry, looked across the gorge to the fortress. There, at the very top of the hill, a jenny[11] was grazing, tethered on a chain held down by a meter-long stake. She paused and turned her head towards me. She was chewing on a tuft of dry grass which slowly disappeared in her mouth.

· 5 ·

WE REGARDED EACH OTHER, each chewing her dry stalk of grass. The shadows on the *kuhendiz* began to fill with crimson: the sun was rising behind the fortress hill. Crimson fingers stretched towards the *shah-ristan* and spilled into the gorge between myself and the donkey. An old road followed the gorge from the mountain villages to Panjakent, where it ended at the market square. It was very quiet, the wind sub-sided, the rocks and the *pahsa* of the ruins prepared themselves for the sunrise, and even the grasshoppers disappeared as if they had never been. High above us, a pair of doves flew towards the city following the twists of the gorge; they were heading to feed on the corn dumped in the marketplace.

The sun rises quickly here. Crimson is replaced with pink, which, in turn, is chased off by orange, pushed into the shadows and hollows, so that the new color can take the highest points of the surface and roll down like hot chocolate over a scoop of ice-cream. The change comes rapidly, one wave after another.

I loved sunrises. I always stood up tall, straightening my back and planting my feet wide on the ground; then I lowered my hands, palms-down, touched the crimson forehead of the hill and slowly, like a sorceress, raised them again. It was important not to rush, to match the sun's pace, so that my hands could cling to its disc and have it push them up, even though it looked as if I was lifting it.

My arms would feel leaden; my fingers would tremble, for the burden they were lifting from the deep well in the citadel is not for the weak. Slowly, so slowly, the hands would rise, and the growing arc of the sun, as if drawn by a magnet, would crawl after them. Once out of the dungeon's cold and into the pure air, the sun began to heat; now it was orange and my hands held it on its sides, like a basketball.

My arms are tired, but they must not tremble. The trembling is inside me, because this ascent I am making is a miracle, and I am proud of my perseverance: my legs are rooted, angled like the base of a tower; my hands are parting now, letting go of the orb. And now it rolls out fully and yellows swiftly; the sun is a lemon on a shuddering branch. All that is left to do is to slap it from below, like a light spank to a baby's behind, and it will continue its march on its own and grow smaller.

My skin could already feel its heat, not yet cruel but warming, like the warmth of an open fire. In an hour, the sun will have the heat of a *tandyr* bread oven, that intolerable heat which bakes your bones if you stand still. In another hour it will be hell, the air will shudder, the haze will curtain off the mountains, and only a tiny pancake will remain, bubbling angrily in the distant and bottomless sky. When looked at straight, through squinted eyes, it immediately turns into a white-hot cross.

I did it then: pulled up the sun, set it free in the sky. My arms and fingers were numb and I squeezed and opened my fists a couple times. It was time to go back to the dig: our team started work at daybreak. And then I heard the scream, and then again. It was coming from the gorge. I looked down.

It was a common jack-donkey, one of the dozens who wait for their masters in a corral at the city's market. He was being ridden by an old *dehkanin*-farmer; a pair of stuffed saddlebags hung on his sides, held together with strong cloth. The old man tapped the jack's neck with his right big toe, just under his ear, which stood up like a smokestack. The jack walked slowly, as if he was carrying a ton. Suddenly, he curled his lips, baring his bluish gums with their strong teeth, shook his head, and let out another coughing wail. The echo bounced around the gorge and flew up, to the top of the hill, where the jenny heard it. She was the one for whom it was intended, this cry of desperation. The jenny rolled a terrified eye to look below; she was protected by a steep slope. The fortress on whose remains she was grazing was inaccessible from the gorge, even for a lusty donkey used to scaling cliffs. Still, his thunderous voice scared her; she jerked her head, and took off galloping away from the edge, forgetting her chain. The chain almost snapped her off her feet, jerking her backward, but the animal had lost its mind from fear. With characteristic stubbornness, she lunged and lunged again, as if attacking an invisible foe and trying to knock him down with her forehead, as stupid rams do to gates. Foam flew off her in great flakes, and it seemed like I could smell her fear on the wind. The jack let out another gut-wrenching shriek and went on hollering, no longer stopping for breath. Jenny echoed him from her terror-filled throat, screaming as if all the merciless furies of the night were tearing her apart with their claws.

The jack, meanwhile, rooted himself firmly to the ground, spreading his legs in a strange impression of a pommel horse. He threw his head back and transitioned to a roar that mixed pain with wild, animal passion. His eyes grew dull and filled with blood. The old man silently dismounted, took the saddle-bags off the donkey, spread them out in the shade of the wall and sat down cross-legged. He pulled out a small gourd from inside his sash, threw a pinch of *nasvai* under his tongue and went all glassy, as if having lost his hearing. He had floated into a different dimension of time and space; his face looked tranquil; his cheek muscles relaxed, his eyelids drooped heavily and almost closed, leaving just two tiny cracks as his window onto this insane world.

The jack kept screaming, but did not move. An appalling pipe protruded from his gut and bit into the earth like a fifth leg. Wild donkeys inspire fear even in mares: the donkey penis exceeds any imaginable size and their lust is proverbial. Once he smells a ripe mare or a jenny, the donkey male will chase after her until he can copulate and pour out his passion. Mares are sometimes saved by their long legs, but the little animal's stamina is boundless, and he is known to chase his unfortunate mate for hours until she surrenders in exhaustion.

The donkey is a symbol of hard-work and stubbornness, but also of lust. One of the frescoes we found depicted a jack with an erect penis and a Soghdian beauty dancing before him. *Akó* Boria, a big fan of dirty tales, told us an ancient legend about a lascivious queen, her black slaves, a mountain jack, and a wise king who eventually had the loose woman publicly executed.

I continued to stand there at the edge of the gorge: the sight both attracted and appalled me. It was the first time that I had seen *that*, and for some reason I felt more sympathy for the desperate jack than for the hysterical jenny thrashing about on her chain. The jack seemed to be about to die right before my eyes: he had strained his voice and could only groan hoarsely, all in a lather, his legs trembling like flour in a sieve. Finally he sobbed, his fifth leg went limp as a piece of intestine and was sucked back into his belly. The monster was instantly transformed into an endearing pet. The little donkey stood—his legs collected back together in resignation—like a senior citizen waiting in line for his single bottle of cotton oil. Twitches and spasms still roamed about his body, spit dripped slowly from his lips, and his ears hung limp, like bug-eaten cabbage leaves, but he was humble and spent. The jenny, as if someone had whispered "Freeze!", instantly calmed down and returned to nibbling on her grass. She did not give the gorge another glance.

The old man returned from contemplating the mysteries of nothingness, expelled his processed weed and black spittle, wiped his mouth with the corner of his robe, and creakily stood up. He piled the saddlebags back onto the donkey's back, hoisted himself onto the saddle, stuck out his right foot and toe-tapped the beast on the neck, directly under his right ear. The donkey took a step, then another, and was on his way to the market. I watched them for a while, and then turned around to face the digs. *Akó* Ahror was standing on the mound of excavated dirt; he appeared to have been there for quite a while, restrained by his natural tact from coming down to me. He was grinning like a boy.

"Vera, come here."

I climbed the dirt. He touched me on the shoulder lightly with his hand, pointing the direction in which he wanted me to go, but on impulse I clung to him, hugged him around the waist, and pressed myself against his chest. He patted my head and said, "Vera, you are like a daughter to me; I loved your dad."

I felt good and peaceful, and I laughed happily, and he laughed too.

. 6 .

WHEN I GOT HOME that evening, we had guests: Mom's brother and his wife, Uncle Kostya and Aunt Raya, had come to visit from Kurgan-Tyube.[12] Uncle Kostya was a construction engineer; he first worked on the Karakum Hydroelectric Station, and later moved to Kurgan-Tyube to build a dam on the Vakhsh River and stayed there. Uncle Kostya was a member of the Party and held a middle management position, and Aunt Raya worked as an accountant at a concrete plant. They came to see us, as Uncle Kostya announced, on the occasion of my mom's birthday, even though it had been a month before. On the table stood bottles of cognac and champagne, Aunt Raya brought all kinds of candy, Mom had baked a cabbage pie, and everyone was making *shashlyk*[13] in the yard.

The day stuck in my memory because such feasts happened very rarely, only when Mom's brothers came to visit. Her other brother, Uncle Styopa, lived in Dushanbe, and could not come that time; he served in the Border Guard Command and it was very difficult for him to get leave, even for his sister's birthday. We feasted outside under the apple tree, and then Uncle Kostya produced an old Radiola and we played records. I devoured Aunt's candy, and she could not tear herself away from Mom's quince jelly; she must have eaten two pints of it at least, and Mom later sent a gallon jar home with them. It was fun; the grown-ups drank a little but it was not a custom in our family to get drunk, and the half-empty bottle of cognac would be shut in a kitchen cabinet for a long time and then disappear altogether, I don't remember where, I only remember that the glass was completely covered in dust by then.

The following day was Saturday; we went to swim in Zaravshan, lay in the water, splashed, and Aunt Raya waded in the shallows looking for gemstones. She wanted to find a real agate, but she never did. Uncle Kostya and Aunt Raya collected rocks. I had never been at their place, but just heard about their collection, which included rare amethyst and crystal geodes. The collection was lost in '92 when we all had to flee together from Tajikistan; Vovka, their son, could not save it.

At the lake, Uncle Kostya recalled how after every expedition my dad would send him interesting samples.

"Most of my collection and its best specimens came from your dad," he told me.

He spoke of my dad easily and joyfully; Mom did not even tear up. When they were young, they roomed together for a while, and they had a lot of shared memories.

Then I asked about *akó* Ahror, since he had said he was Dad's friend, and Mom responded with surprising praise. Ahror Djurayev used to work as a driver for the geological exploration group, but when his wife fell ill he had to look for work in Panjakent. Dad helped him, and his group gave Ahror their decommissioned little truck. Ahror restored the car himself and now it fed his entire family: the Djurayevs had five children.

"Our nurses visit Mukhibá Djurayeva every other day, give her injections, but it is a sad case," Mom said and added that Ahror cares deeply for his wife and children, runs home during his lunch break to check on them, and tends the chickens after work.

Meanwhile, the girl from Petersburg somehow gained Lidiya Grigoriyevna's trust and went to work in the conservation lab, in my old job. Ahror, being a true gentleman, did not say anything to Lidiya. The girl began to pursue Ahror, found pretexts to be alone with him, bathed naked in the *haús,* making sure that he would see her when everyone had gone to the dig and the base camp was deserted. Lidiya Grigoriyevna was not aware of any of this. The little bitch sucked up to her, and then went off seducing her beloved behind her back.

Ahror could not stand it anymore, went to *akó* Boria and asked him to send the girl to the dig. She was called into the boss's tent. There she said that Ahror raped her in the orchard and that she thought she was pregnant. This spelled real trouble. *Akó* Boria conferred with his wife *api* Valiya: in those days, a thing like that could be catastrophic for an expedition. Students from Moscow and Leningrad paraded around the base camp in bikinis and swimming trunks, and the Tajiks, unaccustomed to such frivolity, had long been spreading rumors that the archaeologists were running a whorehouse and even asked *akó* Boria to have his female students for the weekend, "to go for a ride," and offered good money for them.

The girl was transferred to the dig. In the morning, as everyone was loading into the truck, Ahror gallantly offered her his hand to help her climb in. She swung around to slap him on the cheek and screeched:

"Go back to your Lidka! I don't want to see you anymore, you lusty jackass!"

Ahror froze. Silently he climbed into his driver's seat, waited for the last person to load up, and took everyone to the dig.

Lidiya Grigoriyevna immediately got a report of what happened. At night, I accidentally witnessed their conversation: Ahror stood with a stony expression while Lidiya Grigoriyevna passionately talked at him. Suddenly she threw up her hands, and I heard the word "why?" repeated many times. At first he did not react at all, just stood there like a concrete pylon, then turned and walked to his car. Lidiya Grigoriyevna leaned against the wall of her lab, and followed him with her gaze; her eyes, filled with tears, shone with adoration. He walked straight ahead, calmly, and did not once look back.

The girl caught a bad case of dysentery a couple days later, after eating too many peaches from the ground. I am sure she did not wash the fruit, even though we were reminded to do so almost every day. First they took her to our hospital, but when it became clear that her diarrhea was not responding and she needed stronger antibiotics, she was put on a plane from Samarkand to Leningrad.

Akó Ahror was the one to take her from Panjakent to Samarkand. With the same stoicism as when he fasted, he accepted the task, lifted the blanket-wrapped girl into the cab, threw her suitcase into the bed, and drove off. The little truck took several hours in the heat to get there, and they were alone, the two of them in the tiny cab. The girl was very ill, running a fever, and they must have had to pull over many times.

The next morning he was standing there by the truck, polishing it with his rag. They got to the airport without trouble; once on the plane, the stewardesses took care of the girl, laid her on unfolded seats, but it was still Ahror who carried her up the steps to the plane. He answered all the questions with his soft Tajik pronunciation, but there was metal in his voice, metal of that special tempering that makes black Chust[14] knives.

I always got a smile from him, even that day, and I wanted to ask him about Dad and the truck, but was scared. I never asked.

That night at dinner I could not hold it all inside anymore and told my Mom everything about Lidiya Grigoriyevna, *akó* Ahror, and the girl from Leningrad.

"You are growing up, Vera," Mom said. "Women don't just walk away from men like Ahror."

· 7 ·

AKÓ AHROR BECAME my first love. It was a strange love. When my class-mates shared their own love stories I only half-listened. Their kisses and walks home, looks and dances at the Culture Center did not interest me. Boys tried courting me, one even walked me home from school, but we had nothing to talk about, so he walked with me for a while and then stopped. Once I overheard them calling me "Fish." I do not know why, but the name did not seem insulting; let it be fish, especially since it also happened to be my zodiac sign. I made a note of it and that was all; I had no idea that I would yet hear that name many times. I existed outside of my peers' social circle and did not go to their parties.

At the dig, among students and researchers, I was curious and moti-vated, and they treated me as an equal, did not make advances, and left me alone as Ahror and Lidiya's friend. I did not feel jealous. I saw him every day, and that was enough. He would nod at me, say something trivial, I would smile in return, and he would melt into a smile too; what I dreamed of when I was alone was private, and my dreams were enough for me. Curiously, I also fell in love with Lidiya Grigoriyevna. She could feel it and returned my affection; she was always kind to me, and, I suspect, knew my secret, but still I did not have it in me to go back to working in her lab.

In September I became friends with Galya Dolzhanskaya, an archae-ologist from Petersburg. Galya was twenty-five; a small, skinny woman, she could swing a pick-axe at clumps of packed earth for an hour or two non-stop. The four of us—Galya, Asya Rakhimzhakova, a fourth-year Leningrad University student on field-practice, Nar, an Ossetian boy thrown in to dilute the female company, and myself—began work at the Kul-Tepe burial mound, a kilometer from the main dig. Ahror would first drop people off at the *shahristan*, and then take us and little Karim-*boi*, Galya's son, to the mound. Karim's name was Karen in his regular life; he was five, and the locals refashioned his Armenian name to suit their taste. Galya was divorced and had no choice but to bring her son along on the expedition.

Karim messed around in the dug-up dirt, made caves, dragged a tin truck about on a string, and never, never got in anyone's way. At ten, when the sun would begin to get hot, Nar boiled a kettle of tea over an open fire and beat on an empty bucket with a spoon to summon us for a tea break. We drank green tea with flatbreads; Karim-*boi* went to take a nap in the shadow of a canvas lean-to, and we worked for two more hours until the lunch-break, the worst two hours, when the heat was intolerable. At noon, Ahror would come to drive us back to the base camp, where we were supposed to eat, but the heat was such that food held no appeal, and instead we drank more tea with flatbreads and slept through the worst of the day. I did not go home for lunch; Mom was on duty at the hospital anyway.

Just as often, we stayed at our dig: in the heat, one is inclined to languor, and a bumpy truck ride to the base camp seemed like torture, so we just collapsed onto the mats under the canvas next to Karim-*boi*, who was accustomed to sleeping during the day, and fell asleep ourselves. If we had any energy left, we walked to the closest irrigation canal, about half a kilometer away, and temporarily washed the dust off ourselves with warm water poured from a ladle. Our bodies dried off instantly. We came back to the blessed shade of the overhang completely dry, with no memory of the joy of washing, but with a bonus: the endless field that stretched to the foothills was planted with grapes, and we never missed a chance to half-fill a bucket with dark red moscato grapes or the long, brownish-green "lady's fingers." We lay in the shade, mashing the fruit with our tongues, and often that was enough for our lunch. Our faces and hands got sticky. We lined up by the water cistern, washed again, and crawled back to the shade to toss and turn on the hard mats and wait for the heat to subside. We lay around in our swimsuits, which gradually crusted over with salt, and every day after work I rinsed mine out; it dried during the night and greeted me in the morning from the clothesline on the balcony—my uniform. I only put on a dress in town; I got so used to walking around mostly naked that I hated putting it on; it seemed unnecessary in our field life.

Nar and Asya quickly became friends. Of course, the initiative came from the older Asya. Obsessed with sex, she had seen a lot in her twenty short years. Her father, a famous Orientalist, was a very old man, in his eighties. Asya said that people called him "Muallim" (Teacher). In the Soviet years, protected by his degrees and publications, he was essentially a spiritual leader, observed Fridays and the Quran, shaved his head, went to a mosque, but remained loyal and unthreatening to the regime and thus was left in peace. Their home was always filled with young men who had come to absorb Muallim's scholarly words. Asya, his belated and beloved daughter, could do as she pleased.

"Dad is like a little donkey," she would say. "He's kind and harmless, and only cares about his theology books."

She loved him, but still manipulated him; at home she behaved perfectly, so that she could let loose at the university or on expeditions. Men flocked to her: unattractive, but extraordinary lively and spirited, Asya surrendered without a fight. She had just emerged from an affair with a Leningrad-based osteologist, Nikolai, who went back to his family when his stint with the expedition ended. *Akó* Boria, who accepted the inevitable field affairs as an unavoidable evil, had no romantic inclinations of his own. He could tell an indecent joke, always peppered his porch lectures with erotic details of ancient eras, but did not stray from the path of virtue. Instead he watched his troops and tried to keep them within the boundaries of decency, a task at which he, naturally, failed.

Following her affair, Asya was exiled to Kul-Tepe. Nar, attached to the all-female team, had not been considered as seriously as he ought to have been. This fifteen-year-old Ossetian from Zoya Kosmodemyanskaya Street, a son of his mother and an unknown father, had dropped out of school, fell in with a band of thieves and was on the brink of landing in the juvenile reform system. His mother, in the hopes of cutting him off from his dangerous friends, had begged him to take a laborer's job with the expedition. And her plan worked. Nar found a home. He had been working with us since April and shuddered at the thought of the researchers moving back to Leningrad for the winter. He was eager, stronger than an average boy his age, did any work gladly, and earned the expedition's respect.

Asya wound him right around her little finger. Proud of his victory, Nar threw himself into the romance head over heels, moved to the base camp and became such an eager adjutant for Asya, that *akó* Boria had a confidential conversation with her, which, of course, solved nothing. Asya put on her good-girl face, lowered her little eyes, and said in her tiny voice, "*Akó* Boria, we're just friends, and as to the fact that he spends the nights here—well, you know that this is the only place where he is safe from his old gang. I think we must take care of him."

In her mind, she had already worked out a plan to lure the boy to Leningrad and get him admitted to a technical college there;[15] it was a romantic plan, a magical plan, but nonetheless, it warmed their hearts. They were left alone. They were consumed with each other, so I talked mostly with Galya and especially Karim-*boi*. This suited Galya, who worked a lot and, at night, in addition to keeping our records, wrote a dissertation whose strange title I have held in my memory all my life, like the lyrics to a song: "Problems of Migration: The Formation of Cultural Space in the Panjakent Valley in the Early Muslim Period." It was imperative that she defend it and receive the associated pay raise: her ex did not acknowledge Karim and refused to pay her any child support.

I became the baby sitter: I fed the child, put him to bed, gave him baths, played his "war" and "truck" games with him when I could, caught grasshoppers for him. I felt good around him, he clung to me and said in his low baby voice, "Vera, you are my favorite baby sitter, and in Leningrad you will sleep in an armchair by my bed."

He had romantic dreams of his own, and Galya and I did not dissuade him.

In the evenings, the young archaeologists went to the orchard, drank cheap Chashma port and sang along to someone playing the guitar; occasionally Nar procured weed, and they furtively passed around a joint. They offered it to me, too, but I refused: in my mind I pictured the faces of the totem-like figures at the teahouse.

However, those who did smoke did not freeze into a stupor, but instead thought every word spoken was utterly hilarious and couldn't stop laughing. I watched and saw only a silly emptiness in their faces. I stopped going to the orchard with them. I would read a fairy tale to Karim and then run home to Mom, so that I could return at half past five the next morning and do the job I loved. I quit socializing with my classmates altogether, and it didn't seem to make any difference to them or to me. I counted the days, knowing that soon my "cotton-picking" month would be over and that school would start. I was genuinely saddened. When I complained to Mom, she only shook her head; we did not see much of each other during August and September of that year.

. 8 .

THE KUL-TEPE BURIAL GROUND dates back to the early Muslim era. The dead were supposed to face Mecca, but in those times, before the invention of the compass, people relied on the sun. The buried shared a common faith, but Galya found three different types of pottery which suggested separate ethnic groups—the valley was inhabited by a multinational, multilingual community. The ancient cemetery was discovered by accident when the local farmers were digging an irrigation *aryk*. They turned up old skulls and pottery fragments and immediately contacted the archaeologists—the expedition that made Panjakent world-famous had also taught the locals to respect what the earth had preserved.

We had already opened eleven tombs, and there was no end in sight. Nar, the muscle of our operation, worked on the crusty top layer of dirt with a broad hoe. Asya, Galya and I then cleaned the skeletons off with scoops, brushes and dull knives. We didn't find many artifacts except pots with funeral meals—traces of paganism that survived here for centuries, far from Mecca and Medina. Occasionally we'd discover a coin or a dagger that had turned into oxidized wads and crumbled to dust when touched; sometimes there would be a string of beads—the community wasn't wealthy, neither in Soviet nor in the ancient times.

Dehkani[16] farmers often visited us on their trips from mountain villages to town, since the road passed within a couple hundred feet of the dig. They materialized as if from nowhere and climbed the mound of the excavated dirt. Men crouched and silently watched us uncover the graves. Women—wrapped in shawls, and always bunched up in a separate group— did not approach the men, and looked on disapprovingly. The sight of our tanned, swimsuit-clad bodies had on them the effect of a red rag on a bull. More than once in the presence of such shame a mother covered her daughter's eyes and led the girl away to their donkey cart; everything about our place was, in their opinion, satanic and unworthy, and for that reason both disturbing and attractive.

Soon we got used to our visitors, greeted them with a "*Salam Aleichem*," but did not engage in conversation. On the very first day, I managed to distinguish myself. When asked what we were digging up, I simply answered "Muslims" and showed ten fingers for the tenth century. The old man who had asked me smiled excitedly, clicked his tongue, shook his head, uttered a short word and drew his hand across his throat. That's when Asya, who spoke Tajik, broke out in a hurried explanation. The faces of the old man and his two companions immediately grew serious, then they nodded, and the old man even spat on our dirt as if to seal an accord. They sat around for a while longer, and then, slapping themselves on the knees with the customary "*hop-maili!*" stood up, bowed, hands pressed against their hearts, and departed full of dignity and satisfied that they had understood everything correctly.

As soon as they were out of sight, Asya turned on me.

"Are you insane? Muslims?! If they get the drift that this is a Muslim burial ground, we're done for. He showed you how they'd slit our throats. We are lucky that these days they bury according to the compass and not the sun. They could see the difference, so they believed these are pagans. And there are things in the graves, which the Quran prohibits. I told him you made a mistake, meant to say 'pre-Muslim,' but didn't know the word."

She laughed.

"In the future, you'd better keep quiet or you'll end up on a spit."

I didn't talk to the locals anymore, and they did not ask any more questions either; the old man must have told everyone that we were studying pagan graves, which was not considered a sin. In the eyes of the faithful, a *kofir*, a non-Muslim, is just another stranger with no bearing on the life of the local community. *Kofirs* live according to their own rules, whether they are Orthodox and worship Isa and Mariam, or Jewish with their devotions to the wise Solomon. Allah, through his prophet Mohammed, had commanded respect for believers of other faiths who had yet to attain the Truth. That made what we did science, a curious and respectful pastime, and a far cry removed from the sin of desecrating ancestors' graves. The locals still stopped by the dig, mostly in the morning and in late afternoon, on their way someplace else. They had to have been talking about it behind our backs and certainly disapproved, but they didn't interfere, and if they talked in our presence, they did so only in whispers. Science and all things scientific are highly respected in Asia and inspire an almost worshipful reverence in uneducated people. Sometimes they left a flatbread or a cantaloupe for us as a sign of respect, but Dolzhanskaya firmly prohibited inviting the locals to tea.

"We'd never get rid of them if we start. Let them take offense if they want," she said.

And, indeed, the locals' practice of leaving us gifts abruptly ceased. As far as their disapproval went, no one ever said anything to anyone's face. Galya explained this, too: she was Karim-*boi*'s mother, which meant there was a father, and he was the one that was supposed to teach her, the woman, her manners. Asya fawned over Nar, so he was recognized as her boyfriend. As far as I was concerned, I was young and Russian, and thus the locals expected me to be rude. Further, they knew that we were protected not by family and kin but by the Criminal Code, which they despised more than feared.

The guest that one day arrived on a black stallion was different. Asya noted at once that he was an Uzbek. The rider, too, instantly recognized her as a Tatar, and after greeting everyone in Russian, chattered in his own language. Asya responded, apparently having taken offense, and he switched back to Russian, which he spoke relatively well.

I did not look at him, but at his horse. It was lean, black, with a white star on his forehead and white socks over his hocks, the signs of good breeding.[17] The tack was new, with shiny copper studs, but the saddle was that of a collective farmer, and the saddlebags were made from colorful, mass-produced fabric. The horse stood on the mound of dirt, his intelligent eyes looking, it seemed, straight at me. I couldn't hold myself back and climbed the dirt to stroke his warm, flat cheek. He shook his head a few times, nickered softly, and playfully hunted for my palm with his teeth.

The Uzbek was an old man in his fifties or sixties, with a beard dyed raven-black. He wore canvas boots and a padded brown robe tied with a sash. From his side hung the requisite dagger in its scabbard. He dismounted easily, handed me the reins and carried his saddlebags to our little campground under the lean-to.

"Mind the horse, he's quiet," he said over his shoulder.

He had brought us grapes. He spilled a whole mountain of them out onto the table and gave Karim-*boi* a slap on the shoulder. Then he crouched in the shade, clearly expecting a continuation of our interaction. He knew what he was doing: he invaded our little world on his own terms and therefore expected attention and respect. We had no choice but to offer him tea and feed him flatbreads with jam.

Galya, Asya and Nar gathered around the table. The guest's name was Nasrulló; he was the caretaker of the *kolkhoz* vineyards and came to reach a neighborly understanding. I only half-listened to their negotiations—the splendid steed had captured my attention. He stood quietly, with the dignity of a mature creature, and only his sly eye followed me. It took all I had to resist stroking him; I kept touching his neck tenderly with my finger, secretly, so that no one could see.

Nasrulló was asking us not to steal the grapes.

"Why should you steal? Come to me, I'll give you good grapes, sweet, we'll be friends, like neighbors should."

Galya served him a cup of tea; he slurped it loudly, straightened his broad shoulders and shifted into a more comfortable position as if he expected to share the long lunch break with us. Suddenly he looked me in the eye, and winked.

"Drop the reins, come here, let the horse eat, too."

I only clutched the reins tighter in my hand.

"Can I ride?" The question popped out all by itself; I didn't even have a chance to be shocked with my own insolence.

"You want ride? Ride ahead, it's a good horse," he said with a serious nod.

Galya for some reason gave me a stern look, but I didn't care any longer. I jumped into the saddle and pinned the horse's sides with my heels. The horse leapt forward and cantered. Standing in the stirrups, my left hand gripping the saddle, I was speechless with awe. My body fell into his rhythm right away. I'd never ridden such an eager horse before, but we seemed to have understood each other without words. He ran along the burned-out flat, now in full gallop, and I almost let go of the reins. Twice he flew over some ditches and I nearly fell, yet managed to hold on and shouted with the joy that was washing over me. I was galloping on a strong black horse, and he was taking me somewhere far, toward the mountains, and the wind blew into my face, furious and hot.

I don't know how long we were gone. Later Galya said it was no more than half an hour. But they had to entertain akó Nasrulló for that half-hour, which was not the easiest job in the world. The Uzbek smiled with his whole face, smacked his lips and kept trying to switch to his native language, but his pride prevented him from doing so—when visiting, it was the custom to speak the language of the host who set the table. They had little to talk about, however, and kept drinking tea and waiting for me, silently cursing my carelessness.

When I came back, no one scolded me—I was so radiant with joy, they couldn't bring themselves to spoil it. Catching my breath, I handled the reins back to the Uzbek and exhaled, "Thank you."

Nasrulló jumped into the saddle with an ease that did not match his age, wheeled the horse around, made him prance, stopped him sharply and said something guttural to him—the stallion just twitched his ears, absolutely obedient to his master. Nasrulló raised his hand:

"Come ride, come tomorrow, I'll give you grapes!"

"Yes, yes, thank you!"

"Thank you for the tea, neighbors always welcome!"

He shifted slightly in the saddle and the horse took off at a gallop, as if he hadn't just raced with me for half-an-hour. Nasrulló became one with the horse, and they flew above the earth until they disappeared behind a tall hill.

· 9 ·

I SPENT THE following day devising a plan to slip away and ride the Uzbek's steed—Dolzhanskaya strictly prohibited any contact with Nas-rulló; she did not like the caretaker. Leaving work was out of the question. I was helped by an accident.

Little Karim got a headache, and when Ahror came in the middle of the day to drive us to lunch, Galya took the child to the base camp. The three of us said we would eat at the dig. As soon as Galya was gone, Nar and Asya dove into the stuffy storage tent. I knew their trick: the tent stood a hundred and fifty feet away from our overhang and the table, they closed the flap behind them, but opened the one on the other side of the tent, facing the mountains. This way, they had shelter with a breeze from the mountains and only the appearance of a closed tent. I also knew what they did there—Asya spared me no detail.

As soon as I was alone, I grabbed a pail for the grapes and set out for the vineyard. The heat was truly hellish, and I threw a long terry cloth towel over my shoulders—I would wet it in the *aryk,* and it would keep me cooler at least for a little while.

I came to the *aryk* on the path we'd beaten. There, I drew water with my pail and poured it over myself. The water felt like tepid soup. The vines lined the other side of the *aryk* as if standing honor guard. The air trembled with invisible vapors; there was neither sound nor whisper nor movement anywhere. I faced straight lines of blood-red grapes that hung like aiguillettes down the steel rods that propped up the vines. I

took off my clothes and slowly stepped into the *aryk*, looking down
into the clear water. The clay under my feet instantly bellowed up like
smoke, but the slow current pulled the mud away. I sat down as if in a
bathtub, so that the water covered me up to my chin, and stayed there
for a long time, motionless. A snake-like movement caught my eye.
Not too far from me a fat, revolting leech was moving along the far side
of the canal. Thank goodness, it couldn't care less for me.

The water was cleansing my body, blue sky reflected in its surface. Two
large fish swam past me, side-by-side, giving me a lazy once-over. I held
my breath and followed them with my eyes. They nestled close by on the
bottom and released a few bubbles. Taking it as a kind of fish greeting, I
blinked in return, but the beasts were quiet; they must have fallen asleep.
Then I jumped up with a squeal and scampered up the shore; when I
looked back, the fish were gone. It was as if I had imagined seeing them. I
soaked the towel, arranged it into a turban on my head, and, pail in hand,
marched down the path that ran along the edge of the vineyard. Here and
there in the gray dust I could see the hoof prints of my longed-for steed:
his master had already completed his daily rounds. Nasrulló's own tent
had to be somewhere close.

Soon I saw it: a wooden frame covered with weather-beaten, bleached
canvas, an old sheepskin on a pallet, and a sooty kettle over a fire under a
lonesome tree. The old man kneeled beside the fire, feeding it with twigs.
The horse, tied to the other side of the tree, was calmly eating barley from
a crude wooden bowl.

When he saw me, the Uzbek began to fuss, got up, stepped forward to
meet me, spreading his arms and looking at me solicitously.

"Hello. Come in, sit down," he said, pointing to the sheepskin.

I greeted him too, put my pail down and sat—it was awkward to ask
for a favor right away.

"You'd like to ride?" asked Nasrulló, gleaming.

I simply nodded.

"Good girl, pretty girl," he petted my shoulder. I didn't like his touch—
his palm was grainy like sandpaper.

"No worry, we'll have tea in a minute."

He took the kettle off the fire, raised it to his face and inhaled the smell
deeply: stems of some plant floated in the liquid.

"Good, good, you came right on time," he giggled and looked to the
side.

Following his eyes, I suddenly realized that from the hill where he had pitched his tent, Nasrulló had a clear view of the whole vineyard, and—oh, the shame!—of the *aryk* where I had bathed naked. From the fidgety movements that betrayed his embarrassment, I deduced that Nasrulló had seen me. Blushing, I tried to jump to my feet, but heavy hands pressed me back onto the pallet. Nasrulló held out a cup filled with brownish-green brew.

"No worry, no worry," he kept saying. "Have some tea, then we'll ride."

So I had to take a sip of the stuff. That it was not tea I realized instantly—the hot liquid smelled of hay. The roof of my mouth and my tongue went strangely numb as soon as it touched them.

"Is this mint?" I asked, and took a cube of sugar from a plate wanting to cover up the bitter taste of the brew.

Nasrulló left my question without an answer, instead concentrating on his own cup. He took his sip like a part of a secret ritual, closing his eyes and rolling his head slightly backward.

"Oof!" he exhaled. Then he ran his hand against his sweaty forehead and added something in Uzbek.

I finished my cup, and he quickly refilled it. I would have been rude to refuse, and this way he practically forced me to drink three cups of his "tea."

At first, I did not understand the change that was overtaking me. The "tea" flowed through my veins, making my body light and foreign, as if I had floated outside and above it. My self and my body separated and continued to exist without one another. I was seeing myself from outside my body, but also I still perceived myself to be the person sitting there with a cup in her hand. I felt good; a warm current ran down my arms and legs. The world suddenly filled with sounds. I heard each distinct crunch that my horse made as he ground his barley; I heard the ting of his tack when he reached down to the bowl; I heard the buzz and hum of the flies that clouded around his head. I could even hear the rustling of the fabric—sheepskin rubbing against felt—when the man came very close to me, put his hands on my shoulders, and carefully unwound the towel from my head. His hands did not seem repulsive any longer; they were warm, and I could even feel his pulse beating in them—so confidently, with such persistent malevolent force.

Suddenly, I found the color of his watch's wristband—two red stripes on a black background—unbearably funny. It was a funereal ribbon, but on seeing it I laughed out loud and fell onto my back. Nasrulló also laughed, while his hands undressed me with a new boldness, and I helped him, turning around to make it easier to undo my bikini bra. The clothes constrained my body and it seemed right to be rid of them.

And then he was everywhere—his fingers, his hands stroked my skin, tickled me and made me laugh. We chattered in Uzbek non-stop; I did not understand a word, but I was speaking it. Nasrulló was laughing, and only the small black pupils of his oiled-over eyes remained still.

I became dizzy with the flood of words; then hot, then chilly. I felt feverish and wanted to lie down, curl up, and fall asleep right there on the sheepskin under the open skies. But I could not sleep—this I understood suddenly and clearly. The prickly wool of the sheepskin bit into my naked flesh, and the discomfort that it caused kept me awake, in touch with reality. The "tea" had robbed me of my will but not of the ability to reason, and it kept spreading its monstrous tentacles inside my body; I had to, I needed to and wanted to escape its grip, but I could not. It was a terrible sensation. I had long since been reunited with my body. I could not recall how and when it had happened, but I understood that I was myself again, except that I had no command over my body. The Uzbek now materialized as a horrendous giant, whose massive shoulders had blocked out all light. He smelled, like his horse, sweetly of sweat—that masculine odor that drove me crazy, simultaneously seductive and revolting. I saw him bend over me as if in a fog, and I mumbled something about the grapes, asked for something. He was like a mountain, completely naked, with the gleaming body of a fish, and I could see that he was covered in scales up to his chin, to the very edge of his blue beard. I had no strength to scream, fight back, or even to move. I became a doll in his enormous hands.

Even without my will, I knew clearly what he was about to do. He commanded me, and I obeyed, because if I hadn't done what he wanted at that moment, he would have simply torn me apart the way a starved man tears up a flatbread. His weight was incredible; I lay buried under the weight of a mountain. I had no air to breathe, and he kept sucking it out of my lips, prickling my face with his bristly hair, reeking of hay.

Then there was pain. The pain came in waves, bludgeoning me; it seemed it would never stop, but it did. Nasrulló abruptly let out a strange roar, as if he were choking, curved his back, shook his head, and fell beside me, convulsing as if he'd touched bare electrical wires.

I turned away from him, curled up into a ball, and instantly fell into a bottomless pit. I fell and fell, without any sense of time, seeing neither light nor the walls of this endless hole, and when I finally hit the bottom and came back to my senses, the man and his horse were gone. I lay on the sheepskin covered up with a dirty rag. I had a skull-splitting headache, and my body felt wooden and stiff. I could not move my arms or legs; it hurt just to gather my fingers into a fist.

I lay under the lean-to; the heat subsided; cicadas chirred in the tree behind me. I could feel their chirring on my skin, as if hundreds of tiny needles were stabbing me. But, curiously, this pain was also bringing my body back to life. I could already move my arms a bit; then I felt something sticky and hot on my legs and became scared.

I remembered everything clearly, in the tiniest detail, and it *all* repeated itself, rising in front of my eyes again and again. I could not stop the visions; it was as if someone kept cruelly rewinding and replaying a film.

Suddenly Ahror appeared at the edge of the pallet. He stepped toward me, bent down, kissed me on the forehead, gathered me in his arms, pressed me against his heart and kept repeating, "Quiet, quiet, girl, don't scream like that, quiet."

I did not hear myself screaming, but boiling tears ran down my cheeks, burning deep grooves in my skin.

Ahror had brought Galya back to the dig and, sensing trouble, went looking for me. He found me and took me to my mom at the hospital. I stayed there for two weeks. Kind Uncle Davron, the head surgeon, did everything that needed to be done—the animal had torn me like a flatbread.

Mom and Aunt Gulsuhor took turns at my bedside, making me drink pomegranate juice, stroking my hair and talking to me, but I did not respond. My mouth and tongue refused to melt out of the "tea"-induced numbness. I could only grunt, and thus remained silent, staring at the ceiling. It pained me to look into other people's eyes. The women cried furtively when they thought I was asleep and could not see their tears. But I did see them, peering out between the cracks of my nearly-closed eyelids.

Still, my wooden body was softening. At the end of the second week, I got up from the bed by myself and went to the end of the hallway. By the time I came back, I could speak. I did not want to utter whole words, but for my mother's sake, I said, "It's alright, mom, let's go home."

Ahror drove us from the hospital. He had visited me twice while I was there, bringing fruit and trying to talk to me, but I turned away and looked at the wall. I remember very well the way he said, "Forget it all. He must not live." I felt ashamed of myself, and tears flowed involuntarily. Now I understand it was the tears that thawed me out. The tears and the kind words that surrounded me.

Ahror stopped his truck directly before the door to our apartment building. I walked out calmly, keeping my head high, while the all-knowing matrons of Kosmodemyanskaya Street looked on from every window. Ahror did not come into our apartment, but just hugged me outside the door, and I buried my face in his hard chest. He turned and walked to his truck.

I did not go back to the expedition.

The following day they found Nasrulló the Uzbek in his tent in the vineyard. Like a dangerous snake pierced with a hunter's spear, his body was nailed to his sheepskin bed with a sharp metal rod—the sort driven into the ground to hold up heavy vines. The police searched for the murderer, but never found him.

The story made quite a stir. It seemed a Kosmodemyanskaya Street girl had been avenged not by the Criminal Code, but by a man. Everyone, including the police, knew his name, and everyone respected what he had done. The police did not have any evidence: when summoned to the station, Lidiya Grigoriyevna swore that Ahror Djurayev had spent the entire previous day with her and had stayed the night at her place as well.

A week later, Lidiya Grigoriyevna flew to Leningrad on an urgent matter. She was never seen in Panjakent again. Ahror remained with the expedition. He never visited us at home after that. If we ran into each other in town, he walked on, looking through me as if we did not know each other.

. 10 .

AT THE HOSPITAL, they injected me with tranquilizers so I could sleep. During the day, the medicated fog kept me safely walled off from Nasrul-ló's bristly blue beard, his hands on my body, the smells of his sweat and the herbal brew. When my mother's or Aunt Gulsuhor's hand stroked my hair, I felt a momentary relief, but then the shame flooded me anew. It was hard to keep it hidden.

It was even harder at home. I remembered the neighbors' faces with their mixed expressions of sympathy and disgust. I refused to go out. I holed up on my couch. I forced myself to eat; did not want to see anyone. The girls from school came to visit me, but the panic on my face when I heard they were at the door was such that Mom didn't let them in.

I continued to pretend to sleep. Mom tried talking to me, but all I did was turn away to face the wall or look indifferently out our window at our street. I did not notice being talked to. Mom left for work in the morning, came back at night, cleaned up my unfinished lunch and served me the dinners I was also unable to eat. I kept pushing food away. Mom would go into the kitchen or into her room with a heavy sigh. But it was still easier during the day.

At night, the battle with sleep would begin. I'd get up and tiptoe around my room, look at the bright light of the streetlamp where it fell on the floor under my window until my eyes watered from its yellow glare, or would wrap a cold damp towel around my head (Mom thought I was having migraines). For a while, these things helped, but by morning, when the moon waned in the sky, I'd give up.

It all started with the old man. He loomed above me and his eyes with their tiny pupils stabbed at my soul. Then he lay down on me, blocking the light with his body. I was submerged into a closed space filled with murky liquid. The liquid was charged with the pain of a myriad of sting-ing, blood-sucking leeches. I could not see them, yet they tormented me. The murky water pulsed with an unspeakable threat. I knew that this pain and fear would never leave me and that the only way to be rid of them would be to kill myself.

I understood that would be a mortal sin, but couldn't do anything about it. I chased the idea away, but didn't have the strength to resist the pain. The old man was waiting above the surface of the murky water, and beneath it I was besieged by the leeches. There was only one way out—to go to the bathroom and open my veins. Then this torment would stop and all the bile that was boiling inside me would pour out with the blood.

But as soon as the thought occurred to me, as if in punishment for my sinful idea, the space around me would close in, gag me, plugging my eyes and ears. I could no longer breathe, or scream, or see, or hear. I lived a death inside death. My miniscule "I" was squeezed so tightly by fear, that beyond it I could see nothing. My consciousness dimmed.

Some dreadful force would begin to push me forward. I was dead and not breathing, yet I was being thrust through an endless tube. It was not enough to be blinded and senseless—the tube was ripping off my skin.

Just as suddenly, the torment would end. Gasping for air, I would fall out of the tube onto my little couch. Every cell of my body ached, but at least I was alive. The fear broke free, and I must have been screaming, because this always ended with my mother's hands stroking my head and shoulders. Yet every time I thought the hands were someone else's, and I fought them off—I saw the enormous Uzbek. But then my sense of reality won out and, sobbing and shaking feverishly, I pulled myself into a ball and quieted down. Mom sat by my side, patted my shoulder softly and sang a lullaby: "Sleep, my child, go to sleep, let the sweet sleep come to you." She used to sing that song when I was little. I would wake up in the middle of the day, when she'd already gone to work.

Other times at night I was pursued by the sharp fins of man-eating fish. They would surface suddenly—cold and razor-like—and would chase me as I tried to swim to the shore. They sliced the water dangerously close to my body. I could not see the fish themselves—only the blades of their fins. When they sped past me, a cold wave of fear would wash over my stomach, legs and sides. They would circle and catch up with me again. I would wake choking on my own scream.

I don't know what would have become of me if not for Doctor Davron. One morning he came by our apartment building in an ambulance, woke me up and took me to the hospital. I obeyed. I fell silent and tensed, setting up my defensive perimeter. He did not insist on talking to me.

We drove around the district hospital on a narrow road and entered the fruit orchard that stretched behind the main structure. There, hidden from inquisitive eyes, stood a one-story building. Davron led me inside, past the receptionist—a round-faced Uzbek man in a white coat who looked more like a policeman. The Uzbek led us through a handle-less door that he opened with a key. We were in the psychiatric ward. I realized I was done for.

Davron confidently led me down the hall. Strange patients huddled against the walls–bleary-eyed, with trembling hands, young and old, si-lent and giggling and yelling something at us. One of them, an older man with disheveled hair wearing a faded military blouse, blocked our path, saluted us military-style, and commanded, "Battalion, eyes right!"

Davron walked on, ignoring him. I followed on the doctor's heels.

At the end of the hallway, the corner room housed abandoned re-tarded children. When we entered, they were sitting around a large table and drawing with colored pencils. Their teacher sat close-by, clearly suf-fering from lack of sleep, and mostly indifferent.

Twelve faces distorted with Down syndrome turned to us as if on com-mand. Twelve puffy, cross-eyed, disproportionately large heads mumbled, "Good morning!" just as they'd been taught.

I froze. Davron let go of my hand. Automatically, I said good morn-ing, too. And then the fattest, biggest, most awkward boy–he was about ten, with unnaturally bloated, poorly formed fingers–ran up to me, grabbed my hand and pulled me toward the table.

"Look, look, look!" he repeated.

His hand was surprisingly warm and his skin incredibly soft. He was pink as a piglet and smelled of milk, like a newborn baby. Sensing my hes-itation, he stopped abruptly, halfway to the table, and gave me a rushed hug. He laughed irresistibly and kept saying, "Good boy, Dimulka is a good boy." For some reason, his touch made me feel easy and joyful. I stroked his head, covered with soft fuzz, and said, "Yes, good boy, calm down, what did you want to show me?"

"Look-look-look," he babbled again and dragged me on with unex-pected strength.

I came up to the table. The children regarded us with interest and only one of them, completely dissociated from reality, picked his nose unself-consciously. The boy wanted to show me his drawing.

"Look, look, the sun! Yes!" he assertively nailed the picture with his finger.

On his sheet of paper, yellow lines scattered around chaotically; the usual round shape was nowhere to be found.

"The sun, yes, yes!" he nodded solemnly and then suddenly made a movement with his ugly stubby fingers in front of his face, as if cutting through the air with scissors. Then he threw his hands up in the air and laughed happily. The next instant I was laughing with him. I caught myself remembering the doctor behind me, but Davron was laughing as well.

"I'll leave you here for an hour, ok? I have to visit my patients. Could you draw with them? Look how happy they are to have you."

I didn't understand why he was doing this, but nodded in agreement. Aunt Firuza, the teacher, locked the door behind Davron, and went back to her chair. Soon we were drawing and learning words.

"A bird," the children said after me.

Dimulka added importantly:

"Sparrow, chirp-chirp. Yes! Yes!" and slapped his face with his hands in delight.

I got used to them very quickly: the boys were kind. Their faces were no longer frightening to me, and I even wiped their spit a couple times with a towel—two of the boys drooled constantly.

When Davron came to get me, I was reading "The Giant Roach"[18] to them. I don't know how many of them understood how much, but all were listening intently, their faces glowing. The children did not want to let me go. I took my time saying goodbye, patting each boy on the head and holding his hand, and they stroked and touched me back. They needed touch and kindness like air. I promised to come again.

Davron helped me into the ambulance van.

I was silent. The excited, kind, idiotic faces remained in my mind's eye.

"What do you think about my kids?" Davron asked.

"They're nice. It's easy with them."

"They liked you. If you want, you're welcome to come and help out; no one cares about them here."

Davron kissed me on the forehead and told Hakim, the driver, to take me home.

Dimulka saved me that night. I imagined us drawing horses, the moon, a flower, a donkey, a snake, a light bulb. I could hear his laughter and his assertive "Yes! Yes!" I could feel his warm, soft hands on my face and could smell his milky odor. His silly smile was the last thing I saw before falling asleep.

I slept without trouble. In the morning, I got up at the same time as my mom and solemnly declared: "I am not going back to school. I want you to get me a job teaching the retarded kids."

So it was that, having finished only eight grades of school, I started working at our hospital. I lived with my boys for an entire year and could not have dreamed of a better life. The hospital hired me as a nurse's assistant and even paid me a monthly salary of one hundred and five rubles. The hospital also provided meals for its staff, and my mom and I now had enough money. Sometimes I stayed for the night, giving the night nurses a break. This was done, of course, behind the head nurse's back, but she looked the other way.

One morning, just as I entered the hospital's campus I saw a familiar truck. Ahror had brought in his wife. She was very ill.

I put on a white coat and cap and asked my supervisor to excuse me for an hour. I went to the main building; I had to see the woman.

. 11 .

THE TRUCK WAS GONE from the hospital's parking lot. I went upstairs to the third floor into the second therapy unit. Mukhibá Djurayeva had just been brought back from having her X-rays done.

"The cancer has metastasized all over her body," a nurse I knew told me. "If you want to talk to her, hurry up, because they'll give her morphine soon and she'll be out. She'll be in pain until the end. A sad and sorry case. She's in room four, by the window."

I went to the room. Aunt Mukhibá was in the corner, next to a big window. On her bedside table were a plate of fruit and a bottle of Narzan mineral water. An aluminum cup. The blanket was pulled up to her chest. There appeared to be no body under the cover—the illness had eaten it all up. Only her eyes were alive. Her black irises gleamed with an unhealthy sheen. When I approached, the irises turned to me.

"Thank you, I don't need anything," she whispered.

"Aunt Mukhibá, my name is Vera, I'm the daughter of the geologist Nikolai; I've come to sit with you."

"You are Vera, the Russian girl that gave me back my husband?" her lips formed an imitation of a smile. "Go ahead, sit down. It's hard for me to talk, so you tell me about the other woman."

I sat on a chair and took her paper-dry hand into mine. I began to talk, stroking and massaging her fingers all the while. Mukhibá listened silently. Her hands were cold, like the hands of Grandma Lisichanskaya when she is dying. I kept talking and massaging, until what little blood she had left flowed to warm her fingers.

Her doctor came in with the nurse, but when Mukhibá saw the syringe, she shook her head:

"I don't want to, I must stay awake."

The doctor did not try to convince her, just shrugged his shoulders and left. No one disturbed us after that. The other patients did not pay us any attention. I spoke softly for as long as I could, and then I fell silent. Mukhibá had closed her eyes a long time ago, but I knew she was not sleeping. Once I had warmed up her hands, I began to stroke her head, her dry, bristly gray hair. She breathed through her mouth, in short and shallow breaths. I kept running my fingers through her hair, parting it into strands, and trying to picture her braiding it into forty braids as a girl. I rubbed her temple with the pads of my fingers or cupped my hand like a shell next to her ear—my mom played with me like that when I was little. Instinctively, I put my hand on her forehead and mostly forgot about it. My left hand went back to warming her fingers, which were quickly growing cold again.

The hour for which I had been excused had long since passed, but I had no intention of leaving. Signs of discomfort appeared on Mukhibá's face—her pain was returning.

Suddenly, inexplicably, I could feel it throbbing. My hand, which was still on her forehead, received the signal.

Now I know this sensation well; I have learned to seek out this throbbing and to distinguish pain from helplessness, anger or bottomless despair. Back then, the feeling was new, and I almost jerked my hand away from it, as from hot oil spitting in pan. Mukhibá blinked fearfully and whispered:

"Don't take your hand away, may Allah keep you!"

"I'm here, Aunt Mukhibá, I'm not going anywhere."

"I must wait for Ahror."

"He'll come soon," I lied automatically, since I was not at all sure when he was coming.

"He'll meet the kids after school, feed them dinner and then come."

Mukhibá closed her eyes; it was easier for her that way.

We sat for a long time in silence. I could feel her pain, and it was difficult; my hand felt like stone, but it did not hurt. There was just something heavy and cold at the bottom of my stomach, and my eyes were tearing up. Mukhibá's forehead grew warmer; a barely visible blush spread over her cheeks, her wrinkles smoothed out, and her breathing became more regular.

I sat there, afraid to open my eyes, deaf to the outside world, and thought about Mukhibá, and about Ahror who was about to become a widower with three children. I remembered his truck and the old walnut tree in whose shade he loved Lidiya Grigoriyevna. I even thought of the terrible Nasrulló, but the thought did not frighten me, because he was long dead and could do me no more harm.

I didn't feel it right away when someone else put a hand on my shoulder. I finally felt it when I heard my name; I turned and saw *akó* Ahror standing by my side.

"Thank you," he said. "You can go now."

I got up. He was looking not at me but at his Mukhibá, and his eyes were sick.

"Aunt Mukhibá fell asleep," I said. "At night, before bed, they might give her morphine. She refused it earlier—she was afraid that she'd miss you if she were sleeping."

Ahror nodded and sat down on my chair.

"It would be better if she didn't wake up," he said in a muffled voice.

He was not aware of my presence any longer, having pressed his palms against his eyes. And that's when I heard Mukhibá say, soft as a breath, "*Inshallah!*"[19]

Ahror did not hear her. I think he was praying.

I tiptoed out of the room.

. 12 .

There was no need to inform my mom: she knew that if I did not come home at night it meant I was substituting for the night-shift nurse. I knew I had to spend the night with Mukhibá.

At ten, after lights out, I went back to room four. The nightlights were dim. The window was left open, allowing the coolness of the night and the moonlight to seep in. A pack of dogs was howling with many voices in the wasted field behind the hospital.[20] The moon was full.

The fruit and water on the bedside table had not been touched. Mukhibá did not open her eyes. The night nurse told me that, at Ahror's insistence, she'd been injected with morphine.

I sat, very still, at Mukhibá's side all night. For a long time, my hand did not feel anything; the woman's waxy forehead glistened in the moonlight, lifeless. My hand went numb and heavy in just half an hour, but I did not give up. Suddenly, as always, without warning, I sensed a weak pulsing signal. It came again and again.

The pain had not left her. It was hidden, lying in wait, cuddled in the drug like a pot of mashed potatoes wrapped in a blanket. The drug had also stifled all her senses, leaving alive only touch. I had known the same state when I drank Nasrulló's "tea." Mukhibá could feel my hand. The instant I realized this, it seemed that she felt a bit better. Then, I left my body to be with Mukhibá. I had no weight, no awareness, no smell; I submerged into the cotton-wool silence where I could catch the feeble signals of her heart. I gathered other impulses as well: Mukhibá was resigned to her fate, and, rather than suffering, the hidden pain was causing her discomfort, as if she'd been laid naked onto a crusty old sheepskin. The touch of my hand alleviated this discomfort. At some point, I returned to reality and the hospital room: I desperately had to pee, but I forbade myself from thinking about it, and the need disappeared.

In response, as if in gratitude, Mukhibá flooded me with waves of emotions which stretched me thin, like a plastic bag filled with water. For some reason, a single sentence came into mind and kept turning over and over. "It would be better if she didn't wake up." It was a terrible idea. I kept thinking about it, and I was certain that Aunt Mukhibá was thinking about it too.

She did not wake up. Just before sunrise, for an instant, my hand felt as if it were branded with a burning piece of ice. I jerked it away, frightened. All at once, my sight, hearing and smell returned to me. It was all over; Mukhibá had passed. A stone lay upon a stone.

I got up and called for the night nurse. There was nothing more to be done there. I went back to my department, curled up on the couch in the nurses' room and covered myself with a cotton-padded quilt, pressing my numb, slowly melting right hand between my legs. The hand reluctantly returned to life. I didn't notice how I fell asleep, and woke up only when the doctors came to work later in the morning.

Later, Ahror came. Someone came to tell me to meet him at the door; our building was closed to the general public. He hugged me, pressing his whole body against me as my boys often did, but strangely, it was as if I were hugging a rock. I was frigid myself, too, like an iced fish. Ahror started crying. Still, his tears did not melt the stone that had rooted itself in my stomach. I withdrew and stood there with my arms hanging at my sides like a guilty schoolgirl in front of a teacher. I had nothing to say to him.

"Thank you, Vera," Ahror whispered. He peered into my face and drew back abruptly; then, turning on his heels, he walked towards his truck. I turned, too, and went to my boys.

That night I told my mom that I would like to take the exams to study at the medical college in Dushanbe.[21] She had been trying to convince me to do this for a long time.

two

. 1 .

FROM 1969 UNTIL '92—for twenty-three years, I lived in Dushanbe. The city was created overnight, on Stalin's order, out of a mountain village, and development continued the entire time I lived there. Trucks, cranes and construction crews were raising apartment blocks in the center and in the suburbs; they even went back and installed elevators in some buildings engineered in the seventies. Asphalt and concrete advanced against blooming trees and flowers along Lenin Boulevard; the sun heated the building bricks to the cracking point, and the watering trucks that crawled the streets did little to alleviate the heat—everything here was different from little Panjakent. In winter, when the weather was bad, the wind gathered speed on the boulevard and swept through the yards of the apartment buildings. Furious and bone-chilling, it ripped laundry hung out on balconies to dry, bit into people's faces, and rattled window-frames. Little Pavlik, my second child, was so afraid of the wind's howling noise that I invented its agent: Old Man Wind-Blower, a single mention of whom was enough to send the boy to bed with no further discussion. Valerka, my older boy, was never scared of anything, but even he respected Old Man Wind-Blower and would retreat to his perch on the top bunk, in the bed their father had built for them, and promptly fall asleep hugging a boat or a plane he'd been making (he'd turned into a mechanic before he even entered kindergarten). I read them fairytales that I checked out from the hospital's library; Pavlik always listened attentively, but Valerka only pretended to be interested. From birth, the boys were very different.

We don't have such winds in Moscow, or such exhausting heat, but the air here is hopelessly poisoned with exhaust. When my Grandma Lisichanskaya starts to gasp for breath, I use an oxygen bag to help her.

The oxygen clears her airways, and then her cheeks flush with color, the muscles of her face relax, her hands, clenched into tiny fists, unfold, and I massage her fingers and palms for a long time—she really enjoys this. I came up with the massaging trick when I baby sat little Sashenka, the late daughter of Uncle Styopa, Mom's younger brother, and his wife Aunt Katya. Sashenka was born anemic, so I tried to improve her circulation, to warm her cold hands; massage made the bluish tinge recede from her lips and sped her pulse. The girl became so accustomed to this half-play, half-therapy that she wouldn't fall asleep until I "warmed her hands."

I got into college easily. They had some sort of quota for students from Panjakent, and all that we—me and my neighbor Ninka Surkova, the one I used to raid orchards with—had to do was turn in our applications.

They gave us a room in the dorms on the other end of the city, Second Soviet District. That neighborhood had a rough reputation, and Uncle Styopa, who served in the Border Guard Command, said with military authority:

"You will live with us. Our building is respectable; it belongs to the local government, and is not far from the college. And you could help with Sashenka."

I obeyed, especially since Mom fully approved of her brother's decision, and thus I became my cousin's baby sitter. I brought the girl home from daycare, fed her dinner, bathed her and put her to bed. Uncle Styopa often had to travel for his job; Aunt Katya worked as a secretary for the Republican Central Party Committee and it was not unusual for her to be delayed till midnight and driven home in a shiny black "Volga" with a miniature leaping deer on its hood.

Their home was always well stocked with delicacies: Aunt Katya received special rations. It was there that I had my first taste of "Truffles" chocolates, candied roasted almonds, cold-smoked hard sausage and many other things that I hadn't even known existed. From his trips to the border posts, Uncle Styopa brought back wild goat; he enjoyed hunting, and a special rifle with long-range optics was displayed against a Bukhara rug on the wall above their bed. The rifle was a present from a general.

My studies went well; I was good at physics, chemistry and other sciences. I always let Ninka Surkova copy my work. In a big city, she let loose, fell in with a group of older guys, and didn't really connect with anyone at the college—she had little time left for studying. At first, we were always together, and our classmates decided that I was the same kind of girl as Ninka. In fact, I feared meeting boys: I was afraid that they would find out my secret, and so I pretended to be an independent, mature person. To be quite honest, I was bored with them anyway, just as I had been in school back home, and they quickly dropped their attempts to flirt with me. I was polite and distant with everyone; I had convinced myself that I would never love anyone. It was too embarrassing to admit that the reason I had to rush home after classes was because I was earning my keep as a baby sitter, so I intentionally cultivated the mystery that surrounded me. Soon the college rumor mill concluded that I was living with a much older man, which was why I never came to the club to dance and never spent a night in the dorms. Some girls seemed to envy me, but when they asked me questions, I only shrugged my shoulders. Again, I was alone, hiding in my cocoon of secrets and fearing the same old thing—that my biggest secret would be revealed and I'd be ridiculed. It was stupid, of course; I had cornered myself.

I only saw Ninka in class. She was the one with a truly secretive life that she did not see fit to disclose even to me. When I asked her where she spent her evenings, she cut me off:

"Would you like to come to the Café Seagull with me? Oh, but you can't—you have to watch Sashenka, slaving for your kin."

She wasn't making fun of me; she mostly felt pity. She never told me what exactly went on in that café, and if I asked her, she'd just say, "It's great!" At this, her eyes lit up with a special light, and her face became cunning and coy—she was proud to belong to a circle of grown-ups. Her Mamikon, or Mamik, picked her up at the college a few times, riding his trophy German motorcycle. It was rumored that Mamik had done time and that, besides brass knuckles, he carried a small Belgian-made Browning in his pocket.

I heard this from Veronika Svetlova. One day, the three of us left the college building together. Mamik was already there, waiting for Ninka: he straddled his bike smoking a crude cigarette and inspecting the brightly polished pointy toe of his orange boot. When he saw us out of the corner of his eye, he kicked the starter with his heel; the bike's engine roared and blue smoke exploded out of the tailpipe.

"Let's go for a ride, beauty," he pointed to the seat in the sidecar.

"Some other time."

Ninka climbed onto the high seat over the rear wheel, behind Mamik.

"Then you, go ahead, jump into the sack," he leered at Veronika.

"Thank you, but I have to go home."

Mamik immediately lost interest in us, shifted into gear, and rolled away, downtown, to the Café Rendezvous or Seagull, where their circle met.

That's when Veronika whispered to me conspiratorially:

"They say he always carries brass knuckles and a small Belgian Browning in his pocket. Is that true?"

"I wouldn't know."

"Oh, come on!"

"No really, I don't know. I haven't even met the guy."

Veronika gave me a long look, but I don't think she believed me. She looked like she wanted to ask me something else, but hesitated. Soon we parted; Veronika caught her bus, and I walked home: my uncle's apartment building was only two blocks from the college.

I "lived with a man" my entire first year in college. I lived in a large apartment building designed specifically for party officials, downtown, next to the shopping center; I warmed Sashenka's hands before bed, ate chocolates, went to classes, and didn't have a care in the world. Sometimes I would get a letter from Mom and write back saying hello to Aunt Gulsuhor and Uncle Davron, but mostly for politeness's sake—Panjakent was growing more and more distant in my mind. I knew I would never go back.

. 2 .

LIFE MOVES IN WAVES. I realized this a long time ago and have accepted the nature of this flow. If someone had invented a device that told you exactly when it was time to rush down the crest of a wave, living would no longer be interesting. Neither is it true that old people live adrift in a dead calm. My Grandma Lisichanskaya is a great example of this: her rhythms are as unpredictable as a heartbeat during a fibrillating arrhythmia. This morning she was chatty, gave me a double "morning-morning," even laughed when I rubbed her fingers and massaged her temples; her eyes were alive. I gave her a sponge bath, changed her clothes and bedding, and Grandma lay propped on a fluffed-up pillow bright as a new penny. She ate, smacked her lips, and later, after I came back from the pharmacy, listened with obvious pleasure to a chapter from *Smoke Bellew* about the stampede to Squaw Creek.[1]

During the night, Grandma died. I was ironing in the other room, but heard her wheezing, unplugged the iron, rushed to her—and made it. Moist, marble-like skin, cold sweat, feet like icicles. The tell-tale sign: press on the base of a fingernail and the white spot stayed there. Blood pressure sixty over thirty. Pulse that refused to be regular and then disappeared altogether. I pumped her chest, fearing that I would lose her. I didn't. I managed to restart her heart and then mixed a quick IV: dextran and dopamine with glucose. Oxygen mask. Then I lay next to her for half of the night, keeping her warm with my entire body as best I could. Together we surfaced from the depths that are terrible to remember, and it began—the slow, quiet ascent to the crest of a new wave.

I kept repeating my laywoman's prayer; God must have heard it, and didn't let Grandma go. I was the Robinson Crusoe on our island of pain and despair, and she was my Friday, the speechless savage whose mute presence rescued me from loneliness. Later, when she fell asleep, I sat in the armchair, stupefied, drained of all emotion, and leafed through Jack London without putting words into sentences. I remembered how I read "The Stampede to Squaw Creek"[2] by Sashenka's bedside: the room we shared also had a cozy armchair and a table lamp under whose warm orange light I stayed up until midnight, swallowing book after book from Uncle Styopa's library. Their books, like the food, were purchased by Aunt Katya in the special, internal Central Party store.

Sashenka and I became close friends, and that closeness irritated Aunt Katya. I once overheard her complaining to her husband that I was the only person their daughter listened to, to which he sensibly responded:

"Spend more time with the girl; no one's keeping you from her."

Such answers only made it worse for her. I don't mean to say that Aunt Katya became my mean stepmother; she was a reserved, almost terse woman, with military-like discipline and good in her way, but she, too, got frustrated. I could feel this, and tried to stay out of her sight as much as I could.

Our life went on like this for a year—a well-measured, clockwork life from dawn to lights out. Only the night hours in the armchair with a book were my own, like the personal time that the army mandates for every soldier. The little doors opened on the cuckoo clock, the cuckoo slid out on its perch, cuckooed, bowed comically, raised her tail and slid back in to come out again in an hour and cuckoo twice, then thrice, and sometimes I would hear four cuckoos before I went to bed.

At school we were getting ready for finals. May was drawing nearer, and in summer they promised to add us to the construction crew of the Medical Institute students, where I was hoping to make some money. I dreamt of buying something for myself; everything I wore came from Aunt Katya's wardrobe.

Spring in Tajikistan is the most beautiful season, and even in Dushanbe you can sense the aroma of distant blooming orchards. Flowers burst into bright colors everywhere, the grass is green and the river runs full and swift. People smile, children squeal with delight, and even fat bureaucrats in boxy suits with their mandatory briefcases eat ice cream and flirt with women, more in keeping with the general joyful excitement than out of their eternal lust.

That April, Ninka Surkova went completely off the rails. She began to miss classes and then stopped coming to college altogether. The dorm crowd said she was rarely seen there, too. The student president of our class demanded that I find out what was happening: my friend was about to be expelled.

I went to the dorms twice and waited for Ninka, but she never came. Just when I lost all hope of finding her, I ran into her on the boulevard, purely by accident. She was alone, shambling somewhere, badly in need of a bath and a comb, not drunk, but somehow detached—I'd never seen her like this before. I called her name. She turned and looked as if through me, but she recognized me. The skin of her face was deathly gray, as if spring had not come for her.

"Verka!"

"Where have you been?"

She waved me off and cursed. I took her by the arm and led her home, gave her a bath and a meal, and put her up in my bed. I told Aunt Katya that my friend was in a difficult situation, and we had to spend a night together. Strange as it seemed, Aunt Katya let her stay, only saying,

"One night—and that's it."

That Ninka was in trouble was obvious, but she didn't say anything and instead just ate ravenously, like a hungry dog, until beads of sweat came out on her forehead as if she'd stepped into a heated bathhouse. Late that night, when everyone was long asleep, and I—no longer expecting her to talk—was nodding off too, Ninka suddenly shook me awake and began to speak. We sat facing each other on my bed, and she kept talking. From high in the sky, a tiny, oily moon shone down on us, vacant like a junkie's eye.

Mamik, with whom she had fallen in love, wagered her in a card game and lost. Ninka was gang-banged after they pumped her full of *kuknar*, a brew of poppy stems. Men's chins, rough as cheese graters, had scraped up her back. Their bloated flesh thrust blindly, tore, tormented and bludgeoned her angrily and carelessly. She was tossed about like a wet mattress, without a break, turned over and had again: tight muscles pressed against her cold, balled-up stomach, hair as stiff as chain mail rubbed her breasts raw, teeth tore at her flesh, and fat, bull lips slobbered into her ears and neck, drooled and then licked up the spit with rough tongues, like animals sucking up the last crystals of a salt block. The muck, once it closed over her, had no end. The rocking made her seasick, her mangled ribs hurt, and they kept turning and tossing her around, until someone stern and quick, coarsely barking profanity-laced orders, spilled his manly bliss onto her face and her numb lips caught this humiliating rain. Then they poured another cup of *kuknar* down her throat, and left her to sleep on a cot, barely covered, and when she woke up everything happened again. The studs partied all night—they were full of strength, of the well-fed, dumb, restless men's strength that overpowered every cell of her body, plowed over her soul, and raked her memory to tear out, like weeds, everything that was living and warm. They filled her with *kuknar* again and again, and the pain receded, replaced with a warm stupor, as if her body was filled with wax. Then the wax cooled and set into a crust that was now impossible to break, or tear off, or wash off, ever.

She told me all this in a dead voice. I had never seen a face like hers: she looked as if she was walking along an endless railroad track, eyes down, counting the ties like the rungs of a ladder to nowhere. Her hand was cold, and I could not warm it. Ninka did not seem to be looking for sympathy anyhow.

"You know how it is," she said.

"I do."

"Then why do you put on these virgin airs? I don't care anymore. I lie and I don't feel anything. They always want it; we can't refuse them."

At first I was frightened, and I had to will myself to speak, but soon my fear disappeared, and we took turns confessing, first I and then she, except she wasn't listening to me, and later I realized I wasn't listening to her either.

"The girls say it can be different, but I don't feel anything, I don't care, I don't have any pity for myself," she kept repeating like a broken record, and I couldn't tell her anything different. I didn't have the right words. She needed to be chastised and whipped out of her stupor, and instead I pitied her.

The cold that took her over, like a shard of the Snow Queen's ice,[3] was lodged deep inside, and I was not able to melt it. She did not reach out to me; she was already dead, and I think she knew it.

In the morning, ashamed of her tale, Ninka grew restless. It was obvious she couldn't bear to stay. Somehow, she managed to drink some tea but refused the sandwiches; a complete opposite of the girl who had wolfed down food only a day before. I did not understand this, and thought she was ashamed. I suggested that we wait for Uncle Styopa who could protect her from the gang, but Ninka jumped up from the table and said goodbye. She couldn't wait to leave.

"Let's go to class."

"Don't waste your time on me. I need to go back there."

I still had hope, I thought she'd come to her senses, like she did that night. I opened up to her without reservation, scraped up everything that I had turned over in my mind so many times, but she hadn't heard me. And she left.

I felt scared and cold, and wanted to lie down, curl up, see no one, and hear nothing. I hugged Sashenka tight against my chest, and she laughed, thinking that I would tickle her as always, but then she fell silent, put her arms around my neck and burst out crying, desperately, as only children can.

Trying to comfort her, I felt more at peace myself. I took her to daycare and went to college. I spent the day in a fog—the sleepless night caught up with me. I skipped my nursing care class; I knew where I had to go. I set out for the Seagull, determined to speak to Mamikon.

· 3 ·

THERE WEREN'T MANY PEOPLE in the café. A group of Russians, sent here to work in construction, was having a good time in the corner. I did not see Ninka or her friends anywhere, but Mamikon's motorcycle stood by the door like a horse at a hitching post. I took a deep breath, for courage, and asked the waiter for Ninka Surkova.

"From the medical college?" he gave me a curious look. "Wait here."

He left through a door at the back, but soon returned and waved me in.

"Come in, they are waiting for you."

I went through the door. A young man, a kid really, bumped into me in the darkness.

"Hello, sweetie! Mamikon said to welcome you with open arms," he leered, undressing me with his eyes, but he did not touch me, and walked ahead. We passed through a sort of pantry and then along a dark corridor, at the end of which he opened an inconspicuous low door.

"Welcome to our humble abode!"

I stepped inside. Sheepskins with pillows were strewn on the floor, between low tables. The lair was packed; card games were underway. Everywhere there were bottles, plates with solidified *plov* leftovers, gnawed-on *shashlyks*, and wilted greens. A person in a padded coat slept, nose-down in a sheepskin.

Mamikon was sitting opposite the door; Ninka lay spread out beside him, in the arms of some tattooed character. Two other girls looked no different: they were dirty, sleepy and limp.

"Since you came all the way here, take a seat," Mamikon said authoritatively. "Eat with us. Or do you have something to say?"

The whole pack, cards hidden in their fists, watched me.

"I want to speak to you alone."

"Get out of here, bitch! Where'd you come from, I told you, forget it!" Ninka screamed suddenly.

The guy who was holding her slapped Ninka across the face. She fell prostrate and lay still.

"Quiet! The girl came to talk," Mamikon raised himself from his pillow and, leaning forward, stood on all fours, like a baboon.

"You in?" he winked at the guy who showed me in, and he bolted the door with a heavy stick.

I was trapped.

"Let Nina go, or I'll go to the police."

I said that very firmly, surprising myself with my strength.

"Will she go, though?" Mamikon stood up, leaning sideways, and stepped towards me. The pack roared with laughter, but he raised his hand. Instantly, it was quiet. Everyone was looking at us with keen interest; only the sleeping man had not stirred.

"Why would you want to take her away? She's fine here. Sit down with us, we don't hurt pretty girls."

I could feel his breath on my skin; he was looking me straight in the eye, and all I saw were his menacing oily irises. I recognized the drug-narrowed pupils and became scared. For some reason, I thought that he would pull out his Browning and prayed that he would have the focus to kill me with a single bullet.

"Hang on, brothers!"

I turned my head and recognized him at once: Nar, who had grown up a lot in the past year.

"Vera, sister, so good to see you!"

He sauntered up, calmly, pushed away someone's arm that was already reaching for me, and gave me a peck on the cheek.

"What a reunion, brothers. Swear by my fate, I didn't expect it."

He put himself between me and Mamikon. Mamikon waited.

Quickly, Nar pulled a knife out of his pocket and opened the blade with a click. He raised the tip to his eye-level and then, with flair, as if showing off to the other kids in our yard, flipped it so that it stuck straight in the mud floor at his feet. Nar bent down and dragged the tip of the knife around me; now I was in the middle of a circle. Done with the ritual, he pressed the blade back in, and pocketed his knife.

"Blood oath, I'll not let you touch my sister. Mind you," he said to me, "my friends are honorable people, they won't tread on blood here. True ain't it, bros?"

"She's your sister?" Mamikon asked. Everyone waited with bated breath.

"Named sister, Mamik-jan. I drew the circle, and no man shall cross it. We good?"

"Good!" agreed Mamikon.

The gang let out a collective sigh and burst out chatting. The kid that had bolted the door brought me a cup of tea. I declined politely. Nar, pretending at joy overflowing, whistled:

"*Hop-maili*, brothers, haven't seen sister for a year, gotta have ice-cream!"

The Ninka issue exhausted itself. Surkova was back in the tattooed character's embrace, and avoided meeting my eye. Mamik came up to me, kissed my hand, and apologized gallantly.

"We don't mess with blood. Beg pardon, sister."

I squeezed out a semblance of a smile.

Nar nodded to the kid; he opened the door. We went out into the street.

"Vera, really, I'm so happy to see you!"

We hugged again. Nar was big and warm; his almond-shaped eyes shone.

"Please, I have to make sure you don't come here anymore. Mamik and I do business, he won't harm you, but his people are rotten. Forget about your Ninka, she's on the needle, she won't leave; they've strung her like a shoe-lace."

"Nar?"

"I know what I'm talking about, trust me. Asya talked about you often, she loves you."

He walked me home. He had gone to Petersburg with Asya and entered culinary school there, but got depressed.

"Wicked city, it's cold and the people are all harried, run around all day long. So I left. I just do this and that, make things happen."

I offered to take him home, told him that Uncle Styopa could get him a job, but Nar refused.

"It's my fate, Vera."

We hugged at the door, neither one of us suspecting what our next meeting would be like.

Uncle and Aunt were waiting for me. Instantly, I sensed a storm. A golden brooch (a wedding gift) and forty-five rubles that had been on a dressing table by the mirror were missing. Now it became clear why Ninka was so nervous in the morning.

It was my fault, since I was the one who brought her home. Aunt Katya tarred and feathered me, and went through a thorough list of all my sins—there were more than I had ever imagined. Sashenka rushed to my defense, wailing, but was spanked away and locked up in her room.

I cut Aunt's tirade short.

"I will earn the money and give it back. Thank you for the food and board. I am leaving."

It didn't take me long to pack my things. I moved out despite Uncle Styopa's appeals; he did not want me to leave. I left all the gifted clothes behind, too proud to take them.

So it was that I went to live in the dorms, practically naked and without any means of supporting myself. But it took me only a few days to get a job as a night nurse's assistant in Dushanbe Central Hospital. Never again was I to enjoy the kind of carefree and cozy existence as I had with Uncle Styopa, except maybe in recent years nursing Grandma Lisichanskaya. This is a quiet, steady situation; Mark Grigoriyevich pays me well, and I can afford whatever I want. But life taught me to save. On the other hand, how much had I saved? When Valera and his Zulia visited last month, I gave them twenty-five hundred dollars to buy a car. They need one and I don't, I'm used to getting around on foot.

· 4 ·

BETWEEN MY JOB and my classes I did not have time to hang out with other students my age. There was only one guy I saw every day: Viktor Bzhania, who worked part-time, like me, in the same hospital. I got hired in the second internal diseases unit, and he went to work in the morgue, where the pay was better, which was important for him since his family couldn't support him. Vitya spent a lot of time reading specialized literature (he would graduate with high distinction) and was torn between his dreams of becoming a pathologist or a surgeon. A pathologist is privy to the mysteries of death, it's a purely scientific path; on the other hand, a surgeon is a practitioner who saves lives. Somehow, working in the morgue must have helped Viktor make his choice, and he became a cardiac surgeon; he works in the Bakulev Institute in Moscow now and has defended his doctoral dissertation.

We'd set off for the hospital as soon as our classes were over; our true motivation was to get there in time for the dinner served to staff in the hospital cafeteria. I spent very little time in the dorms, eating and sleeping at work—the senior nurse, when she learned about my circumstances, offered to put me up there. On our walks from the college, Viktor would make me laugh with stories from his department; traditionally, most assistants at the morgue were complete winos. I was not afraid of corpses: after I witnessed Mukhibá's passing, I knew that the dead are far less frightening than the living.

The discipline and hierarchy at work were strict: the senior and managing nurses were like the apostles to the Almighty Unit Chief. I was treated well: everyone knew that I was a student. Gradually, they began to trust me with the simplest tasks: preparing catheters, administering enemas and shaving patients before surgeries, distributing thermometers—I volunteered for everything, I was curious about it all. At first, the nurses sheltered me, and didn't want me to work with terminal patients, but once they learned that I was friends with a guy in the morgue, they began to give me the dirty work. I attended to hopeless patients, and some people were terrified—why would a young girl want to mess with the dying?—but others, like Chief Doctor Marat Ishakovich Karimov, made me feel special. I did whatever work I had to do and spent my free time on my studies and my comatic patients, but I didn't tell anyone about my gift. Often, I sat at their bedsides until after midnight; I don't remember when I slept, I never did learn to sleep more than six hours a day, and I don't seem to need it. I must admit, I rarely made real contact with those patients; most of the time, I just sat beside them, held and stroked their hands, and often that was enough to relieve the hospital despair. I had no favorites; they were all equally important to me. The pockets of my white coat were always filled with candy, treats, cookies, or apples: the patients gave me small presents whenever they could, and I put everything on our table in the nurses' lounge at tea time. That's probably why Marat Ishakovich nicknamed me Candy, and that's what everyone began to call me.

In July and August I arranged for a leave from the hospital, to join the coveted construction crew, eventually going to work at a community center in the mountain village of Djuma-Bazar. I earned good money there. I got the kitchen job and learned to cook. Once the project was over, I went to Panjakent with five hundred rubles in my pocket and ran straight home from the bus station to surprise my mom.

I opened the door with my key and went in; heavy, stuffy air hit me like a brick wall. Mom was lying on the couch; an unfinished bottle of Chashma stood at her feet. Before, she couldn't tolerate even the smell of alcohol, and now she was sick. Doctor Davron said she sometimes even came to work drunk.

Mom had changed: she was tearful, nervous, often hysterical. She screamed that everyone had abandoned her and called herself "cursed by God." I nursed her, begged her to get treatment, asked her to come live with me in Dushanbe, where I could easily find her a job, but she refused.

One night I came into her room and lay next to her. Mom was sleeping on her back, with her head tossed back and her mouth open: she was struggling for air, gulping spasmodically with her dry lips and snorting through her larynx. I pressed my body against hers, put a hand on her forehead, and started gently massaging her temples. Intoxication had put her into a stupor, like anesthesia; her muscles contracted reflexively; she must have been having a nightmare, because her face looked like a marble mask carved into a disgusting grimace. I could not sense anything, couldn't reach her through the walls of the alcohol-induced fog. She was in a different dimension. My helplessness filled me with cold terror. I got up, shuffled back to my own bed and tucked myself in like Mom used to do when I was little. A weary silence filled the apartment; I left the door to Mom's room ajar, and yet I couldn't even hear her breathing. Helplessness bore resentment, and my resentment turned into anger. All night I tried to convince myself that my mother was ill and needed medical attention, and was scared because I hadn't been able to pull her out of her pit.

Inside me, something important snapped. I, who was not afraid of dead bodies, felt repulsed by my own mother. She would go to work and come back intoxicated; eyes to the floor, she'd slip into her room and later, after she'd drunk some more, she'd come back out and begin declaring something incoherent to me. She thumped her chest, confessed, cursed her fate, cursed people, and asked me to forgive her for not watching me better, not preserving my "purity."

The hint was enough to make blood run cold in my veins, turn me into stone, make me deaf and unresponsive. I had nowhere to go from home: I didn't want to visit the dig, and when I stopped at the hospital to see my boys, they didn't recognize me, having forgotten me in the year that I had been gone. Dimulka gave me a suspicious sideways look and didn't run into my open arms. Their old teacher had been replaced with another, even sterner and colder woman; whether I had changed somehow, or whether the boys were completely repressed, I couldn't tell, but I felt like an unwelcome stranger.

I don't know how I managed to stay on there for a week. Then I gave up. I fled. I cursed my weakness, but I could not live with my Mom any longer. Apparently I could find a way to connect with the most desperate patients, but when it really mattered, I didn't have what it took.

I rode the night bus to Dushanbe, feeling as cold as the insides of our fridge, which I had filled with food. Then I left a note on the table, kissed my sleeping mother, and left. Most of the passengers were asleep; the headlights cut through the darkness and the tiny lights of the villages that clung to the highway passed by outside the windows. Then the mountains began, and the howling of the engine on the serpentine road echoed in my soul. I sat still, my teeth clenched, hands gripping the armrests, and watched the sunrise.

· 5 ·

IT TOOK ME a long time to realize that Vitya Bzhania was in love with me. I ran to see him whenever I had a spare minute, and in his free time he came upstairs to our unit. We did homework together; we traded books. Vitya borrowed books from the Central City Library. I liked adventure stories and so did he. *The Headless Horseman*, *The Heir from Calcutta*,[4] *Captain Daredevil*, *Moonstone*—these favorites were always in high demand, but Vitya made friends with the librarian, and thanks to him I enjoyed many beautiful books. Sometimes, I would close an unfinished volume and imagine the rest of the story, out loud, to Vitya. He listened, never interrupting, and looked at me as if he was afraid to miss even a single word I said; I liked that. Later, he told me that's when he fell in love with me, but at the time I thought of him only as a close friend. I seriously convinced myself that I would not be able—would not have the right to—love anyone.

Gennady Bystrov was brought to our hospital when we were finishing our second year in college. A junior sergeant on the police force, he had miraculously survived a shoot-out: his lungs and abdominal cavity had penetrating wounds, there were slash wounds on his chest and back, and his knee was shattered by buckshot. His night patrol had stopped a truck coming down from the mountains; it was smuggling a load of poppy straw, and the load was too big for them to give up without a fight. Gennady was immediately shot in the knee, and then the smugglers set to finishing him off with knives. But they didn't get the job done. Of the three policemen in his patrol, he was the only one to survive. A border patrol that happened to be returning to its barracks by the same route joined in the fight and eventually detained the traffickers. One of the four smugglers arrested was Nar.

I learned the details from Gena's friends, who visited him regularly. The sergeant lay unconscious, strung up in an apparatus after an eight-hour surgery; Marat Ishakovich pulled him back from the other world.

"He'll live, but do keep an eye on him," he said to me.

I kept an eye. Gennady was very weak, and I checked on him every fifteen minutes. It was convenient, too—I also cleaned, part-time, in the ICU unit. For the first four days he hardly said anything, only kept asking for something to drink. I soaked gauze in tea and let him suck on it; he was not allowed to drink much. The nurses, seeing that I doted on him, did not pay as much attention as they otherwise might have done. The wounds on his back became infected from lack of movement, and then he got bedsores.

At night, I sat by his side, held his hand, and felt the force that his body was using to fight, to heal, even though he was as helpless as a baby. I don't think I was helping him much; I mean I would have given all my power to him, but he managed the pain and the weakness on his own, and this was new for me. He would open his eyes, as if he had not been asleep just a moment before, whisper, "Candy," and I would give him the tea-soaked gauze, and he would smile. He smiled, said nice things to me, and always joked with me. When I washed his body with a sponge, I only had the bath on my mind until Anya Steblova, one of our nurses, noticing the size of his member, said, laughing, "Look at that stud!" and I suddenly felt my cheeks burn. Anya was the first one to tease me.

"You must've fallen in love; you don't leave your Bystrov for a minute. Better go wash the floors in the hallway."

I washed and thought, "She is so full of it, and I am just feeling sorry for him, the way I would for any other patient." And then I caught myself thinking that I thought of him all the time.

When Gennady began getting better, we talked often and at length. He had a single fear: that he would be left with a limp, would be decommissioned, and would no longer be able to catch bandits. I reassured him that everything would be all right, and he believed me. It was funny: he was like a kid, so grateful for the sympathy.

"Hello, Candy!" he would shout as soon as I entered his room. I felt at ease with him; he was strong. When he learned that Nar had rescued me from the bandits' den, he said: "Don't fool yourself; he wouldn't have let any other girl go. They are all like animals; drugs destroy your brain once and for all."

Gennady also insisted that I go to court and then report back to him in detail.

Nar sat calmly on the accused bench, gave monosyllabic answers to every question and curved his lips in disdain. I tried to catch his eye, but he pretended that he didn't know me; he just glanced around the room once, then turned away and did not look back at anyone.

The ringleader got the death sentence—he was the one who had gone berserk and finished off the policemen. For Nar, the prosecutor requested a fifteen-year sentence; the judge gave him twelve. The convoy took Nar away through a special door. I did not run after him—out into the street where the van would be waiting for him. This was not a named brother, my rescuer, but a cold-blooded criminal.

When he heard my report, Gennady praised me: "You got it all right, Candy. You are alright, through and through."

I suddenly felt an urge to cry, jumped up from the chair and ran out of the room.

At night, I thought about my sergeant. He was a hero, just like Maurice Gerald from *The Headless Horseman,* fearless and honest. Vitya Bzhania, by the way, shared my opinion.

Bystrov was awarded a medal, but he laughed when I asked him if he was going to wear it.

"Why would I? It's just a button, a toy."

He wanted to have children, which nagged at me. He talked about the children he would have one day, pierced me with his hot eyes, smiled warmly, and… did not say anything else. At moments like these, he was suddenly tongue-tied.

Later, the doctors sent him to the rehabilitation sanatorium in Kislovodsk and after that to Moscow, to the Trauma Institute. Gennady had to have complex surgery on his knee.

"Ta-da, Candy! Thanks for everything. You going to wait for me?"

He pressed me against him and kissed me hard on the lips. My head spun.

"Yes."

I did not know I would give him such a simple answer.

He left, and I waited. For a whole year. He did not come back and did not write.

. 6 .

BUT, OUT OF THE BLUE, my Mom wrote. Apparently, thank God, things had straightened out there. *Akó* Ahror, who must have been put on earth for the sole purpose of saving our family, rescued her. One day he stopped by her place and had a long conversation with her. "It was as if he poured a tub of ice-cold water over me," she wrote. After their talk, Mom never touched wine again. Ahror had left the expedition and was working for the hospital, driving his truck around and "doting on it, as always." Mom also wrote that Ahror had married a young woman and they were expecting a baby. He was especially curious about me, and Mom told him that I was studying to take entrance exams to the institute.

She asked me to forgive her, wanted me to come spend the summer with her, and, most importantly, informed me that she had met and was now living with a wonderful man, Viktor Petrovich, a doctor's assistant who had one year left before he could retire from his job at the clinical hospital. He owned a small house with a garden, and Mom was planning to move there with him.

Everything had fallen into place, but for some reason, the news did not make me happy. I remembered this Petrovich—he was a nasty little man, a pedantic bore, and I could not imagine my Mom finding happiness with him. And yet she did, and she lived with the old crone for eleven years, part-wife and part-nurse: with age, Petrovich succumbed to ferocious asthma and she nursed him like a baby. By the time my kids were old enough to visit, she did not invite us for the summer—she could not manage two boys and a sick man.

Foolishly, I was offended. Our lives simply went their different ways and I had no desire to go back to Panjakent. The news of Ahror's new marriage did not seem to affect me in any way; I do remember dreaming of him for a while after getting the letter, but soon I did not think of him at all. On the other hand, I never dreamt of Gennady. Rather, he would appear in my mind's eye, as if he were right there and had only stepped away for a minute. I waited for news from him, but there was nothing. His mother lived in Tver oblast, in Vyshny Volochok—perhaps he had gone there? He had stayed in Dushanbe after he served there in the army.

My year—the last academic year in college—dragged on. Viktor was set to graduate with a gold medal; my grades were a bit worse, but still above average. Viktor finally decided to become a cardiac surgeon. Trying to get into an institute in Tajikistan was out of the question: money was the key, and we had none. Marat Ishakovich advised me to go to Kalinin, where the medical school had a good reputation and where I could try to get in without a bribe. Viktor aimed for Moscow and only Moscow and wanted me to come along.

"We'll get in, I swear—you know this stuff as well as I do."

We studied together every night. On the weekends, Marat Ishakovich drilled us in Chemistry, and his wife, Olga Romanovna, an academic director at a high school, critiqued our essays. I dreamed of becoming a physician. Now, letting that chance slip is my only regret, if I even have any.

In May, on the eve of graduation, Gennady appeared in the doorway of the doctors' lounge. In civilian clothes, with a light wooden cane. A new, serious man, one I had not seen before.

"Candy!" he opened his arms, and the next instant I was at his chest, hugging him back.

"Let's go, I have to tell you everything!"

I left my shift, and we went to the orchard. Gennady was visibly limping—the Moscow surgery did not help, and to this day he cannot completely flex his leg.

From the orchard we went to our dorms. Gennady bought champagne and chocolates. I was not walking—I had wings. His troubles seemed trifling to me now. The main thing is that I told him everything, I gave him my horror in exchange for his little fears. Gennady then held me tight against him:

"You silly girl, you're not denied anything. You need to be loved, loved forever! Let's go somewhere—I've been dreaming of you for a year."

The fool did not write because he was afraid I would not have a cripple. And before he left—he did not say anything because he did not want to upset me!

My fear and doubts vanished in an instant. My mind, which had tormented me all my life, went mute. His strength, his awkward tenderness, robbed me of all reason. There was that moment when I felt his hand closing over my mouth, kindly but persistently: I was moaning and screaming, and the dorm walls were thin as cardboard. Afterwards we lay there for a long time, mute, on a wet sheet; I pressed against his back, strong and supple, like a stallion's croup, smelling sharp and sweet of sweat. My palm sheltered his shame; the way a mother guards her sleeping babe. The empty space around us crackled with the electricity released by our bodies: tiny grains in the drywall sparkled green and blue and the moon that peeked in the window was flushed, coy and generous, like the face of the old Tajik I bought milk from when I was little. When the bottle came out of his fridge, its neck was beaded with sweat, like Gennady's shoulders. I wanted to pick up the beads with my tongue, but had no strength left to reach them; I could not even fall asleep.

My dream of becoming a doctor instantly evaporated. In the morning, we applied for a marriage license.

The next day, they brought to the hospital a badly burned young construction worker. The pain would not release him. Even drugged with dimedrol and promedol, he screamed and woke, his eyes filled with horror, his forehead bathed in cold sweat. I sat by his side several times and held his hand, but could not catch the signal; I was thinking of other things.

· 7 ·

THE SHOT THAT smashed Gennady's knee cut short his career: he had dreamt of big cases and big stars on his shoulder straps, of studying at the Academy, but it was not to be. He was offered a job in the police archives, but he could not stand the boredom. He fought with his bosses, was fired, and left. No job, no place to live. I was pregnant. One could get an apartment by working in construction, but what good is a cripple for mixing concrete and laying brick? The meat-packing plant was also building its own apartment block, and Gennady, without a second thought, went and got a job on the floor there.

He came home and announced proudly, "I got a job at the meat-packing plant; comes with an apartment."

"Can you handle the work?"

"Piece of cake. They pay for output, up to three hundred. We'll be fine, Candy!"

We were put on the waiting list, and a year and a half later we moved into a two-room apartment—Gennady earned it.

A floor man killed up to two hundred head of cattle every shift. I was the one who got him ready for work, who washed his uniform, exorcised the smell of death that had seeped through his underwear, ironed his overalls, pressed sharp creases in his trousers, all the time straining to think of him and not of the terrible things he told me, bragging, with a smirk. In his hospital bed he could not brag and strut—there he fought for his life and won. Now he was fighting against himself. Sometimes his eyes would grow dull and distant, like the eyes of an old horse waiting to be sent to slaughter. Often, after dinner, he would sit staring into space, and not respond to anything I said.

I tried to convince him to quit, but every time he would cut me off with, "No! Am I worse than others?"

"You are better than they are; that's why you have to quit."

"Shut up!"

He would raise his voice. He would turn and go to the other room. After these skirmishes, he would not respond to my touch at night. Gennady was as stubborn as a Panjakent donkey.

When I was in the eighth month of my pregnancy, I went on maternity leave and stayed at home, waiting every day for Gennady to return from his shift. I would sit at the window, not wanting to miss him. As soon as I saw him limping across the yard from the bus stop, my head would start spinning. I would rush to the door, and he would come in: first stepping over the threshold on his good leg and then heaving in the bad one. He would say a tired hello and go to the bathroom to wash his hands. I would hand him a clean towel—that was our ritual. When I snuggled against him at night, I could feel with the full breadth of my soul how quickly the invisible force that had raised him from the hospital bed was transforming: he was growing a protective shell, and I could not pierce it. He became capricious and demanding and delighted in finding fault in me. I took offense, but he did not apologize, and would only pat me on the shoulder in the morning, as if I were his cow or horse. That was supposed to be his "I'm sorry."

At the hospital, even though he had survived a furious battle, he never had nightmares, but at home Gennady often screamed in his sleep, bolted awake, and went to the kitchen, where he would sit smoking for a long time. He was ashamed of this weakness; if I followed him, he would turn on me, "What do you want? Go to sleep!"

"Gena, what happened?"

"I said, go to sleep!"

He would be glowering at me then, his whole being filled with some unknown, malicious force, as if he had to restrain himself from hitting me. I would return to bed and bawl into my pillow. He would return, too, a mute stranger, turn to the wall and go to sleep without a word.

He developed another unattractive trait: suddenly, everyone around him was a terrible person; everyone was against him, trying to short his wages or trip him up. This was impossible to deal with.

"You are making this up; you must trust people more."

"You idiot, what have you seen in your village!"

He called me worse, too. My Mom never cussed at me; even if she called me "Porky," it was lovingly, in jest.

The first time he came home drunk I was making eggplant ragout, which Gennady loved. He went straight to the bedroom, shook out of his clothes, tossing them into a heap on the floor, collapsed onto the bed and blacked out, snoring. I covered him with a blanket, put a glass of sweetened water with lemon juice on the night stand, and went back to the kitchen. I ate supper alone. Finally, I had to go to bed and had to figure out how to perch on the bed without touching him: I could not stand the smell of alcohol on his breath. The sheets were wet. Somehow, I shook him awake enough to pull him off the bed. As many times as I'd had to change bedding for hospital patients, I never seemed to mind the sharp smell of urine, but here, at home, I barely swallowed the urge to vomit. I carried the bedding to the bathroom and soaked it in a bucket, then dragged the mattress to the balcony and put down clean sheets. He watched my maneuvers silently, sprawled on the floor. He blinked and did not say anything.

"Go to sleep, you stupid drunk!"

He stood up, swaying from side to side—skinny, naked—put his hands behind his head and suddenly stuck out his fingers like horns, bent over, rested on his knees and crawled towards me. His drunken face came close to mine, mooed, snorted at me with rancid breath as his cheek slid against mine and he sank into a pillow, head first. Then he made a sound resembling a laugh, lifted his face from the pillow, moved his horned head back and forth miming a bull, and, still on his knees, crawled to the kitchen. I lay down quiet as a mouse; the blanket could not keep me warm. No sound came from the kitchen. Later, Gennady came back, cautiously slid into his spot next to the wall and instantly began snoring.

In the morning, he patted me on the shoulder and did not say anything. Sat down to his tea. Picked up the knife to slice sausage for a sandwich, but stared at the blade dumbly and then put the knife aside.

"Cut the sausage."

His hands were shaking violently.

"You should have a beer; tea won't do you much good."

"I said, cut the sausage!"

I made him a couple of sandwiches. He ate silently and went to get dressed. When he was already at the door, he said casually over his shoulder:

"We celebrated a record—two hundred and fifty bulls in one shift. Soon I'll be a model of communist labor."

It was after that night that he started drinking regularly.

. 8 .

HE WOULD COME HOME exhausted, eat without enjoying the food, down a glass of vodka in one gulp and collapse onto the bed or stare at the TV.

Once he learned the ropes at the plant, Gennady began "transporting": he would come home wearing an overcoat (in that heat!) concealing various cuts of meat wrapped around every inch of his body. His personal record was fifty pounds in one go! I was afraid that he would get caught, but he had his answer ready, "Everyone does it! I've had enough of catching thieves!"

He bought a Ural motorcycle with a sidecar, and was very proud of it. When Valerka was born, Gennady picked us up at the maternity ward with flowers, seated us in the sidecar and drove around the dorm three times. He solemnly carried Valerka into our room. For two months he did not touch wine, bathed and swaddled the baby, but then his interest to the new toy cooled, and everything returned to the way it had been before our son was born.

"It's important to me that you not worry about anything," he would declare meaningfully after his nightly drink. "You take care of the home, and I'll earn enough for you."

The money didn't bring me joy; he came home as if it were a boarding house, never went out with us, but led his own separate existence, even though at first he was the one who wanted to have children. I remembered that, he really did. The men in our yard respected him, and their company, their herd became the most important thing for him. The street cops he used to work with were paid little and often came to buy the stolen meat; in those days, a butcher was an important person. However, gradually they stopped coming. But he still had enough clients in our dorms, and later, when we moved, in our new apartment building. Gennady liked to boast about his earnings and always compared how much he brought home to what I made, but I knew that the pride was superficial; underneath, his suspiciousness grew painful, and he was convinced that people were staring at his stiff leg. It was impossible to persuade him otherwise.

I got my diploma and started working in my old unit as a nurse. He ordered us around at home and I obeyed as was proper. Our neighbors lived the same way. He rarely had sex with me anymore, and when he did, he was rough, as if punishing me for everything life had denied him. At first this scared and offended me, and I constantly dwelt on his coolness. The girls at the hospitals liked to talk about sex, and I listened, taking note of ways to arouse his interest, his tenderness, if not his love. It was in vain.

He did not act the bull any more, and I never reminded him of that night, but the sheets did have to be changed on a couple of other occasions. I even learned to do it mechanically, as I did at the hospital. Many women would take their husbands to task, but I never raised my voice at him. He took that for granted. Once, as I walked across the yard past the picnic table where the men were playing dominos and drinking, I heard Gennady say boastfully, "You gotta hold your bitch in your fist, man! As soon as you loosen your grip, she'll get you under her heel!"

The men agreed in unison. I walked along quietly; they did not notice me. At home I had the laundry waiting for me. I fed my son and put him to bed, and then took up the washing. Gennady was still not home. I do not know what came over me, but I washed and washed like a ferocious robot. I kept rubbing his heavy, dirty overalls over the washboard; soap foam and dirt splattered all over the floor. I could not stop; my fingers, softened by the hot water, gripped the thick canvas and would not let go. I fought the overalls, beat them, shredded them, tore at them and wrung them, twisted the legs and whipped the whole wad against the metal bathtub as if I could beat the living soul out of the dead fabric. Sweat, water and tears ran down my cheeks; the little space was hot as a steam room. In the end, I had no more strength; I threw the overalls into the tub with the dirty water and walked, swaying, to the kitchen where I leaned against the door jam. After the heat of the steam, I shook with chills, as if I had come in from the cold; my body had lost all feeling. The wrinkled, unnaturally white pads of my fingers were cold as ice. Somehow I made my way to bed, climbed under the blanket, curled into a ball and pressed my hands between my legs. Finally, I sensed the tiny needle-pricks in my fingers; they returned to life. I was so drained that I could not even turn to lie on my other side. Thank God, Valerka slept calmly through the night, and I did not have to get up to comfort him. My husband didn't come home that night; as I learned later, they got drunk and fell asleep in the Polenovs' garage—no one had to go to work the next day, and they drank until late, finally crawling home in the dark.

He came home disheveled and menacing and began to pester me. He was trying to make amends, called me Candy; his hands, which smelled of herring, groped my body crudely and shamelessly. I did not respond. I was ashamed. He could not finish what he had started, cursed, rolled over and fell asleep. His right hand still grasped my breast possessively. I slipped out from under his grip, went to the bathroom, and washed myself with lye soap. In the morning, he left for work without eating breakfast or patting me on the shoulder, just left. At night, he reappeared and shoved a large red rose into my hands. I kept that rose, dried, for a long time in a bottle on top of the wardrobe, where it stood with its head slightly bent, like an apologetic schoolchild, gathering dust. The overalls that I roughed up soon tore, and I had to buy new ones.

· 9 ·

Valerka was still a newborn when we moved into the two-room apartment in a new brick building with all the modern conveniences. Gennady patched up the poorly installed plumbing, built in a storage closet in the hallway; we bought furniture and a refrigerator. That was it. Over the next sixteen years we did not add anything except a basic TV. Gennady felt he had fulfilled his duties, of which he would never tire of reminding me, so now he was free to let loose. His drinking became serious. Naturally, he did not quit his job at the slaughterhouse.

Aside from haphazard sex and the money he brought home, little connected us. I often heard women say, "It's our own fault when men turn to drink." I don't believe that. They drink to fill their emptiness and out of their infantile laziness. Gennady's life contracted to the domino table and "purely men's talk." At least I never joined in the "purely women's talk" on the bench in front of the building. I do not like a world divided into "the men's half" and "the women's half."

I started using protection, because I was afraid of having another child with him, and he certainly didn't express any desire for one. But I must have slipped, and Pavlik was born. This time, there were no celebratory rides around the building. Instead, there was the drunken husband screaming at someone in hospital admissions. He had an argument with one of the nurses and railed on about this offense the whole way home, while I carried Pavlik in my arms.

I nursed the baby, held him upright and waited for him to burp, then put him down in his cradle. Gennady sat beside me and waited, and as soon as Pavlik's breathing deepened in sleep, he dragged me to bed. He did his thing and lit a cigarette.

"I thought you missed me too."

His voice was so full of reproach, there was no point in explaining anything to him; he didn't care about my condition at all. Then the doorbell rang; his pals had come to congratulate him. He dressed right away and said over his shoulder, "Candy, I won't be long."

"Pick up Valerka from daycare."

"Uhu!"

And he disappeared. At six, knowing that the daycare was about to close, I left Pavlik on his own and rushed to get my other son. Valerka and the teacher sat on the floor alone; the boy was building something. Gennady showed up after midnight, wordlessly collapsing on the bed.

I could not help it: my fear that I was sinful and soiled returned and tormented me at night. Often, as I lay by his side, I looked at the moon. It was as small and cold as the night I had talked to Ninka, its disk the same as the polished coin that lured me in the hospital in Panjakent. I thought I could hear Ninka whisper, "I don't feel anything anymore." I did feel, though—Gennady's touch was so repulsive that it made my throat clamp shut, and I was mute in the performance of my matrimonial duties, choking with disgust on the cold lump in my throat. He would whisper angrily, "What's your problem, cat got your tongue?" Unhappy and lost, he would roll away like a loose log from a poorly built stack of firewood. The soft night breeze played with the lace curtains, moonlight streaming through, and I could almost see my husband's body becoming wrapped in tree bark.

The children saved me. Pavlik's cry would break the silence and I would jump up to rock his cradle, or Valerka would start tossing violently in his sleep. He slept fitfully, rolled his sheet up into a rope, and liked to sleep crouched on his knees with his head stuck straight down into the mattress. I would lift him, still asleep, off the bed and remove his shorts. His weenie stuck up like a carrot, and I would grab the night pot and whisper "pss pss." Without ever opening his eyes, he would release a vigorous stream and then sleep calmly, with a fist under his head. It was touching to watch his face wrinkle up with the strain, as he tensed up to push out the extra liquid. Then I would go back and lie down with Gennady. By then, the insults would be fading, sinking from the surface. My hands held the warmth of my boys' touch, and that warmth spread through my body, sanitizing my poisoned being. My throat would loosen up. I would have no desire to recall the stupid things he had said to me, and I would gradually fall asleep.

I tried to talk to him many times, tried to find out the root of his alienation, but he would not respond, or, if I really irritated him, would curse at me vulgarly. I could sense there was something that oppressed him, but it was impossible to reach him through his defenses. Now he drank with the men in the yard; he did not even notice that he drank away his motorcycle, and he was not beyond tossing his earnings into my face. I have seen and heard all sorts of things in my life, and thank God he did not beat me or reach for a knife when he was mad. He was generally bad-tempered and got into fights impulsively. He often came home with bruises and scrapes, but obediently let me disinfect them and answered my questions with a single, "It was just a thing."

I, woman, was not supposed to nose around in the lives of the men.

One day, out in the yard (they were playing, as usual) Styopka Polenov, our neighbor, a quietly alcoholic excavator operator from the roads department, came up to me.

"Verka, give me cash for a bottle."

An aging bruise grew dark on his insolent face.

"You have your own wife—ask her."

"You stupid bitch, I'd die here and you'd just step over my body."

His usual talk, but for some reason Gennady decided to defend my honor. He jumped up from the bench as if stung by a bee; in an instant he was above poor Styopka holding him by the collar of his shirt and twisting it in a choke grip. Polenov's face went blue, veins bulged on his neck.

"What did you say?"

"Let him go right now!" I interfered.

I had no desire to be later accosted by the hot-tempered Mrs. Polenova.

"Yeah, right! Go home!" he barked, and hit Styopka in the teeth with his fist.

Styopka flew about ten feet away, grasped his face and howled. Gennady jumped at him and set to his task for real, as they had taught him in the police: he hit him on the kidneys, then in the stomach, then in the kidneys again and again in stomach. Polenov, helpless and disoriented with pain, could barely stand up. Then Gennady felled him with a single terrible blow to the jaw. Polenov fell like a cut tree. The men at the table roared with laughter.

"What are you still doing here? I said, go home!"

His knuckles bloodied, his eyes glowing, Gennady must have felt like an honest-to-God hero.

Without another word, I left.

"That's right, Gena, you gotta give him a lesson. If you lose, you're buying, and don't be rude to your neighbors," one of the men said.

An hour or so later, I looked out the window. They were still at the table and Styopka Polenov was back with them, only now his entire face was one large bruise. He must have bought his round of drinks and been accepted back into the gang. Gennady came home drunk, of course, and expounded at length about his ability not to let anyone bother me or our sons.

I did try to take him to a doctor. It was in vain; he did not consider himself an alcoholic. Vodka, by the way, had a strong effect on his manliness, which, I must confess, worked just fine for me. One night in bed, when he could no longer contain his bitterness, he said to me:

"Look at you—you're like a fish! A cold fish!"

I got up and went to the hospital. Of course, I ran back in the morning, to get him ready for work and to send the kids off to daycare. Gennady kept screaming at me as if he were being stabbed. Figuring that the best defense is to cause offense, he accused me of having a lover, even though he knew perfectly well where I had spent the night. He had called the hospital, but I asked the nurse to tell him I was too busy to answer. On his way out he slammed the door so hard that it shook plaster loose from the frame. After that night I slept in the kids' room. All in all, we had eleven years of married life.

That night, during my shift, I cared for a critical stroke patient, an old woman who had been difficult during the day, whined, blamed the doctors for everything, was ridiculously demanding and did not engender any sympathy in the staff. I made myself sit at her bed. I looked at her heavy, swollen face, filled with stagnant blood. Her dirty, fat body smelled. Suddenly, a shadow of something different flittered across her face. She smiled in her sleep, and then again there was only her strained face and the blue lips forcing stale air out of her chest. I pulled up a stool and put my hand on her forehead; gently, I began to massage her temples. I was silent, but I was not thinking about her—I thought about Gennady and absent-mindedly, mechanically shared my own feelings with hers as my fingers rubbed her fat-filled skin. And that is when I suddenly felt everything: the endless contempt others showed her, the shame she felt in her awkward, easily lost shape, the loneliness and the fear of death. My hand was now glued to her forehead, fingers like leeches, attached to her temples. My hand went numb, but I did not dare take it away; then my fingers sensed a weak pulse, and her forehead grew warmer and her face relaxed. I sat like that for three or four hours, deep into the night, when everyone else who was on duty had gone to sleep. Afterwards, in the nurses' room, I ran hot water over my hand for a long time, exhausted, drained and ecstatic. Thank goodness, no one caught me in the middle of this strange procedure.

The old woman slept through the night, and in the morning she looked comforted, and even a bit chastened; she stopped bossing people around and quickly got better. She treated me especially well, calling me "daughter." Once she grasped my hand in her frog-like paws and whispered,

"Don't despair. God gave you a kind heart, and you won't see any kindness from those asses—I know."

Her skin was hot and shiny, and her eyes—helpless and beautiful. The daylight lamp above her bed flickered and flashed uncommonly bright; the flash caught my eye and I winced. In the darkness of my closed eyes a red-hot dot glowed. The blackness around it pulsed and billowed like smoke; the dot multiplied and finally burst into a myriad of dancing sparks. I felt dizzy. Confused, I drew back my hand, turned around, and left the room. We did not say anything to each other that night.

The girls in the unit teased me, asking how I had managed to charm the old witch. I did not answer, they would not understand or believe me anyway. I took night shifts more often, so I could sit up with the worst cases: the patients liked me, the doctors and nurses avoided me, and only the unit head, as always, supported and encouraged me. Karimov loved me and I loved him back; nothing could change our lives.

Gennady reacted quite simply to my move to the nursery: he went on a drinking binge so severe he did not see daylight. I still do not understand how he managed to keep his job. For the next seven years we lived as neighbors. He paid almost no attention to the kids; I did his laundry; I cooked for him. Sometimes he gave me money. Other times, I pulled it out of the pocket of his pants when he collapsed in a dead heap in the hallway. We were never hungry; he kept stealing meat. I was busy with the children and with my work. At the hospital, I could relax. My coworkers did not suspect what my home life was like, and I preferred to keep it that way. Everyone mostly gave up on making friends with me. No one called me "Candy" any more, only Gennady did when he wanted something, and his coy tone made my stomach turn.

The old witch—her name was Olga Davydovna—died a year later. Her son, an inconspicuous little man, found me and gave me a tiny toy donkey: apparently, his mother insisted that it be given to me after her death.

The donkey was made of sturdy plastic, his legs attached to the body on screws, and a string with a heavy ring at the end could be pulled out of his chest. If you set him on a table and pulled the string, the donkey began walking after the ring. He trod slowly, rocking side-to-side, but he never stumbled or fell—he'd reach the edge of the table and stop above the abyss, where the thread hung loosely, no longer exerting its pull. Pavlik fell in love with it. The sight of the little donkey working his way steadily across the table and freezing at the edge made him giddy—a small miracle. Sometimes, after everyone at home had fallen asleep, I would pick up the toy and pull once, and again, and again. The donkey clambered to the edge and stood there, helpless, lonely, and beautiful. The toy was eventually lost, and no one knew what happened to it; I was sorry for the loss, but the wily old toad had achieved what she intended: I remembered her for the rest of my life.

. 10 .

I DID NOT TALK MUCH to our neighbors. It did not take Gennady long to begin selling meat in the courtyard, and once he started, of course the money did not make it all the way home. Things got tighter, but I was not unhappy. I am no good at sales and always feel embarrassed when I have to sell something. Gennady by then was drinking so hard that sometimes he, too, would forget about his meat; he lost his good clients and would trade his "grab" to anyone for a bottle of vodka. I suspect that he used my nickname in the yard, and after a while everyone called me Fish behind my back.

The women who at first hadn't welcomed me soon came around. One needed her blood pressure taken, another had me give her a course of injections, and they began to think of me as the building's medic, but the nickname, once it stuck, would not be forgotten. I pretended I did not hear it and did not try to make friends. With Farshidá, it was a different story. Born the same year as I, in some godforsaken mountain village, she was betrothed as a girl to her Sirojiddin. He went to the madras in Bukhara, graduated as a mullah, and served at the local mosque. Trim, sharp, tactful and excessively polite, he automatically inspired respect, and for some reason the ladies on the bench were afraid of him. Farshidá stayed at home and had babies; by the time we had to flee Tajikistan in

'92, they had ten of them, and Farshidá was pregnant with the eleventh. They lived on the same floor, in the three-room apartment next to us; it was quickly too small for them. They never had much. Farshidá was constantly saving for the circumcision of their next son, and I always helped at their *tui-pisars*. Of course, I could never think of taking money from them. The mullah's children went to the same school as mine; Valerka was in the same class as their eldest, Avzaleddin—or Afi, as everyone called him, and they were friends. Farshidá was illiterate, and I often helped her kids with homework and otherwise; in exchange, they shared with us fruit, nuts and highland honey, which their rural relatives sent in abundance.

By this time, I straightened things out with Uncle Styopa and Aunt Katya, and visited them on holidays. Gennady—if he happened to be sober—refused to come with me and the children. He did not like "the Colonel," as he called Uncle Styopa (who, in fact, was only a major then), or his "General in a skirt," and openly envied them. My return to the embrace of my family could not have happened without the intervention of beloved Uncle Kostya and Aunt Raya: they came from Kurgan-Tube twice a year, and on one of these occasions they got me to join the family feast.

I had quickly paid back the money that Ninka had stolen; the brooch, strangely enough, turned up on its own ("must've fallen behind the dresser"). We never reminded each other of that particular conversation. Sashenka had matured into a beautiful girl, and was always happy to see me. Our rare family celebrations were pleasant. We missed my mom, but she could not leave her Petrovich even for a minute and had not had a chance to visit Dushanbe since I had left home. Her grandchildren did not know her; they each got birthday cards and shared New Year's cards from their two grandmas—one from the faraway Volochok and the other from the not-so-distant Panjakent. They were closer with our neighbor Farshidá, Aunt Raya, and even Aunt Katya than with their own grandmothers.

Vovka, my cousin from Kurgan-Tube, studied for a while in Dushanbe, majoring in mining engineering. He often stopped by and I fed him, since he was a student. He and Valerka became pals: they both loved messing around with motorcycles. Pavlik, who was four years Valera's junior, had a completely different personality—he wanted books. I spent all my spare change at the bookstore and shopped at the Central Committee's distribution center with Aunt Katya's party card. Sometimes I would also receive books as presents from my patients. Books and meat back then were better than money. By the end of our stay in Tajikistan we had accumulated two large bookcases, sixteen shelves in all.

In fourth grade, Pavlik contracted tuberculosis. He was diagnosed accidentally, when everyone in school was given the routine Mantoux skin test. He went to the hospital. His doctors suggested surgery: the upper lobe of his left lung was completely affected.

Unexpectedly, Gennady insisted on accompanying me to the appointment with the surgeon. He even shaved, put on a clean shirt and a suit. In a word, he was unrecognizable. He did most of the talking; all I had to do was sit there quietly. The surgeon insisted on the operation. Gennady refused.

"All you want to do is cut! I won't let you do that to my son, I'll cure him myself!"

It was said with great power. He was capable of that, when he wanted to be.

The surgeon finally agreed to wait and see, but refused to take Pavlik off ftivazid, an anti-tuberculin drug. So it was a tie.

The story of his leg engendered in Gena a deep hatred of surgeons, whom he blamed for everything that had gone wrong in his life. The men in the yard gave him the idea to visit some old native medicine women in the mountains. He went into the country, to a Doukhobor village,[5] and came back with some dried herbs, then made the poor boy drink disgusting bitter concoctions. I did not see how the herbs could do any serious harm, but instead studied the x-rays and hoped that the trusty ftivazid would do its work.

We began home-schooling. Mom by then had buried her Petrovich and was living alone; I wrote her a letter asking her to come and stay with us, since I needed help. The reply came from Dr. Davron: Mom had suffered a severe stroke that had left her completely paralyzed; she was in the local hospital. I had to go to Panjakent, but I could not leave my sons, and Mom died there, without me. I barely made it to the funeral. No one blamed me, of course, but I caught certain looks from the hospital staff and from our old neighbors, and they did not make my three days in Panjakent any easier. *Akó* Ahror came to the funeral as well—it was his truck that carried Mom to the cemetery.

Afterwards, at the wake held at the strange home on the edge of the city, where she had lived with Petrovich, I went out into the orchard, and stood under a tall walnut tree, leaning against its coarse bark.

The walnut grew next to an earthen *duval*; on the other side fruit trees framed a dusty pasture. Fields stretched beyond. In the distance, very far away, through an opening in the trees' canopies, I could glimpse the blue mountains. It was midday, hot and silent. A homeless donkey, unkempt and skinny, shuffled along, barely moving his feet: old, unwanted invalids like him were often just set loose, free to roam the countryside until they either died or were captured and slaughtered. There was a truck with a boxed-in bed that people called "Oswiencim."[6] Two Tatar brothers drove it about unhurriedly, hunting stray dogs and old donkeys to be turned into soap. The donkey in the meadow walked as if he were pulled along by an invisible rope with a heavy ring at its end. It was not as hot in the shade of the walnut tree, and soon I tired of staring into the distance and instead focused on the intricate patterns of the tree bark. No human hand could have produced such rhythmic, fierce beauty.

Akó Ahror came up to me there, in the garden. The years had left no trace on him. In simple words—in his speech he was always miserly and precise—he expressed his sadness. I listened, silently, and nodded. It seemed as if I were listening to a stranger.

"I'm sorry, Vera, that you left."

I shrugged my shoulders and went back to the house. Ahror followed me silently; there was nothing more to say.

We returned to Dushanbe in Uncle Styopa's government Volga. After that, nothing linked me to Panjakent. Now I often remember things from there, but back then I was certain I was erasing it from my memory forever. When my grandma Lisichanskaya stares intently into the shadows drawn on the ceiling by the Italian lamp, she stares as if trying to glimpse the nocturnal angels that stand between her and the other world, and I know she is remembering. Her face changes—first it is warm, then it is stern and distant. She must be engaged in some unfinished conversation with the past. When people tell me that all my efforts are meaningless and that it is time to stop nursing the life in this half-dead body, I do not argue with them, but keep my peace. How could I convey to them what I know from being at her side? I look at her little dried-up face that has become part of my family and sometimes I am ashamed: I did not get to my mother in time, did not have time to help. Mom died alone, although the kind doctor Davron stopped by her bed after his morning rounds.

"She left quietly and gracefully," he said at the wake.

He said what people always say on such occasions. I kissed him and went to the orchard, to stand in the shade of the old walnut tree. I stood there, alone and quite, until *akó* Ahror came.

. 11 .

FTIVAZID DID SLOW the progress of the disease and Pavlik's tuberculomas calcified. Now the doctors insisted on a change of climate. Pavlik needed time in sanatoriums, places such as Abastumani or Teberda—the high-altitude facilities where, it was believed, the lung disease could be completely cured. I could not possibly send him away for a year on his own and entrust him to the nursing staff at the sanatorium, and Gennady also would not hear of it. Incredibly, my son's illness had changed my husband. He quit drinking, left his job, and spent all his time traveling from one folk healer to another and having lengthy conversations with them. I could not begin to list all the disgusting things Pavlik had to force down: from *mumije*[7] dissolved in water to melted badger fat and all manner of herbal brews. Gennady prepared these salves with his own hands, in our kitchen, based on the recipes he had written down in a large ledger.

My husband endlessly expounded on the topic of sin and, despite the fact that he did not go to church himself, became vehemently opposed to me interacting with the mullah and his wife. He hung crosses and icons everywhere, and procured from somewhere a large, thick Bible, that he read from in the evenings. All his interpretations yielded the same conclusion Satan was everywhere, hidden, biding his time, and as soon as one stopped praying, if only for a minute, he would sneak into one's thoughts and there lie in wait. Demons were constantly watching. Any word we said, any thought that occurred to us, they would snatch up and use in their battle against our Lord for the corruption of human souls. Gennady now constantly mumbled something inaudible. I quickly got used to this new habit and stopped noticing it.

This new life (on top of everything, he also became a vegetarian) stoked his lust, previously drowned in vodka, and he was constantly after me, either threatening me with divine punishment or begging in a disgustingly unctuous voice. I could not go back to bed with him; I continued to sleep in the children's room. He got angry and accused me of having affairs; in the end, I also became the Whore of Babylon, for whose sins our baby was paying.

I also did not stop seeing Farshidá. And I learned to listen to Gennady's fire-and-brimstone rants with just one ear, as they say, and initially I was simply happy he had stopped drinking. I decided I could earn enough for both of us for a time; perhaps, he would come to his senses. I wished he would go to church like normal people, but he had a special theory for that, too: the Church had sold out and God had abandoned it. Personally, I never had the habit, but people I knew who were regular church-goers—the old nurse Aunt Shura, the night watchman at the dormitory, the aging ophthalmologist Shmelev—were all kind and completely harmless people. I understood that my husband needed to find a foundation, a pivot on which to build his life, having lost the one that serving in the police had given him. I even offered to go to church with him, to speak to a priest. But he instantly turned the conversation into a rabid argument, in which he referred to some special knowledge he possessed, and when he saw that I had lost interest in his rubbish, he became angry again, screamed at me and called me a cold, coarse, empty fool.

Listening to him was tedious, and besides, I did not have time for it. There was one positive thing: Pavlik, sensing that his father cared, reached out to him. Gennady became an advocate of cleanliness and gave the apartment a twice daily mop-down. He opened the windows even in winter. Air, water, sun, herbs—these were all the right elements, but they were mixed in the wrong proportions in his twisted mind.

One of his fresh-air spells mowed down Pavlik: he ran a high fever and I took him to the hospital despite Gennady's objections. Pavlik had pneumonia. At first, the doctors were afraid that one of his tuberculomas had burst, but thank God, that did not happen. Nonetheless, the attending put his foot down—surgery was unavoidable. Pavlik had the upper lobe of his left lung removed.

Gennady brought a million curses down on me. He raved all night, and I went to work on very little sleep, tired and frustrated. I stopped by Pavlik's room: the boy was a fighter and the doctor promised to take out the stitches very soon. In the doctors' lounge, there was a surprise for me: Vitya Bzhania had come to visit. He invited me out to a café later that night. I was happy to see him.

. 12 .

VITYA BELONGS TO the same breed of men as *akó* Ahror: not especially tall, but slim and sinewy. His appearance was also almost untouched by age, except that now his hair was completely gray, which, in my opinion, is very attractive. Even now he never forgets to do his morning exercises and takes ice-cold showers. Only on a few occasions had I ever seen him tired, and never depressed. He is good at hiding his feelings and at the same time is always attentive to others, a great listener. Patients in his unit adore him, and he always has time to spend with them. He can be militarily stern with them as well—sometimes that is what a patient needs, a bit of reasonable discipline that can inspire respect for another person and distract one from anxious thoughts. Nowadays, when specialist surgeons have little time for patients, preferring to dump them, with all their fears and suffering, into the laps of the attending physicians, attention from a unit head is rare, even though care, in my opinion, is the foundation of therapy.

With his family and friends, Viktor is kind and soft, his eyes radiating warmth. He uses words as a last resort and would rather listen and watch; he reminds me of a purebred horse whose eye, whose mere look fills you with the power, warmth or joy of your encounter with him. Viktor speaks with extraordinary precision that sometimes borders on curtness, and this often makes people who do not know him well feel uncomfortable, sending them into long-winded apologies.

That day, in the café, Viktor gave me a bouquet of scarlet roses, opened a bottle of champagne and said simply, "Here's to seeing each other again, Vera. I think about you often."

Gennady and I never went out on the town, and I was pleased by the attention. I relaxed, even though I knew Vitya would get to his point very quickly.

He reported his grief as if at an evening check-in in the barracks.

"I buried my Mom four days ago. I will stay until the ninth day,[8] and then I'm going back to Moscow, my patients, and my dissertation."

His mother had died of a heart attack, and he, a cardiac surgeon, could do nothing to help her; she had refused to move to Moscow.

"You say I've become stern. That's nothing; my mom, now *she* was stern. It's a pity you didn't get to know her."

He smiled imperceptibly. I could not help myself and took his hand into mine; almost mechanically, I began to massage his fingers just as I did hundreds of times for frightened, worn out patients. I talked for a long time, telling him about Pavlik, about Valerka, about the aging Karimov who was being pushed aside by the young and the bold. Suddenly, he interrupted me, jerked his hand back. Looking me in the eye, he came straight to the point.

"You must come to Moscow with me. How can you live with that worthless slime?"

He drew Gennady's portrait with a few simple, medical strokes: "An alcoholic is the same as a drug addict: the changes in the brain are irreversible."

Something invisible had passed between us: his pity, up till then masked with rationality, put a chill on our conversation. I could feel my limbs stiffen involuntarily, my temples grow cold. I felt an approaching headache and winced; Viktor interpreted it as a sign of my being offended, and it made him go on the offensive. Never before had he said so many words to me. He had a place to take us, a two-room apartment in Moscow. He promised a job for me and the TB hospital for Pavlik, the best clinic in the country. He had thought it all through down to the smallest details. At the end, as precisely as he had laid out his previous arguments, he dropped the bomb: "Vera, I have loved you all my life. I promise you—the boys will be my sons."

He fell silent then. I could see he did not know what to do with his hands and busied them with a paper napkin shredding it into little pieces, then rolling up each piece into a ball and throwing it into the ashtray.

"Vitenka, I can't."

"Why?"

"Fate."

He took a sip of his coffee and began talking about his institute and his dissertation; he even made me laugh with a joke. He walked me to my apartment building. We walked silently through the surprisingly warm winter night. I remembered Nar, someone who had also walked me home and who also destroyed many dreams with a single word.

At the door, Viktor gave me a piece of paper with his phone numbers, work and home; I noted that he had to have prepared it in advance. I felt sorry for him. I kissed him on the cheek and dove into the building. I stopped on the second floor landing and looked out; the window pane had frosted over. I breathed on it to peek out. Viktor was standing by the sandbox, looking at my windows. Then he turned around and marched away.

The apartment was quiet as I slipped into the kitchen. I still had the headache and needed to take something for it. Gennady stood silently at the window. He turned to face me slowly, and I realized right away that he had seen it all.

"That was Vitya Bzhania; he came to bury his mother."

"Go to bed. It's late," he said, and without another word, went to his room.

I swallowed a pill, sat down on a stool and held my head with my hands. I badly wanted to cry, but could not. I do not know how long I sat like that, but the headache eventually retreated. I went down the hallway, slowly, as if to the gallows, counting my steps. At my husband's door, I stopped. Put my hand on the brass handle. The metal was cold and heavy. Everything was quiet; the children were asleep. I did not open his door, even though I was sure he was awake; I just stood there a moment and then retreated, stumbled into the nursery. I lay down in my own bed and stared at the ceiling as it stirred with the shadows from the nightlight.

The silence was so deep, deeper than at any time in my life, but for when I was very little, and my Mom, having tucked me in, would kiss my forehead, make the sign of the cross over it, as if salting the breading for the cutlets, and say, "Sleep, Vera, God will shelter you." I strained to hear God—not even His words, just a breath—but everything was swaddled in silence, like in a thick blanket. I thought about the strange word "shelter," and in my mind a big God walked over the world, like Santa Claus, and built shelters around people's houses. These shelters were made of dense clouds, and God would knead them with his hands, stretch them and toss them like they slap wet *pahsa* at aging *duvals*. And these cloudy walls would instantly harden into the same incredible shapes their kin had in the sky. When God was in a good mood, the walls were funny, and if he were tired after a sleepless night, the walls came out lopsided and mis-shapen, like the doodles of a small child who had only just discovered crayons and paper.

Why do I have to be afraid of something invisible, non-existent, something from a different dimension? In my mind, all the horrors were here, around us, on Earth. The silence surrounding me was lulling me to sleep, relaxing me, filling my body with pleasant warmth. I even uttered my own simple prayer: "Father-God, help my unfortunate husband, my children Valerka and Pavlik, and all the people I love, especially Vitya Bzhania, and do with me as you see fit. Amen of Holy Spirit."

. 13 .

SHOULD I HAVE opened that door? Rationally, I realized that Gennady, like me, hoped to turn back the clock. That night, at the window, he was his old self, the one who captivated me with his strength while lying in a hospital bed, his leg in a cast, helpless. Then, he was someone who knew how to conquer his own weaknesses and did. Now, he had fits of jealousy about my imagined lovers, but when a real competitor came around, Gennady was quiet. I, in turn, was lost and kept expecting him to act.

I told myself that I was trying to keep things together for the sake of the children; I lied to myself; I still expected something better. Vitya Bzhania, with whom I could have probably had a peaceful and sheltered life, remained my friend, selfless and loyal; Gennady was my husband. The wall between our rooms kept us apart; the door had not opened.

In the morning he was glum, refused to eat slightly burned, "carcinogenic" eggs, and, in front of the children, unable to control himself any longer, spewed out everything he thought about me: I was again a heartless cuckoo that abandons her children, a cold, self-absorbed fish.

I floated away to work with a twist of my tail, deaf to his hysteria, and spent my day with the patients. In the evening, the emergency crew brought in a jolly old man, a gnome with critical asthma. I volunteered for the night shift and stayed with the old man until morning, sleepless, cutting short his coughing fits and stroking his small, wrinkled face, which resembled a dried-up pumpkin. I bowed to him from my stool like a little wooden cuckoo from its perch on top of the clock, counting the hours—not years—that he had left to live. The gnome wrinkled his nose comically, much like Pavlik used to do when I nursed him.

Naturally, the antagonism at home had its effect on the children. Valerka seemed to have been bred by cuckoos—he hardly lived at home, spending all his time first at the plane-modeling club and later with his motocross buddies. I did not really want to know exactly how and what he rode, and he never bragged about his victories, instead locking up his trophies and medals in a cabinet. He was out late at friends' garages and showed up dirty and exhausted, but if I were prepared to listen, he would share with me important news about how they increased the torque on Andrei Grin's "Yava" or what kind of carburetor they installed for Dimka Moskvitin. He was attracted to nuts, bolts, springs and patched up mufflers, all of which were quickly filling up his room. Gennady's lessons, icons, prayers and conversations about the purity of the soul bounced off him like gravel off the belly of retired colonel Didenko's jeep, which they had covered with three layers of protective goo.

Pavlik was a different matter altogether. His father told him stories from the Bible, in his own interpretation, and from the booklets supplied to him by his new healer-friends. Under his influence, Pavlik even tried to become a vegetarian, but lasted only a week. I hoped that the boy's interest in the occult would dissipate by itself, but Gennady had him thoroughly confused and intimidated.

One day I could not stand it any more. They were sitting in the kitchen and discussing something that had to do with seals and a trumpeting angel, and Pavlik's voice trembled with fear.

"That's enough. You have got the kid's head full of the Apocalypse. Look how frightened he is—that's a great bedtime story. Are you trying to turn him into the same sort of Jesus freak you've become?"

A chair flew back with a thud. Gennady was on his feet, eyes charged.

"You, woman, vessel of evil! What do you know with your chicken brain?!"

"What I know with my chicken brain is that this child is too young to think about these things and you ought to be committed, which I will do if you don't stop traumatizing my son."

I am pretty sure he would have gone after me—his jaw was clenched—but Pavlik jumped up and stood between us.

"How dare you insult mama, stop!"

Large tears rolled down the boy's cheeks. He gave each one of us a long, probing look. Gennady shut the Bible and went to his room. Pavlik fell into my arms.

"Mom, he doesn't mean harm; he was just trying to explain it to me about the end of the world. Do you believe it?"

"As far as I know, the end of the world is not coming for a long, long time. It is silly to fear it and to keep trying to predict exactly when it will happen. One should live, go to school and enjoy life. It seems that your father has forgotten how to do that."

I put the boy to bed and stayed with him, stroking his head for a long time. He kept wanting to tell me about those damn seals and what would happen when they fell open. It made my head spin. When he finally fell asleep, I quietly stole the Bible that was under his bed—his father had given it to him for his thirteenth birthday—and tried to read it, but did not understand much. I could sense that my son was very scared and had no words to articulate his fear.

"Let's go to church, and you can talk to a priest there."

"We can't, mom. Dad doesn't want me to, and I don't want to upset him."

Something had to be done. It felt as if my youngest had been infected with the insanity bug and I was on the verge of taking him to a psychiatrist, when Pavlik, as if sensing danger, lost interest in the Scripture for a while and went back to reading books that I was more than happy to talk about.

The boy grew older, and I hoped that he no longer needed to cling to his father's nonsense. But they still spent time together, and Gennady did not abandon his dream of converting his son. The Bible took up residence under the bed again for some time, and then quietly disappeared. So it all went, up and down, in waves, until the end of the world came. For a long time I was determined not to acknowledge its approach, but eventually I had no choice—it had arrived.

· 14 ·

THINGS BEGAN CHANGING in Tajikistan immediately after the military withdrew from Afghanistan. Officially over, the war had merely moved a thousand kilometers deeper into the USSR and swallowed Tajikistan.

"The first principle is: don't enter. And the second: once you're in, don't leave," Uncle Styopa said.

He had seen action and was lightly wounded, then went back to his unit, was wounded again and after that decommissioned for good. By the time he retired, he received the "People's Friendship" medal and colonel's stars. He solemnly flushed both down the toilet. The war had changed him; he now hated with a vengeance everything that he used to love.

He was the first to declare about the events, "Time to flee to Russia. They won't leave us be here."

Riots and violence in the streets in February of 1990 scared the whole city, but we still believed that things would be alright. Aunt Katya was promoted and worked now for Mahkamov, the Party's first secretary. She did not refer to her husband's prognostications other than as "defeatist," and they fought constantly. Thank God Sasha by then had left Dushanbe to study at the Krasnodar Polytechnic. In her very first year she fell in love and, without asking her parents' permission, married a local. She still lives in Krasnodar, has two kids and is doing just fine.

Tajikistan's first president, Nabiev, elected in '91, swept Mahkamov's people out of every office, and Aunt Katya barely found a job in a neighborhood library. Instantly, she too was filled with defeatism and the family entered an era of peace and harmony. Together, they cursed and blamed everyone else, and I tried to stay away from their home, all the more so because Uncle Styopa's brother from Kurgan-Tube was staying with them. Uncle Kostya and Aunt Raya escaped the front lines only by a miracle and were hoping to sit out the worst in Dushanbe. Of course they had to leave behind their things—their apartment and the famous gem collections—there was no way it could all fit into Volodya's dorm room.

The Opposition and the People's Front divided the country; the Leninabad and Hodjent groups (that initially came out on top) found themselves under attack by the Kuliab contingent, united and hungry for power. A civil war erupted. Nabiev abdicated the Presidency.

The streets were no longer safe. Militia fighters grabbed young men and sent them to the front in Kurgan-Tube. Students were holding demonstrations and protests. Food prices rose. The new Tajik rubl seemed a mere parody of the old Soviet ruble. The hospital began seeing people hurt in street fights. Everyone was involved: Tajiks went after Tajiks, settling old clan scores. The Exodus began.

Gennady acted as if he did not notice what was going on around us. He rarely left the apartment, where he prayed and fasted. We fasted, too, but not for reasons of faith. To buy bread one had to venture out before the curfew and navigate through checkpoints at a crawl. We queued up and still did not get the bread—sacks would be tossed over our heads, people taking care of their own. For a while, we were able to draw upon our pantry and ate pasta and cereals.

Farshidá and Sirojiddin disapproved of the unrest and tried to keep their kids off the streets, but their eldest, Afi, joined the militia and was almost never home. Farshidá prayed to Allah for his safety, just as she did for my children. During that calamitous year, we became very close and even Gennady stopped treating her like an enemy. He had one simple reaction to all my fears: "If you want to run—run, I won't stop you." Fear, doubt, anger and distrust took root in people's hearts. Every day, trains of containers filled with household belongings left for Russia.

Uncle Styopa developed the plan for our retreat. He procured from somewhere a decommissioned diesel Ural truck and, together with Vovka and Valerka, they went over it, bolt by bolt. They re-painted it, built a cabin over its bed out of particle board, and welded and installed a primitive stove in it. Jokingly, I christened the truck "Noah's Ark."

I was afraid just like everyone else, but kept working. As long as I was paid, no matter how little, I had to work. Pavlik kept going to school, too, but Valerka dropped out and hung out in Uncle Styopa's garage. I worried about him more, since he, at seventeen, could be forced to go to war. But the trouble found Pavlik instead. He was ambushed outside of the school.

I was at home when he returned. His face, shirt and pants were covered in blood. There were four Tajiks. They sliced his shoulder with a knife, and with a sharp metal rod pierced his cheek, gum and tongue. He could not speak, only cried and moaned, dark red spit bubbling and dripping from his mouth. His classmates rushed to his defense, and the Tajiks ran off, but the boys were too scared to chase after them.

I called the ambulance. The shoulder wound was not deep—doctors closed it easily and then cleaned up his cheek. In the evening, Farshidá came to visit, and brought Afghan *mumije*. In five days, Pavlik could speak again. Gennady came home late that day, looked over the sleeping boy and suddenly said firmly, "Vera, you are right. Pack up, we're going to Volochok."

I went to the hospital to pick up my paperwork and say my goodbyes. When many people cried, it took me by surprise, and I started sobbing myself. Old Karimov hugged me like a father.

Sirojiddin gave us the money to rent a railroad container; he and Farshidá promised to look after our apartment. I am sure they are still looking after it, and I would be happy if it became theirs. Many people sold their apartments for pennies; even more just abandoned theirs, and I sort of gave mine away as a present. Without the mullah's money, we would not have made it: Gennady refused to sell the apartment—he believed we would come back.

Time took off at a gallop: two weeks were taken up by packing the books, the pots and pans, the furniture. Then there was waiting at the cargo station, bribes, nights spent in the lines of people waiting to send their things away. Finally, our container was shipped off. Uncle Styopa set the date for our departure. We were still of two minds: we wanted to fly and were saving up for plane tickets. And then Aunt Raya died. It was instantaneous, a cardiac failure; she went to sleep and did not wake up. We buried her in the Dushanbe cemetery: Uncle Kostya, Volodya, Uncle Styopa, Aunt Katya, Gennady, Pavlik, Valerka and I. The wake was held in her luxurious party apartment, which the war had stripped bare and turned into a refugee camp. In three days, the new owners were supposed to move in: Uncle Styopa had sold the place for two thousand dollars, which at the time was considered very fortunate.

"So, my dear," Uncle Styopa said, "I give you one more day to finish packing; we leave the day after tomorrow."

There were no tickets at the Aeroflot ticket office; we got on the waiting list. Someone had introduced me to a speculator—for three times the face value of the ticket we could fly out the same day. We did not have that kind of money, and that was that.

On an early March morning, the diesel "Noah's Ark" loaded with three families left Dushanbe. Uncle Styopa drove; nestled behind his seat was the carbine with the optical sight, a present from a general who had visited in happier times.

What I did not know, a fact carefully concealed from us women, was that the men had also hidden a sub-machine gun in the truck. They equipped themselves for the worst, and it turned out they were right.

The rabid March sun shone brightly, the air was cool and clean, and a flock of wild pigeons raced ahead of us towards the mountains, like the Biblical doves. We hated those mountains—they had taken everything we had given them. And we dreamt instead of the Russian steppes, of the unknown greenness of the woods, of the earth not dried by the sun, and of people who did not shave their heads. We fled under the bright spring sun, but the fear had not yet left our hearts.

The plastic windows of the living quarters were open; I stood by one of them, and Pavlik took the other. The truck shuddered over potholes: tanks and heavy artillery had ground down the old Soviet asphalt.

three

. 1 .

THE SKY IN TAJIKISTAN is endless. The higher in the mountains you climb, the higher its dome rises over your head. When you think about it, the indifference of the blue is no less threatening than pitch-black darkness. Silvery-grey and black—together, they make a mirror, the amalgam and the base. Only the mirror of the sky is not like common mirrors: it absorbs instead of reflecting, and watches instead of showing. Clear air, sparkling snow, melting ice caps. A human fleeing from point A to point B. The night's silence and the day's silence in the mountains had witnessed this thousands of times. I stood by the window gazing upwards, as if looking for a sign, a prediction of how our journey would go, but did not see anything. I accepted the inevitable with my heart—the mirror of the soul, as the Muslims call it, and grew more relaxed; I could then focus on other things, on the strained roar of the truck's engine as it climbed the serpentine road. The Ural continued to move towards the distant point B that lay under a different sky.

The country was in the throes of a civil war. The Ural crawled from one pass to the next on mountain roads. Few cars came in the opposite direction. We were stopped twice at checkpoints, but each time the former colonel of the Border Guards quickly reached an understanding with the soldier who could have been one of his own. The truck's paperwork was in order—uncle Styopa paid well at the Dushanbe motor vehicle bureau, and we passed without further bribes.

We crossed the Anzob Pass, passed the turn-off to Panjakent, and drove without stopping through Shahristan. Ahead lay Ura-Tube and

Zafarabad on the border with the Syr-Darya region of Uzbekistan. That's where they got us.

A lonely car, a Zhiguli, was parked across the empty road, blocking traffic. It was guarded by two Tajiks with Kalashnikovs. The older one, with a large white beard, raised his, and the other one kept his weapon trained on the truck.

"Gena, red alert. Put everyone on the floor," Uncle Styopa ordered.

He had Volodka in the cabin with him; everyone else was in the back.

Gennady, to give him credit, was instantly transformed, pulled the machine gun from under a mattress, made us all lie down, and stood by the left window. He held the gun low, so that the people on the road could not see it. Uncle Styopa stopped before the car and asked peaceably:

"What's the problem, *akó*?"

"Checkpoint, everyone out of the truck."

Uncle Styopa floored the gas pedal. The Ural charged ahead, mangled the younger man, and pushed aside the car. The older one managed to jump aside. Four more men rose from the ditch and opened fire. A few bullets flew over our heads; one cracked the windshield. I did not see anything. I was lying on top of Pavlik to keep him down and shield him with my body. They told me later that Gennady shot the leader.

The Ural raced along the road. Gennady stood by the opened back door until it was completely dark, on the lookout for pursuers, but apparently they were afraid to chase after us.

We went through Ura-Tube slowly and carefully, as if on parade, in order not to arouse any suspicion, but as soon as we reached the edge of town, Uncle Styopa stepped on the gas again. It was a miracle that neither we nor our truck were harmed—not counting the four holes in the walls of our makeshift home and the cracked windshield. The bandits had not expected any resistance.

We passed through Zafarabad at night. The police post with its detachment of fresh-faced recruits took a bribe and wished us a safe trip. We left Tajikistan.

We stopped on the side of the road; Gennady made a fire. The men discussed the fight; Aunt Katya and I cooked and did not take part in their conversation.

While we were eating, Uncle Styopa, for no apparent reason, said that Gennady's round blew up the bandit like a rotten watermelon, and added with a smirk, "I can't imagine how those poor *houris* in heaven will put his brain together again."

Gennady finished his meal quickly and went back to the truck. When I peered in, he was kneeling in prayer, but once he noticed me, he pretended to be digging in his sleeping bag. That night, I lay down next to him, but he either slept or pretended to be sleeping—his breathing was almost too even. For the rest of the trip—nine difficult days—he was taciturn, responded in single words, and maintained his watch by the window, calm, alert, alone with his thoughts.

Guliston, Baht, Sirdare, Tashkent, the flat Kyrgyz plains—Shymkent, Kyzylorda—the road ran along the shores of the muddy Syr Darya, along fields, orchards, uncultivated wasteland. Dust and sand squeaking on the teeth. Aral, Aktyubinsk, then a downward turn on the map towards Oktyabrsk, Sagiz with its eponymous river fed by melting snows, ferocious and shallow; Guryev, the bridge across the Ural, and the last two hundred and fifty miles to the Russian Kotyaevka.

Later, I would look at the map and try to recall what happened when on our trip. But days blended together, faded and bled into each other: empty roads, infrequent cars, people, gas stations, carts and tractors, oxen, horses, camels, flocks of sheep, skinny foxes on long legs, watchful prairie dogs standing still near their dens, and the steppe eagles soaring in the sky. Cooking over open fires, water from aluminum canisters—warm with a metallic aftertaste, the shaking floor covered with dirty mattresses, my boys excited and exhausted, taciturn Gennady, Volodya and Uncle Styopa taking turns at the wheel, anxious and dispirited Uncle Kostya and Aunt Katya.

There is nothing special about the village of Kotyaevka. Having crossed the border, we stopped at the Border Guard post, tumbled out of the truck, and, on impulse, shouted "Hurray!" The local policemen were momentarily taken aback, but once they learned who we were, they laughed with us and wished us good fortune and much happiness. Noah's Ark moored in Russia.

. 2 .

FROM KOTYAEVKA, passing through Astrakhan, we went to Kharabali, a small town on the Akhtuba River. The head of the fire brigade there was the retired colonel Arkhipov, Uncle Styopa's friend and brother-in-arms from Afghanistan. He took us under his wing.

They put us up in a makeshift barrack that already housed other refugee families; we had tiny rooms without a bathroom. There was an outhouse, and on Saturdays one went to the city *banya*. At night, when everyone had gone to sleep, I would boil a bucket of water in the kitchen and wash, pouring water from one tub to another, in a corner curtained off with a quilt. The availability of hot water in Dushanbe had spoiled me; I could not go to bed dirty.

Within a week, Uncle Styopa got a job at a local school as a military skills instructor, seduced by a small house that came with the job; woodworking lessons were held in an added room. He took on those as well, happily, fixed up the abandoned house, and now boasts that he never dreamed of living out his old age in his own "mansion." He planted an apple orchard, built a fireplace in the living room, and traded his Ural for a small jeep. Aunt Katya went to work for the library. Valerka and Volodka got themselves hired at a small business that fixed tires along the side of the highway. On their days off, they were allowed to use the space and tools to repair cars, and got to keep all the earnings. Uncle Kostya took up fishing, and Pavlik liked to help him. The Akhtuba was full of fish, and soon this enterprise became profitable for all of us. Uncle Kostya founded a cooperative, "Three Rivers," the first in Kharabali. Arkhipov, the fire chief, joined in as a partner and helped them get a loan. They bought a small truck and built a brick house on the shore of the river. The loan was quickly paid off when money was devalued in the monetary reform. But all of this came later, and at first they operated out of an abandoned railcar, delivered fish and fuel for the boat in an ancient Zaporozhets,[1] and paid for an old aluminum boat out of Uncle Kostya's savings.

The Akhtuba, Mangut and Kharabalyk were the three rivers that came together at the cape where the co-op's railcar stood. The Kharabalyk connected the Akhtuba to the Volga. Strong currents stirred the sand on its bottom, forming many deep holes where big fish liked to rest. Some places on that river were truly extraordinary: steep banks and shallow beaches would suddenly trade sides and appear on opposite sides of the river, the sandy beach teasing its brother from across the water with its yellow tongue. The current would carve a deep pool between them, an abyss. Babkin Dip was especially dangerous. The current was restless there, changing directions suddenly, and a motorboat on a still day could easily become trapped in whirlpools spinning the heavy, oily water. The pull of the abyss at once seduced and frightened us. It was here that fish came to winter, to wait out the cold at the bottom. Uncle Kostya told us that fish filled the Dip in layers, sleepy and still. There were catfish weighing more than two hundred pounds, big-headed, monstrous, with live colonies of leeches on their faces. Above them large *sazan* fluttered their fins and pursed their lips, making them look like the fat cherubs painted on the ceiling of the town's church. Fanged pikes, always ready to strike, shared the next niche with quick chubs, the fish that comes dancing above the surface on the hottest days.

From the middle to the end of June, when the water begins to retreat from flooded meadows, the wet grass becomes the breeding ground for gnats. Dark clouds of them fill the air. People have to wear dense clothes and special netting about their faces, but even so there is no relief from the bloodsucking gnats—all you can do is get used to it. First bites itch cruelly and turn into blisters, but soon your body builds up an immunity. The gnats, in God's great scheme of things, are the fishes' main food. The short season, when the year's hatch finds its way from the meadows to the river, is the feasting time: newborn fish feed on the gnats and the bigger fish feed on the throngs of hatchlings. Catfish slide into the shallow streams that wash through the muddy meadows and open their maws—the current fills them with prey. In the river itself, saber carp comes alive and instantly the surface boils with their tails and bodies: the fish turn and dive straight down, hunting the fry. Their sides, like silver coins, glisten across the water; their tails beat like a giant steamboat wheel, and above the river seagulls shriek rabidly. That is when the chub come up and circle at the edge of the carps' feeding frenzy. Here and there, chub begin to dash out of the water, splitting the surface with their speedy bodies; their scales shine in the air as if suspended in a net. Chub pools—an enraptured Pavlik showed me how the fish flex and spin in the water—are very beautiful.

But chub dance only in this short period of time nature gives them. For the better part of the year, the water does not share its secrets with the air but keeps its world safely separate. Only the fishermen know what goes on in the river's depths. Close to the surface float sleepy zander and perch. They roam the river even in winter—in quick raids like warring Tatars and Kalmyks of long ago—and devour everything they can find before returning to their pools to doze in the deep, below the whirls that guard their sleep better than the thick concrete of a bomb shelter. If the flooded meadows are the spawning and birth sites, the deep pools are the fish's shelter, its winter quarters, although the massive catfish enjoy them just as much in the heat of the summer. On moonlit nights, the catfish come to the surface: the slime on their backs glistens in the silvery light, and the water pushes up each behemoth with a sound resembling a rueful sigh. The fish pauses at the surface for a bit, floating above the abyss, and then—a slap of a flat tail, and all that remains are circles spreading across the water. I caught a glimpse of this when Pavlik and I went out to check the nets. He stopped the engine and we were drowned in the pre-dawn mist. At the shore, facing our boat, a bearded face appeared from the bushes: a camel had escaped his pen at the Kazakh farm and was nibbling on wet willow leaves. He stilled and watched the spreading circles on the water with the same delight in his big round eyes as I felt, having never seen anything like this before.

When I could get away to spend the weekend with the fishermen, I preferred to sleep less and to go out with them to the nets, learning to set seines and thirstily breathing in the air saturated with river vapors. To me, born and raised in Tajikistan, this abundance of water seemed like paradise.

Those rare weekends on the river were holidays; in the meantime I took every job I could—cleaning the Culture Center at night, selling trinkets out of a kiosk, selling the fish we caught door-to-door. That year, Kharabali took in thirty or forty refugee families; jobs were scarce, and people kept coming.

"Where are you all coming from?" we heard more than once. The locals were inclined to give us a cold shoulder, did not welcome us, and if not for Uncle Styopa's Afghan ties, it would have been even worse. Kharabali's Russians were different: they never made soup and *kutya*[2] for wakes, said "carret" instead of "carrot," "yesteryear" instead of "last year," and "taters" instead of "potatoes"—this was even true of the kindergarten teachers.

I never went to church in Panjakent or in Dushanbe; Aunt Katya, on the other hand, became pious in her old age, perhaps in spite of her communist past. Her grandfather was a priest, and had been executed sometime in the twenties; her mother observed church traditions and the calendar her entire life, and even though Aunt Katya became a party member as a young woman, it turned out she remembered quite a few old ways. Now she set about educating the locals in the proper observances—her training as a Komsomol organizer was not in vain. In Kharabali, it was customary to visit the cemetery and remember the dead on Easter, but according to the holy books and church rules, the correct day is the ninth day after Christ's Resurrection, Radunitsa. Naturally, Aunt Katya was at first treated with suspicion. The priest, Father Andrei, supported her; on every church holiday he mounted large posters with descriptions and explanations of the day's meaning, but no one ever read them, preferring to live according to old habits.

Of course, we were stunned by the drunkenness. In Dushanbe, very few people allowed themselves to drink as much as Gennady did when he left the slaughterhouse at the end of the day. Deep, constant drinking was considered a great shame. Here it was accepted as a normal part of life.

Strangely, some even envied the refugees and accused us of taking work away from the locals by agreeing to do menial jobs. I always responded by saying, "Who's keeping you from working? Go ahead, wash floors at night and man a kiosk for three kopeks a week." Who did I think was listening? What I did not like was their philosophy of "God, please kill my neighbor's cow, then mine can die, too." Of course, not everyone felt that way, but the envy was palpable and irritating.

The newcomers worked like bees and drank little. Gennady, it seemed, had seen the light: he smoked fish from morning till night and gathered firewood. It did not bother me that he spoke little with me, I was used to it. We knew we had to put down roots and earn the locals' respect. In ten years they would get used to us, but first we had to survive for ten years.

We were granted refugee status as soon as we got Russian citizenship, exactly three months after we filed the paperwork. Uncle Styopa was in charge of this for all of us; the local administration respected his military past. He and Aunt Katya were the first to settle and find some stability in their lives; they lived simply but with dignity. They were paid their small salaries regularly, albeit late. They also received pensions. I gradually began to sell fish full-time: I took it to the railway station and sold it to the passengers in passing trains, not the easiest job in the world. At night, I washed floors. This went on for almost a year, until Uncle Kostya could increase his catch and replace Pavlik, who had to go to school, with two boys from Kazakhstan. We added drying to our smoking operation, in order to handle more fish; it was more work for everyone, but we could sell it to dealers wholesale.

In September, Pavlik entered ninth grade. He had always been a good student, and here, trying to earn some respect, he tried even harder and never got any poor grades. The spring and summer on the river had made him stronger, but he had no intention of fishing for the rest of his life. He had only one choice: to get good grades and go to college. Valerka, on the other hand, never graduated from high school. He loved cars from the bottom of his heart and was certain that his life had to center on them. When the fall enlistment came, we sent him off to the army.[3] They packed him off to Chechnya, to war, from where he sent us short letters every two months. He became an armored vehicle driver, and, silly me, I thought I could worry less because the armor would protect him. Later, when he came back, he told us that those vehicles burn like candles, but during his entire tour of duty, he was never close enough to the fighting to get a scratch, thank God. He has always been the lucky one.

Gennady and I worked, and Pavlik helped us as much as he could. We went on living, or rather, carving out a living from the Astrakhan steppe, like many others. With time, I realized that piecemeal jobs—at a kiosk or washing floors—were not the answer; they only slowly sank us deeper into poverty. It seemed we lived like everyone else, and yet, we were worse off. Containers with our things traveled to Volochok, where Gennady's mother received them and piled everything at her *dacha*; we had neither the money nor the energy to go get the stuff. Should we part ways with the rest of the clan and move on? It seemed we were constantly busy, but money evaporated despite all my efforts to save; the only purchases we had made were an old fridge and a TV set.

Gennady held up well, did not drink, but was still reserved and taciturn. He slept on a daybed in his tiny room and prayed a lot. He went to church often, too, and spoke at length with Father Andrei. A new era had begun in our lives. Any time I brought up one of his old pronouncements, he would raise his hard eyes and look at me in a way that made me genuinely frightened. At the local hospital, all the nurses' positions were filled; to work as a nurse's assistant meant, basically, working for free, since the wage would last only for four or five days. We smoked fish and pinched pennies. We ate fish, bread and potatoes that year.

Those of us who bet on a free apartment and sold themselves into debt for the sake of having a place to live—those who went to work as milkmaids, machine operators or fitters—lost in the long run. The winners were the ones who saved up their pennies to open a little business or fought for a well-paid job. Had we stayed in Kharabali for longer than a year, my Valerka would have done something like that. Volodya owns his own repair garage now; it's small, but it feeds him. He left his old boss a long time ago, took out a loan at the right time, and has already built a house for himself. He found himself a jolly Kazakh woman, Zulia, a trim orphan who nonetheless put herself through technical school and got a degree in accounting. Zulia has a mouth full of golden teeth, two wonderful little boys, and they live with Vovka like peas and carrots. Our wandering tribe that roams from land to land is used to marrying non-Russians; above all we value loyalty and an easy-going nature and we do not worry too much about the children being half-bloods: the more different genes they have in them, the tougher and smarter they are.

Uncle Kostya's co-op fell apart under pressure from taxes and harass ment by local racketeers. When he had enough of fishing, he went to work as a manager at a new fishing hotel opened on an island by some visiting Muscovites. He became an administrator and manages the rest of the staff; he is happy with this life and does not complain about his pay. He met a widow, Aunt Olya, but didn't move in with her, instead putting her up at the hotel where he hired her as a cook. On weekends she bakes outstanding fish pies—they have become the signature dish at Three Rivers—and Uncle Kostya washes them down with beer; he doesn't care for anything stronger. I'm happy for him; I envy him, in fact, with well-meaning envy: I would never be able to recover from poverty so easily.

I had saved up some money and bought my first American dollars, four one-hundreds that I hid in the wall behind a loose strip of wall paper. Perhaps if we had stayed our relationships with the locals would have changed for the better. Perhaps. But it was not to be.

A year passed. We celebrated by gathering at Uncle Styopa and Aunt Katya's little house; we made *lagman*,[4] real *plov* with lamb, and fresh sterlet *shashlyk*. There were many toasts; Gennady warmed up, drank a little—just keeping up with everyone else—and became quite drunk, noisy and cheerful. It had been a long time since I had seen him like that. At night, he asked me to come to him.

I surrendered and came, but he had no strength. At first, his persistence awoke a tenderness in me. Then I felt sorry for him. Then pity was replaced with indifference. He got up from the bed, naked and crazed; he trembled, and a chill spread from his body across the room. His lips parted and uttered one word, "Fish!" It flew at me like the crack of a whip, and tears suddenly burst from my eyes. I had never cried before. The tears made Gennady irate. He hit me once, but so hard that he split my eyebrow and blood instantly covered my face. Cursing dirtily, he dressed, grabbed the TV set and threw it hard against the wall. Not quite understanding why I was doing it, I stood up suddenly and went at him, naked, covered in blood. I walked silently, with my head held high. Gennady brushed me aside like a feather; I flew into a corner and slammed painfully into the door frame. He stepped over me, took the money out of the hiding-place and left. Fortunately, neither Pavlik nor Volodya were home: had they tried to defend me then, lots of blood would have been spilled.

I lay with my smashed face pressed into a pillow. As my blood coagulated, its pounding in my split eye-brow subsided, and I cooled too. The chill spread throughout my body, it was going numb and crusting over with a single scab. I lay like that for several hours, until Pavlik came home. He washed the blood off my face, treated the gash with iodine, and changed the pillowcase and the soiled bed sheet. He wanted to run and get a doctor, but I stopped him with my eyes. The shame had paralyzed me. He covered me with a warm blanket. Seeing that the light hurt my eyes, Pavlik drew the curtains on the window and turned off the night light.

Even the tiny crack of light that sneaked under the curtains was enough. The thin ray of sun that drew a wavy white stripe on the windowsill gave me a migraine and I turned my face to the wall. Noise, just like light, tortured me. When the neighbors' rooster crowed in his coop before dawn, I thought the pain would burst my head open. My forehead was awash in sweat; I went from chills to fever and back again; I suddenly started to choke, as if someone had pressed a solid cotton wool mattress against my face.

Irrational fear took root somewhere deep at the bottom of my stomach and now slowly crawled upwards, like water filling a bathtub. My chest began to burn, then blotches covered my neck and face. My tongue would not turn; it did not want to let out the words that were buzzing in my mind. I took my muteness as a blessing: if I had lost my gag in that instant, I would have whimpered, whined and screamed for help.

Sleep had fled me. I lay staring at a single point in space or letting my eyes, watery with sleeplessness, follow my son's caring hand as it dabbed me with a cold towel. His touch and the cool fabric soothed me and fought the fever better than aspirin.

Pavlik intuitively found the same method as I used with my patients: he kept stroking my hands, head and neck, whispering kind words to me. I used to comfort and lull him to sleep like this when he was little, and now he was paying me back, fighting his own fear with tenderness and love. His therapy worked; it gave me peace, it chased away the demons of shame and fear that had made a nest in my stomach. When he stepped away, having chastised and bound them with his words, they woke again and sucked thirstily on the last juices of my crippled soul.

Fears that had lain forgotten rolled back, wave after wave. The damned old man rose again, I could feel his forceful, powerful hands gliding over my unresisting body. Muck clogged my every pore and crusted over my skin. I felt my body begin to wither, to shrink; I needed water and compulsively licked my lips, which had dried shut. If my son was there, he gave me water to drink from a mug, holding up my head. At night all I could do was pray for dawn to come sooner.

I could not sleep; all the normal functions of my organism had been derailed. Mute, sealed shut, I battled my horror alone. If it had not been for my son's care, I do not know when and how I would have found my way back to the surface.

The word that Gennady threw at me burned worse than his blow. If I were like that, then why should I have this life, for what? I wanted to dissolve into the sheets, to evaporate without a trace, to the last drop of sweat, so that in the morning someone would just wring my remains into the toilet and toss what was left into the trash with the ruined bedding.

I could hear everything that went on in the household: Pavlik and Vovka talked about Gennady's behavior. He had not been home for a week. He was drinking. There was no one to smoke the fish; the family business had come to a halt, life was careening into disaster. Gennady caroused about the town with prostitutes for all the world to see, with no shame at all, while I, hearing about his escapades, stayed in bed and burned with shame, unwanted and slandered, like a faulty part that no one wants to fix. Kharabali is a small town; everyone knows everything, and I realized it would be beyond me to show myself in public.

On the fourth day, something in me began to soften, the tension in my body disappeared, the numbness in my arms and legs loosened and I could move them again. I made my way to the bathroom unaided. Pavlik opened the curtains, and the light did not slice into my eyes; I could calmly look out the window. The street noises no longer tore at me like they did the first couple of days, but I still had choking fits. I had no strength whatsoever in my body, but my skin regained its sensitivity; a thousand tiny needles pricked at my fingers and toes, signaling that circulation had returned. In the evening of the fourth day I drank some chicken broth for the first time and ate two spoonfuls of broth-soaked white bread.

My sickness retreated in waves. On the sixth day I felt I could speak again but did not, for fear I would jinx it. My split eyebrow ached and I welcomed the pain as a sign of life—a happy change from the spell of lifelessness.

Vovka ambushed Gennady somewhere in town and gave him a serious beating. I heard him tell Pavlik about it, but felt no pride in my defender. Secretly, I worried the scab on my eyebrow to cause myself sweet pain. I was embarrassed to admit it to myself, but I wanted to see Gennady; I needed to look into his eyes. I was not afraid of him; this was a different, passionate need that could not be put into words. The thin scar on my right brow—my memory of Kharabali—remained for the rest of my life.

After a week's absence, Gennady crawled home; he swayed with exhaustion like a sexed-out tomcat. Whether because Vovka had taught him a lesson or because he understood something on his own, Gennady begged for forgiveness as soon as he stepped through the door, something he had never done before. He mumbled something about humility, about demons, cried hangover tears and reached out his arms to me. I had not eaten in seven days, but I got up from the bed, put on my robe, went to the stove and put a kettle on. He dragged after me into the kitchen; I turned to him and said calmly, looking him straight in the eye, "When my bruise disappears, we are going to Volochok. Sit down and eat."

I took some fried fish from the pan and ate a piece with great pleasure. The fool, he interpreted it as a sign of reconciliation and tried to kiss me, but I put the food on his plate and went to my room. I knew what had to be done: I had to deliver him into his mother's care. I did not want to live under the same roof with him any longer.

· 3 ·

MARK GRIGORIYEVICH LEFT yesterday. He makes sure to come to Moscow several times a year: he plays concerts at the Conservatory, teaches master classes, and mentors young musicians. Every minute of his two weeks in Moscow is scheduled, but he finds time every day to pop into his mother's room, and talk to her about something or other. Grandma lies very calmly and often falls asleep, happy and peaceful. Their conversations are one-sided, but every time he feels that his mother, finally, heard and understood him. It must be easier for him that way. He leaves the room (I am never there when they "talk") and smiles at me, "Vera, today, Mom and I reminisced about my childhood. I could see she enjoyed it, she was smiling until she got tired and fell asleep."

"Yes, Mark Grigoriyevich, she often falls asleep with me, too, when I read to her. It's a good sign: it means that nothing is bothering her."

We are playing a game that is not entirely a game, when you think about it.

He does not waste time on ceremonies with me, glances at his watch, throws up his hands and runs out: he is always very busy in Moscow.

Grandma has two nieces, old pensioners themselves. They are entitled to part of the apartment in the will; Grandma Lisichanskaya never made a secret of it. At first, when she became ill, they visited, fussed over her, sighed ruefully, and stroked her head, but clumsily and with evident fear. Grandma reacted badly to their visits; at their touch she seemed to congeal, to become as wooden and unyielding as a post. When they really annoyed her, she would pretend she were dying: her blood pressure would fall, she would breathe heavily, or would suddenly clutch my hand in a death grip and not let go until the door closed behind the visitors. Once I overheard their lamentations, "What is the point of this all? Sofia was such a strong-willed person; it is terrible to see her lose her mind. It would be better if this did not last long."

Grandma was lying right there. They treated her as if she was ignorant, deaf, lost to the world, and were not shy when expressing their feelings. I complained to Mark Grigoriyevich, and the nieces' visits stopped.

During this visit, they broke his ban, showed up and tormented him behind closed doors for a good hour. I only heard it when he shouted loudly, "Don't even hope for it, she will not go to a hospice, you will not change my mind!"

They left soon after that, red and steaming.

I was sitting up with Grandma. She was very worried, clasped my hand in her avian paw and would not let go. I stroked her hair for a long time, but she could not fall asleep. No, I would never call my Grandma senseless; I spent half of the night telling her about my life in Kharabali and I think it helped take her mind off things.

Gennady, once he lost it, deteriorated. His binge with the prostitutes in Kharabali even made me happy in a perverse way, because it showed he was still capable of something. But when he came crawling back home, all my hopes came crushing down: it was not me whom he begged for forgiveness but God. I could no longer be responsible for him in this world.

Gennady, once we took him back into the family, seemed to understand this. He talked more to all of us and called me Candy, but when I kept my distance he instantly lost his taste for it and had difficulty controlling his anger.

In our last month in Kharabali, we worked a lot to earn money for our tickets. By letter, Valerka agreed to come from the Army straight to Volochok; there was nothing in Kharabali to keep him there, either. Packing was easy. We gathered for the last time as the big family, joyless and solemn. We listened to everyone's wishes and admonitions, and reassured them that as soon as got there we would send word. Things that had been left unsaid and our mutual embarrassment made the meal tense; our parting resembled a wake.

They helped us board the Astrakhan-Moscow train; we climbed into our soiled third class car which reeked of sweat, coal and cheap wine. I took the window seat and my eyes followed the passing steppe, the infrequent horse herds, the tiny stations and low-roofed huts cordoned off from the world with fences of straw and hay, the sentinels of the front line: crippled tractors, trailers, metal shafts aimed at the sky, kids and dogs who played tag as far as they could get from the frail homes. Occasionally we flew past a village splayed over the edge of a bluff. A pair of cemeteries—the Orthodox and the Muslim—always clung to the edges of these, separated by a brick fence; together but apart, just as people lived their lives here. Sometimes I would see a few graves in the steppe, next to the railroad line, strung along a long-forgotten road. The brass half-moons mounted on poles stuck into the graves indicated that these were the most recent nomads; their families alone knew why this deserted place had been chosen as the final place of rest. From the window I sometimes saw the great *kurgans*—dirt mounds, half plowed-under, where slept the ancestors of those who inserted lopsided poles with the rising Muslim moon into concrete-bordered flower beds.

Before Saratov, we crossed a long bridge over the Volga, and then crawled along its shore, pock-marked with boat stations that looked like beehives. After Saratov, the view began to change, but then night fell.

In the morning, a green sea of leaves washed both sides of the train. It was May, and the ground still had plenty of moisture in it; large puddles reflected the blue sky with the clouds inching across it.

We spent a harried half-a-day in Moscow, riding the packed subway and watching our bags lest they get stolen. It took us two trips to move all our things from one railway station to another. We were as exhausted as supply-train horses when we finally loaded into the new train and collapsed into slumber. In Volochok, Aunt Raya met us at the station, a skinny, not-yet-old woman, complete with a live-in mate, Oleg Petrovich, who was clearly under her thumb.

We packed our things into a van and drove to their house. It was at the edge of town, built next to a slow-flowing, grass-clogged canal. The town was small, with neighborhoods extending in every direction. Our new family lived in one of these settlements. Far away, above a pile of roofs, shone the golden dome of the nunnery church. Now I think it was one of the mountains of gold that my mother-in-law always promised me in her letters to Dushanbe and Kharabali.

· 4 ·

I SAW ALMOST IMMEDIATELY that we could not all live together, and, to tell the truth, I did not have a burning desire to do so. My mother-in-law was completely out of touch with her son, did not care for his piety, and they instantly had a huge fight about it, in which I, thankfully, had no part.

Gennady left, slamming the door behind him. He came back late at night and announced that he had arranged to be a liturgy reader[5] in the local church. His mother, at first, did not think he was serious; Oleg Petrovich, as he had no say in much of anything, did not express his opinion.

Raya and her old mate lived a slowly paced, retired life; they were within the city limits, but had a plot of land where she grew her own potatoes, and a greenhouse which produced cucumbers, tomatoes and sweet peppers. In the fall, she made jams and canned, storing her jars in a well-equipped basement with labels like "Harvest of such and such year, Curr." or "Goosebr." or "Compote." The place she referred to as "dacha" in her letters, and where she had stored our possessions, turned out to be a simple cabin in the woods, about a hundred kilometers from Volochok; it was Oleg Petrovich's inherited fiefdom.

They went there two or three times every summer to pick wild raspberries, blueberries, currants and mushrooms to fill the basement jars, and to gather apples from three lush apple trees that were looked after by the neighbor, Aunt Leyda, one of the Estonian colonists who had settled in the area. Oleg Petrovich was also Estonian on his mother's side, but for some reason he did not like to talk about it, was embarrassed by being Leyda's distant relative, and tried to go as infrequently as possible to the village of Karmanovo, where their families' original homes still stood.

The job situation in Volochok was even worse than in Kharabali: fifteen round-the-clock shifts (one day on, one day off) manning a food stand were valued by the owner at 300-400 rubles, and there were always plenty of willing candidates. The two hospitals in Volochok were fully staffed, as were its walk-in clinic and its pharmacy. It was the same with the mental asylum in Burashevo, nearby sanatoriums, and group homes. Aunt Raya quickly took measure of my relationship with Gennady and within a week of our arrival declared, "I cannot possibly feed you all. Find jobs and a place to live, or go live in Karmanovo. The house is fine, and the linen plant in Zhukovo always needs workers."

So it was that we went to Zhukovo and registered in the local rural council[6] without any trouble; there was no reason to give us the runaround, since everyone there knew Petrovich. The important stamp in the passport made us instantly "local" and we could start our lives from scratch. In the former central *kolkhoz* office I was told that, yes, indeed, they needed workers, especially at the linen factory, but the pay was nothing to brag about. I did not press the issue, knowing full well that no place that paid well and on time would ever have a vacancy. After the offices, we went to Karmanovo to pick up some of the things we would need. All our stuff was piled carelessly on the bed and the table, and the rats had had a good go at it. I spent a lot of time later laundering and mending our quilts, bedding and towels, and eventually restored them to decency.

I got lucky. I met an old lady in the street and helped her carry her groceries home. The grandma lived alone; her family rarely visited her. We started talking, I frankly told her everything about myself. Grandma promised to help, and did: she got me a custodial job in a big apartment building at 500 rubles a month (the maintenance manager was a relative of hers). With the job, they gave us a basement apartment: two tiny rooms, a bathroom, hot water, gas—it was perfect. We built wooden cots and hammered together a wardrobe. I spent half a day scrubbing the old two-burner stove clean and giving it a fresh coat of white enamel, and my men cleaned and reset the burners. We even managed to tile the bath and the toilet stall and to change the faucets, eating up the last of my savings. There was only one thing that upset me terribly: Pavlik refused to go to school for what would have been his last year, and instead hired himself out as a laborer at the local sawmill. He had his father's stubbornness in him; once he made up his mind, it was impossible to make him change his course.

"You should work yourself to death, while I study? Don't even try to talk me out of it."

I talked at him incessantly anyway, but to no effect. He was often in low spirits, and began reading his father's books again. Our life headed for another nosedive no sooner than it seemed to have straightened out. Gennady was always at church, taking his meals there, and soon he began to spend the nights there as well, every other night; they had him doing penance as the night watchman. When I asked him about a wage, he answered honestly: he was not working for money.

"Then go to your mother's."

He went, but came back a week later, spent a night on one of the cots, disappeared again, then returned. I stopped talking to him; I placed all my hopes on Valerka, who would be returning soon, in two or three months.

We wandered around our basement like three shadows. Pavlik left early, returned late, was very tired, ate his supper silently and went to bed. He began to resemble his father a lot. The sawmill employed refugee

Uzbeks and local ex-cons—he didn't associate with them, and made no friends at all outside work.

The storm clouds were gathering above our heads, but I did not sense anything. Aside from the custodial duties, I also roasted sunflower seeds at night and sold them in paper cups at the bus station during the day. Money, filthy money—it made me blind and I lost my son.

Sometimes it seemed to me like Pavlik was coming home drunk. I would smell him, but would not catch a whiff of alcohol. I asked him about it, but he just waved me off.

"Leave it, Mom, you know I don't drink."

When he became suspiciously lethargic, I chalked it up to his depression and begged him to go back to school, even if it meant just taking a correspondence course. He promised he would, but that was the end of that, and gradually I left him alone; Pavlik had become an adult without me noticing.

Valerka was a different story. He returned from the Army in proper style: with golden veteran's aiguillettes on his dress uniform and sporting brand-new box-calf boots he had bartered somewhere. He wore his service cap with its clipped beak cocked dashingly over one ear, was carrying a thick scrapbook and had corporal's stripes on his shoulder straps. He also brought us ten thousand rubles and when I asked him about it, answered lightly, "I earned it, Ma, no worries! In the Army, if you're smart, you can do well."

He instantly found a job as a mechanic at a car repair shop on the Moscow-Leningrad highway, as though they had been saving a spot especially for him. For a thousand rubles, he bought a Zaporozhets, messed with it for a week or two, and began giving evening rides to girls and friends he had acquired as easily as if he had lived here his whole life. Occasionally he came home a bit tipsy, but I mostly saw him in the mornings. Valerka was having his fun easily, happily, the way Pavlik never could. Two or three times the big brother took the younger with him—"to air out," as he put it—until they both came back scraped up. Pavlik had a good-sized shiner under one eye.

"We taught the locals a lesson for calling us 'Tajiks'."

The nickname "Tajik" stuck to Valerka, but after the fight it became a sign of respect and he didn't resist it. Pavlik did not go to "air out" with his brother any more, and Valerka left him alone.

"No, Mom, he is not made for this sort of thing. Maybe the Army would set him straight; guys make fun of him."

It was not hard for me to surmise exactly how Pavlik disappointed his brother. His shyness must have put a damper on his brother's good times. Unfortunately, the boys were never particularly close.

Valerka met Sveta at a New Year's party and began to bring her home. They lived separately for the time being, but were completely inseparable. Both stopped by our place to get a bite to eat, or she would wait for him to change out of his uniform after work. I liked it that she was reserved around me; I am suspicious of people who immediately act like your buddy. Sveta's mother was a hopeless alcoholic, and the girl never mentioned her; she never knew her father either. Valerka was the light of her soul; it was obvious she loved him.

They did not date long. In March, they came and told me that they rented a room from the old lady who got me my job and would live on their own. I was happy for them. Our life in the basement reflected our environment: little light, low ceilings and musty air. Sparrows were chirping with the vigor of the new spring, but their joy could not enter our home: the windows were painted shut.

Pavlik had a disagreement with the other workers at the sawmill. Apparently they argued about divvying up their profits. He was very tense for a couple of days, said he would leave the job, but then things settled down and peace was restored. It seemed as if he had been taken back into the fold. He mentioned a few men by name, stayed out late a couple of nights, and once came home a bit drunk.

The days were growing longer, the sun shone warmer, and I had to work less with the snow shovel and more with a heavy crow bar with a hatchet welded to its tip. I used it to break up and clean off the ice, then sprinkled the walkways with sand mixed with salt. I kept up the yard; all the dirt and debris that had accumulated under the snow had risen to the surface. My men, too busy with their own lives, did not help me out.

On the evening of April fourth, cold and exhausted, I was returning from the bus station; I had sold thirty-two cups—sixty-four rubles worth of sunflower seeds—and bought a pound of sausage and a bottle of milk on my way home. Pavlik had loved milk ever since he was a kid; I thought of buying some cookies, too, but for some reason decided to be cheap instead. I still had to check the refuse chutes in the building, but I was so cold that I decided to clean them in the morning. Gennady was not home; Pavlik was sleeping. I fried the sausages, made some macaroni, and put the meal on the table.

"Pavlik, dinner is ready."

He did not answer. I went to him and saw it instantly: the colorless face, the waxy heaviness of the hand pressed into the pillow. He was already cold. An empty disposable syringe lay on the blanket.

I rushed into the street as I was, bare-headed. I ran across the dark city; I gasped for air, I choked, but I kept running. People stepped aside, made way for me. I reached the church and banged on the door; a dog exploded barking in the back yard. Finally, a passerby saw me and showed me a small side door. I dashed there. The iron bolts on the inside of the door clanged loudly enough to raise the dead. The door opened; there stood Gennady in a black cassock. I fell into his arms.

Then there was police, paramedics, the morgue. Gennady fetched Valerka. I hid in the depths of our basement, in its darkest corner, and could not utter a word, and, stranger still, also could not cry. Gennady and Valerka took care of everything.

We buried Pavlik three days later, on a frigid and rainy day at noon. Gennady insisted on a church liturgy. The old priest swung the censer at an empty, cold church and sang out the words in a cracked falsetto. His fluid, solemn chants rose and disappeared under the sooty dome. The incense had an oily, sickly-sweet smell. Finally, the priest pulled a sheet over Pavlik's face, sprinkled sand over it in the sign of the cross, and Gennady and Valerka picked up their hammers to nail the coffin shut. Next we drove through a pine forest somewhere, past a canal, to the edge of the city. The cemetery was large and new, almost treeless—there were only the fences, the crosses, and the plastic wreaths, rain-bleached and snow-shredded. A strong wind blew; my mother-in-law threw a warm shawl over my shoulders. She was crying loudly for the grandson she had barely met, and I could no more part my lips than if they had been sealed shut with contact cement. They used towels to lower the coffin into the shallow hole. Barely conscious of what I was doing, I squeezed a lump of wet clay and tossed it in; it fell like a rock and stuck to the red fabric. Someone gave me a bottle of water; I used it to thoroughly wash my hand. The wind chilled my wet fingers and, mechanically, I wrapped them in the hem of the shawl. Gennady was fully in command; if not for his self-discipline, we would not have been able to give Pavlik such a funeral. He made arrangements with the cemetery office, he paid the grave diggers, he gave orders in a crisp, commanding voice, and for some reason I knew that he would not get drunk that day. He, Valerka and Petrovich each drank a shot of vodka and left the rest of the bottle to the cemetery workers. With his eyes fixed on the fresh mound, Valerka said, "I'll teach those sons of bitches at the sawmill a lesson. In the army we had a way to deal with druggies."

"Swear to me here and now, in front of everyone, that you will do nothing of the sort."

I did not raise my voice.

"Don't worry, Mom, I know what I am talking about."

"Swear—or I'll die."

Suddenly he understood. The anger bled from his face and he hugged me.

"Alright, if that's what you want, I swear. But I'd fry them alive, fuckers."

That's when I started to cry.

My mother-in-law and Sveta had the meal ready at home, but as soon as I dragged myself back into the basement, I dropped onto a cot and fell asleep. I woke up in the middle of the night; Gennady was sleeping next to me, on his cot. I stared at the ceiling until dawn, like a dumb beast. I knew that this had been my boy's way of escaping the pain. I did not doubt for a second that Pavlik had known exactly what he was doing. I remembered only too well my own pain and the pulsating pressure that pressed on me from all sides, and the inner voice that whispered, "Go to the bathroom, take the razor, free yourself, release the pain." The drugs robbed him of his will so that he succumbed to the temptation, and I—the fool!—missed it. Night was all around me. My mind churned with the words "forgiveness," "understanding," "consolation." I lay in my basement and I was alive.

In the morning we got up. I made breakfast. Gennady only drank tea and then suddenly said, looking me in the eye, "Our life, Vera, did not work out. I am not worried about Valerka—he will be fine. He will take care of you too. I cannot do this any longer; I am going to a monastery, I got the Father's blessing before Pavlik's death. If you can—forgive me. In the old days, if this happened to the faithful, the husband and wife entered monasteries on the same day, but now it's not like that. File for divorce."

He left for his church with his familiar rocking gait, slightly dragging his unbending leg, and I bore him no ill in my soul. I washed the dishes, took my broom, dustpan and bucket from the closet and went to clean the yard.

· 5 ·

SO ON TOP OF EVERYTHING, I also had to file for divorce. It went through quickly: a month after I filed, I was summoned to court, and a large woman at the desk there asked me, "Where is your spouse?"

"In a monastery."

"What do you mean, in a monastery? In what kind of a monastery?"

Her face came to life; she must have never seen a case like ours before.

"My husband has entered a monastery and is preparing to take his vows."

"And you agree with his decision?"

"Yes, I do," I said and added in my mind, "Amen of Holy Spirit!"

The stamps in the passports cost me another four hundred rubles, two hundred from each divorcing party. I gave Gennady's passport to Valerka, and he took it to his father. He just took it and did not comment on the event. I felt a bit irked; my Pavlik would have found the right words to say to me.

Valerka and Sveta refused to move into the basement with me, so I lived alone for three weeks. I tried to be home as little as possible; my yard and the trash chutes all but gleamed. I got up at five and began by sweeping the yard and cleaning the playground. At night, young people gathered there and left behind bottles, cigarette butts, paper cups, spit. Then I went to the garbage chutes, cleaned them out and sorted the trash. During the day, if there was enough to fill my backpack and a wheel-bag, I recycled glass bottles.[7] In the afternoon, I worked on the flowerbeds, dug and planted, whitewashed the trees.[8] I occupied myself any way I could. The residents of our big apartment building treated me with respect and said hello; I always greeted them back, but did not engage in conversation. I generally did not feel like talking—not to anyone.

And then another thing hit me. The Director of the maintenance service called me in and said sternly, "Vera, you are a great worker, but my relatives are coming from Latvia, so I'm going to have to fire you. You have to vacate the apartment—you have a week."

She gave me a bonus, a thousand rubles. The relatives later paid me another two thousand for the repairs and the furniture.

Valerka and Sveta took me in and curtained off a corner in their room.

"That's alright, Mom, we'll find you some work. Don't worry," Valerka promised.

But there was no work to be had. I spent the month of May roasting and selling sunflower seeds. I did it at night, banging the frying pans in the kitchen and keeping the young couple up and waiting in front of the TV for me to go to bed. Sveta, under various pretexts, peeked into the kitchen every few minutes to see how I was doing and if I were about finished with my enterprise. To make matters worse, I could not fall asleep right away and lay in the dark, quiet as a mouse, listening to them. For some reason I was unable to take any comfort in their happiness. I would start to toss on my bed, then I would suddenly have an urge to pee and get up, shuffling my slippers across the floor to the creaky door. A tense silence would gather behind the curtain until Sveta's whisper would break it, "Will she settle down already? No life here, we can't even fuck in peace."

Their happy giggles trailed me to the bathroom. I was not upset; I knew I had to move on, yet I continued to hesitate. Finally, the occasion presented itself. Sveta and I had a fight: I found fault with her fish cutlets and wanted to show her how to make them better. It ended with her yelling at me and then running off into a corner and crying until the evening. I went to the store and bought a bottle of Isabella.[9] When Valerka came home from work, I placed it ceremoniously on the table.

"Go get Sveta, son. We had a fight and now we'll be making peace. I have something important to tell you."

Svetka instantly came out of her corner, puffy-eyed and wary. Suddenly, she sidled up to me shyly, hugged me, and whispered, "Mom, forgive me."

"No, you have to forgive *me*. I shall be moving to Karmanovo; my mother-in-law said they need workers there at the linen factory."

They didn't try very hard to talk me out of it. We ate together. We drank a bit of Isabella and had sausage salad and my unfortunate fish cutlets. Sveta, the fox, praised them.

The next day Valerka and Petrovich loaded the car; all my earthly possessions easily fit into the trunk. I took some groceries to hold me over until I could plant a garden. My larger items—pots and pans, old clothes, winter coats and books—were still stored in Karmanovo. Raya swore that she had not taken a single thread from our container.

I dove into murky waters with my eyes closed and floated to the bottom in search of a safe lair.

I moved to Karmanovo on the 25th of May. Valerka and Petrovich borrowed a tractor and ploughed the vegetable garden and the potato strip, twelve furrows. I stuck some onions and garlic into the ground, sprinkled carrot seeds, dill and parsley, added turnips and zucchini. The idea of starting a greenhouse with cucumbers and tomatoes did not appeal to me at all; I decided I could do it next year if it turned out that I liked poking around in the dirt.

. 6 .

THAT EVENING, Aunt Leyda invited us over—her house was close to mine. There were really no other homes in Karmanovo; it was not, in fact, a village but a small homestead. A few other tiny settlements nestled in the woods, in the remotest parts of Firovo district, far from the main road between Firovo and Volochok. It was all that remained of the Estonian Nurmekundia.

After work, the men drank a little vodka, and we, the three women—myself, Aunt Leyda, and her daughter Nelya, who had come to visit for the weekend—had tea with cream cheese biscuits. Nelya had graduated from Kalinin University and was the Director of Studies in a school in the village of Yesenovichi, fifteen miles away. She filled me in on the local history.

Tsar Alexander I,[10] when he came back from Paris after defeating Napoleon, decided to set the peasants free. And so he did, but only in the Baltic provinces; the rest of Russia had to wait quite a bit longer. Each peasant received a small plot of land that he could pass on to his eldest son. As the result, by the 1880s, Liflandia and Estlandia, as Nelya called the provinces, swarmed with impoverished landless peasants—the middle and younger children who could not inherit their father's rights. A mass exodus began.

Whole families pulled up roots, herded up their cattle and loaded their possessions onto ox-carts. They sought the protection of the great Russian Tsar. Only a ridiculed few booked passage in the hulls of steamships and sailed for America, Canada, or Australia. It was not until much later that it became clear that they were, in fact, the lucky ones. At the time, sailing to the other side of the world seemed like pure folly: the Russian Empire was strong and full of priceless virgin lands to which the poor flocked in hopes of starting their own farms. They settled in groups, close together, which, of course, helped them to survive.

Estonians went to the warm lands on the Black Sea shore, or to the places in Siberia and in the Altai mountains where, it was said, the mere scent of the blooming herbs cured any ailment. Some of them made their way to Pitsunda,[11] a small Abkhazian settlement bordering the ancient Colchis.[12] They pitched their tents and studied the land. It smelled of Artemisia and rotting citrus. There for the taking were plentiful persimmons, tangerines and figs; their sweet juice attracted swarms of flies and one had to chase them away with aromatic mimosa branches. At night the merciless mosquitoes attacked—the areas inland were rife with stagnant pools of rusty water. With mosquitoes came malaria, previously unknown to this Northern people. The settlers perished by the hundreds; mosquitoes banished the Estonians from their Abkhazian paradise. Those who still had money set out for Tver province. There, Brandt's Lumber, an offshoot enterprise of the Ryabushinsky millionaires' empire, gave volunteers tracts of unbroken land and an interest-free loan. That was where they finally settled—in a familiar Northern landscape, at the tip of the Valdai river basin, in woods rich with mushrooms, wild game and malaria-free mosquitoes, on rich, loamy soils yet to be claimed from the forest. They put down roots amidst the three Russian villages—Kuzlovo, Skomorokhovo and Konakovo—that dotted the road from the forest frontier to the provincial market.

The Estonians staked out homesteads, burned the woods and pulled the stumps. In the first year, they built low, sturdy barns for cattle and wintered there alongside their animals, keeping each other warm. By the beginning of the 20th century, the land of Nurmekunde (Nurmekundia in Russian), which means "a union of homesteads," stood firmly on its own two feet. Almost everyone had learned the local language, while, of course, retaining their languid tongue and native habits. People continued to correspond with distant relatives from the old country, places like Yanni, Antsl, Lavassaare or Kallaste. One could boast to them of their newly-raised *kirik*,[13] of their Estonian school for which their relatives had sent books in the native tongue, of their veterinary and medical clinics, flour- and sawmills. The Baltic cattle grew larger and fatter on the Tver meadows, grew stronger and more vigorous and, crossbred with fresh bloodlines brought from the old country, produced the creamiest milk in the whole province.

Like their cattle, the people breathed easier and prospered. Mail regularly brought news of flaxen-haired, industrious Estonian farmers flourishing in the Altai foothills and in Siberia, on the Volga steppes, in Pitsunda, and even in faraway Australia. They began to marry locals; love has no rules, as everyone knows, and does not follow bloodlines like a cattle herd. Two orchestras were started in Nurmekundia—a brass band and a folk-instrument group. Trombones, clarinets, trumpets, contrabasses, cellos and violins were mail-ordered from Europe via Petersburg and mandolins and balalaikas could be found at the Tver Fair. The Nurmekundians played at holidays and weddings, adopting, rather than neglecting, local accordion tunes, whose simpler harmonies they found more pleasing than the louder, flashier voices of the German accordions. The Estonians bought the latest in agricultural machinery: seeders, winnowers, steam-powered thrashers, and even the first tractors to be owned by anyone in Tver province.

Then came the revolution, followed by collectivization. Homesteads were to be no more. The NKVD rake thinned out those not agreeable with the new way of life and, for the sake of fairness, those who did agree to join the *kolkhoz* as well. Those who were left learned to sing revolutionary anthems, organized an Estonian Komsomol, and began to print a newspaper, *The Voice of Nurmekundia*. Like all other *kolkhoz* workers across the great country, they, stripped of their passports and returned to the new serfdom, overproduced daily norms of the Socialist plan, went to war and, if they returned home, were laid in the ground of their graveyard surrounded by an aged wrought-iron fence with a square Protestant cross above the gate.

Passports were finally issued in 1980. Even before that, however, many who had secretly continued to sing Lutheran psalms managed to slither back to Estonia. Men, when they finished their military service, would sign up for the fishing fleet and receive fishermen's passports, which radically changed their status. They went back to their ancestral lands, settled there and immediately arranged for their families to join them. With *perestroika*, everyone was on the move—a mass exodus began. Some found homes with distant relatives—not in vain had they written letters for more than a hundred years—others relied on the help of those who had left before them. In short, by the end of the 1980s all that was left of the lively province was empty fields and random rows of moss-covered logs where the houses once stood; the Russian neighbors, thrifty and descending into poverty, quickly squirreled away everything else that could be of use.

· 7 ·

IN '94, WHEN I MOVED to Karmanovo, an old Latvian man Krastin and an ancient Estonian lady lived in the neighboring village of Pochinok. No trace remained of the Russian Skomorokhovo and Kuzlovo, or of any other villages. The distant Konakovo, ten miles from us, still counted about twenty families. After the demise of the *kolkhoz*, people lived hand-to-mouth, surviving gypsy-style. They relied on their elderly parents' pensions or aid to families with multiple children,[14] stole lumber or aluminum wires, harvested mushrooms and berries, cut and dried beech bark to sell as a raw pharmaceutical, trapped beavers and sold fur to dealers for kopeks. Money was converted into ethyl alcohol, which burned the residents' insides slowly but surely, until it delivered them to the moist Tver soil of the ancient graveyard.

Leyda Yanovna Kyart, my neighbor, spent her working life as a mail carrier, mapped all the Nurmekundian homesteads and villages first with her feet and later by bicycle, sent three children to universities, buried her husband, and had no intention of moving anywhere.

"I was born here and here I will die. My grandmother told me what it's like to move the whole family. There's enough work and trouble for me here."

I understood Leyda's grandmother very well. Someone had painted her portrait in white zinc on the wall of a hand-built wardrobe: a white woman in a lace dress sternly regarded anyone who entered the Kyarts' bedroom. Next to it stood an old, worn-out piano with the word "PARIS" written in gold letters on its lid.

The homestead possessed many useful implements: a hand-operated milk separator, a meat grinder of vintage design, an ingenious line saw, the likes of which you could not find even in a museum, a sharpening stone the size of a barrel lid, kerosene lamps, drills, chisels, bits and other tools whose names and uses were obscure even to their owner. Still, everything was in working order, oiled, sharpened and ready. The Kyart fortress was equipped to withstand electricity shortages as well, which happened all the time—the lights would go out and not come back on for several days.

There was no hope of a phone. Instead, a combine, a bailing machine, a two-horse mower and a tractor trailer were parked in the street outside the house: Leyda's youngest son Viktor lived in Zhukovo, and he hid his share of the divided *kolkhoz* property here. Now that the *kolkhoz* was rising again, this time as a joint-stock enterprise, Viktor had joined it as a simple laborer and rented out the machinery. Basically, he worked for free, since you could not really call what he was paid a rent or a salary.

I learned all this gradually—Aunt Leyda and I now had plenty of time. Under her tutelage, I learned to live in the country. This turned out to be no easy task. There was the silence and the endless woods, the wild animals who left tracks on the road, the large Russian stove and the warm loft atop it, and the smaller Dutch stove next to the bed. Then there were also two cows, chickens, a horse, a piglet, a dog and three cats, and Leyda Yanovna took care of them all. The vegetable garden required regular hoeing; every morning, when I pulled up weeds, a cloud of gnats would burst out of the wet grass into my face and sting me until my eyes watered. I cried in the garden without embarrassment, just as I did in the kitchen when I chopped small, pungent onions. But I had no tears at other times. With my sleeves rolled up, I helped muck the barn stalls and even learned to milk the cows—it turned out to be just as easy as squeezing off my own excess milk. When Pavlik was born, I had so much milk that I shared it with Farshida's baby.

. 8 .

KARMANOVO AND ZHUKOVO are five miles apart. The distance we had covered so quickly in a car, I had to cover daily by bicycle or on foot. The bicycle, an old, heavy "Ukraine," was in the shed; Valerka made a special trip a week later, took it apart, oiled it, put it back together and fashioned a carrier over the rear wheel, so that I could bring groceries back from the store. Having thus fixed my life, he left; communications were broken off.

When the rains came, the clay road became impassable and the trip became a form of torture; I had to walk part of the way, leading the bicycle alongside me. Two hills to climb and one steep one to descend. The mile and a quarter in the middle, where the village of Skomorokhovo once stood, were sometimes impassable even on foot: massive tractors had ground deep ruts in the road and I had to step so carefully on the narrow, slippery shoulder, it was as if I were training to take a tight-rope walking exam.

I got up early, at five, had some tea and bread, and set out to make it to work by eight. The linen factory was an old, long shack, clogged with dust, its dirty windows never washed. The conveyer belt ran through different machines and implements along one wall and back along half the length of the other.

Twelve people in the shift. The supervisor, a local girl named Nadezhda; three men of indeterminate age; an ancient stoker in the boiler room and seven women. Duties assigned regardless of gender. Number one unwinds the rolls of washed and dried linen and, with the help of number two, feeds them into the maw of the brake. Raw fibers begin their ride on the conveyer. They crawl along slowly, through a series of rolls and combs on their way to the shaker (numbers three, four and five). The machine bangs like a machine gun, kneading and combing linen stalks. In the end, it produces low-grade fiber and soft wool, weightless as cotton. This was packaged separately and shipped off for more refined processing. The factory performed cheap, uncomplicated operations. Our product was of the lowest grade, since the prehistoric line was not designed for quality.

At eight-fifteen, when they started the line, the thunderous racket, the moaning and screeching of the machine, the vibrating and clattering, drowned out everything; the greedy conveyer demanded more and more food. Our monotonous, noisy work destroyed any desire to talk; people stiffened and retreated into themselves, became robots whose only purpose was to perform certain functions for the insatiable machine with its rumbling iron guts and clanging, polished ribs. For the first two weeks, the merciless noise haunted me and wore me out worse than the physical strain, stifling all thought. Eventually, this passed.

In exchange, I learned to appreciate silence in a whole new way. On my way home, I would listen to the wind whistling in the electrical wires, the brook burbling under the vast canopy of a pine tree, the tiny birds chirping and cheeping in the bushes. There was greenery and water and the kindly non-burning sun, the skies always swaddled in clouds and the chirr of grasshoppers, not nearly as irritating as the choruses of Asian cicadas. I hated flies and gadflies, but I soon got used to their persistence and tried to dress in light colors: darker clothes attract bloodsucking insects. The only thing I could not get used to was the morning swarms of gnats, but no one can get used to those. I saw mowers go out to the fields dressed in white robes with scarves tied around their heads. They covered their faces completely, only leaving an opening for their eyes, making them resemble our Turkmen girls from the marketplace who insisted on veiling their beauty, even in the Soviet days, and it was probably the right thing to do: only *houris* in the Muslim heaven are more beautiful than young Turkmen girls.

I came home by five or six, helped Leyda with the chores, fired up the stove, boiled some potatoes (from the two sacks the *kolkhoz* rationed me) in a small cast-iron pot, peeled an onion, made a simple vegetable soup, ate it hot, and lay down on the lumpy sofa by the lamp light. I would stare thoughtlessly at a book for a while and soon fall asleep.

In the morning, I washed in a tub with water kept warm on the stove from the night before, brushed my teeth, drank tea and set out for work. My clean skin eagerly absorbed the intoxicating scents of nature, but also soaked up the stench of burning motor oil and the sweet fumes of the factory's diesel fuel, mixed with the heavy smells of damp hay and the sour notes of linen fungus. This repeated day after day. In exchange for my nightly help with her chores, Aunt Leyda gave me a pint of milk every day and a dozen eggs on Sundays.

On Saturdays, Leyda let me use her bathhouse, which had to be stoked, heated and supplied with twelve buckets of water carried from the well. Leyda's children, who visited regularly, chopped the firewood. Only a steam bath could rid the skin of the factory dust. The daily ablutions in the tub alleviated the problem, but did not solve it completely, and by the end of the week my skin itched and scratched. Only the bathhouse steam and the heat from the rocks could purge the dirt and ash that clung to my body after a week in that industrial hell. Soft water and soapy potash revived my hair and returned elasticity to my skin. Wearied from the heat of the steam bath, on Saturdays I fell asleep on fresh linen sheets, feeling weightless—freed from my voluntary servitude. Sundays were all mine: I mended clothes and linens, cleaned the house and baked pies and cheesepuffs in the large oven from the dough that had been rising since the day before. Leyda Yanovna also mentored me in culinary arts. By dinnertime I had changed into clean clothes, walked the two hundred yards that separated our houses and knocked on my neighbor's door. On Sundays we dined together, and if she had guests (she sometimes hosted hunters), everyone sat down to the table together; that was the custom. I confess I looked forward to those Sunday dinners: lonely evenings had begun to depress me; my books, read two or three times, no longer helped, and the mumbling of the radio only added to the white noise, I could never focus on the words.

Leyda Yanovna, of course, knew about my loss, but never mentioned it, instead always finding something to praise, or telling me about her life with her husband, or sharing the settler stories she had heard from her grandmother, who sternly watched over our conversations from the bedroom wardrobe. My neighbor was so kindly and so wise that soon I began to share my troubles with her. The elderly Estonian only shook her head at my accounts of Gennady's doings.

"Fancy that. Peter and I never fought. He liked to drink, and I always poured him some, but he listened to me: if I said that's enough, he smiled and went to bed. Although I have seen what you are talking about, and not only from the Russians. Estonians, they also learned to drink vodka, and to beat their wives, and I saw children suffer, I saw all kinds of things."

She spoke Russian as if she were chanting, and her slight accent only added to the charm of her speech; listening to her was like listening to a fairytale. She peppered her sentences with "oi" or "fancy that!" and liked to begin with "I'll tell you a tale now, you listen," which might be followed by an account of her battles with the notary to divide the property among her children. She never lost heart and never feared her isolation, saying only, "Wait till the blizzards come howling in winter, then you'll come running to my stove."

Her words and practical advice comforted me.

"You were right to leave, that was the thing to do. You can't meddle in young peoples' lives, and when your Valerka doesn't visit—well, he's working, he's busy, he'll come when he can. Don't mope around, go play with my little chickens."

She loved her "little chickens," and her "little cows," and her "pony," and "doggies," and "kitties." On her advice, I would go to visit the "little chickens." Stupid, evil-eyed, and quarrelsome, the chickens appalled me, the way they dashed so greedily after bread crumbs, choked on their food and shoved each other. Naturally, I did not share these observations with Leyda. Mustang, the old gelding, was the one who became my friend. I could brush him endlessly. I would bring him treats of salted bread and rub his powerful, knobby hocks. Or I would just stand there, pressing my face into his dark neck and inhaling the sweet smell of horse sweat. He also came to love me—instantly and forever; he neighed every time I walked or biked past his barn, stuck his head out through the half-open door, scissored the air with his ears and swished his tail to convey his horsey delight. Aunt Leyda welcomed our friendship. I took over looking after the horse, shortening her list of daily chores. She now rarely stopped by the barn, only to visit the gelding and to remind him who his real master was. Still, Mustang adored her as did all the other animals. "A horse gives wings to a man," she liked to say as she watched me curry Mustang's shiny sides. I could see perfectly why she did not want to live anyplace else.

In the middle of August, the factory paid me my first wages, two months late. It was not much of a salary either: a hundred rubles in cash, a hundred-rubles' worth of bread from the *kolkhoz* store, another hundred in soap, laundry detergent and butter, and the last hundred in tiny potatoes, also deducted from the cash payout. The linen factory seemed to have a complicated barter system with the *kolkhoz*. It was useless to object, that much was obvious; the system was maintained by the bosses, and if you did not like it, you were free to go back to your warm stove at home. Which many did, creating constant labor turnover on our production line. People would just disappear one day. New people would replace them; they were just as faceless, gloomy, empty-eyed and fond of gossiping during lunch break about the goings on in the district.

Local news washed over them like soft dew over fields of linen. The dew moistens the plants' yellowish-green stalks and spreads the invisible fungus that breaks down the cells between the bundled fibers and the bark. The straw—*trestá*—must then be dried in bundles and rolled into heavy round bales by a special combine. Some of it would be left in the field to rot under the snow, some would be stolen by the quick locals to insulate their homes or use as bedding for cattle; some more would be lost under the wheels of the heavy machines. The whole operation hinged on accident and custom, and the local news was the same.

Whether I liked it or not, I caught snippets of the recent goings-on: Kolka Myagi had come unstitched again[15] and went drinking, sold all his sheep and ground his wife's face into the floor when she tried to defend her flock. Someone stole Sergeyev's Minsk motorcycle, but it broke down and the thieves left it in a roadside ditch, where the happy owner found it, fixed it, and now rides it to the forest farm as if nothing happened. Mahonia from Staraya village found some extra-special Estonian clay in the woods near Skomorokhovo, the kind they'd been searching for but could never find. You don't even have to mix it with sand, it practically sticks to things by itself and dries better than plaster. He found it, fixed up his stove, but isn't telling where the spot is, but give him a drink and he'll crack like the Swedes at Poltava, and he's about due for a binge, since he's been dry for three weeks.

I tried to ignore the gossip, but later at home Leyda always asked what was going on in Zhukovo and what was being talked about.

"Oi, oi, what a nasty story: you say Antoshka Gutyonov went carousing with Olga the nurse again? The devil, he doesn't care—he's got plenty of money from the sawmill, and money, it makes you stupid. Olga's got three little kids and a husband; her husband, he's quiet but solid. And this Antoshka's like the devil, it's all fun for him. Although, Vera, sweetheart, this has been going on for a long time, must be eight years now they've been squeezing each other in barns. I don't understand this foolishness. It's all because of idleness. Love your own, leave the other's alone. I wouldn't say my Peter was the handsomest man out there, but when he'd hold me tight in a bathhouse, he'd set my soul on fire. The rest is foolishness. Take you and your Gennady—I'm sorry to say—you should have worked towards each other more. The fault is not yours alone, and the grief is not all his, you just lived too much each on your own. You say, the fire of love, the chill of love—that's nothing. I say what I think. You should have submitted more."

Her philosophy was tested by life itself, and most of the time I agreed with her, but this submission thing—no, thank you, I don't buy it—not now, not ever. Leyda habitually smoothed over sharp corners; so taught her wisdom, the wisdom of her mother, grandmothers, and great-grand-mothers, and I did not argue with it. It's just that I don't know how to swim with the current: fish spawn and sleep upstream and that's just the way things are.

When I recounted to her the news tidbits I picked up at work, she listened with a lively interest and always commented. Even though she was isolated where she lived, in the middle of nowhere, she knew the entire district, and I realized that maintaining a connection with this invisible community was as important for her as talking to her little chickens and cows. For the first time in my life, perhaps, I came to appreciate the local "telegraph." Information flowed the same way through the chatty women on the bench in front of our apartment building in Dushanbe. Back then I despised them, and now I was learning the value of their talk. Oral editions of "Nurmekundia's Daily" came out regularly and circulated widely, adding meaning to life and strengthening the bonds that threatened to collapse in front of our very eyes.

And still, when I got my pauper's pay from the factory I became depressed. It was clear that I had become part of the local life, that this place had swallowed me like a garter snake swallows a frog. When Leyda learned that I got a hundred rubles in cash for two months of work, she said, "It's not much, but it's good that they paid something at all. Last year they paid in grain. Put the money away; there is no place to spend it here, and if you start eating sausage and other fancy food, you'll just get gas."

I had no taste for sausage anyway; I had no taste for anything. By September, my potatoes were ready, the apples had ripened, and my dill stood thick as a wall. I cut it and dried it on cookie sheets on the stove. In the woods, mushrooms and berries abounded, so I made jams, dried mushrooms for soup and pickled some more in jars according to Leyda's precise instructions. New to pickled mushrooms, I quite liked them. Generally, I craved salty foods more than meat. Out of the blue, Valerka and Oleg Petrovich showed up, dug up the potatoes, sorted them and layered them in the basement, for food and for next year's seeds. They each took three sacks for themselves, which left me four sacks of large ones, much more than I needed. They stayed for two days, not reporting any special news, except that Gennady took his vows, was named Germogen and sent to Valdai monastery. I felt nothing when Valerka told me. It seemed much more important that he had managed to save enough for the Moskvich[16] he had driven here, which meant he was living smart. Sveta sent her greetings; I sent her pies. The men did the harvesting, horsed around, had a steam bath, drank a bottle of vodka and left. And again, I was plunged into silence. And again, a throbbing, thundering hell awaited my free labor in Zhukov.

One day, on my way from work, I sat down under a pine tree and lost touch with the world, as if I had fallen asleep. For some reason I envisioned Gennady in a black cassock with a beard and a big golden cross on his chest. This pulled on something, like a vein that had lain heavily in a tight, cold coil in the pit of my stomach. Drink like the locals, and neglect my children? I could not release my will: it had happened once under Nasrulló's tent, and for the rest of my life I would remember the groping tentacles of the monsters that prey not only on the body but on your very "self." Empty, unpaid work was another such monster, and I had almost been sucked into a vortex like Babkin Dip, into an abyss from which there was no return. I sat there for a long time; a familiar chill began to creep up from my stomach toward my mind, but then I spotted a strange little bird. It sat within an arm's length of me. It was small and cartoonish: two long, spindly legs with sharp claws, a puff-ball of a body, a pair of round eyes and a funny beak, half-sunk in feathers. Suddenly, the bird hooted, rolling its eyes madly and making itself bigger—it was very angry—in order to scare me and chase me away. It was so full of comical bravado that I burst out laughing. It was an owl, the smallest of the species that we had in Karmanovo. The bird became even angrier and hooted at me with great ferocity. I laughed still harder, until tears rolled from my eyes and—I do not know why—the next thing I knew I was wailing like a banshee. The little owl startled and fled, and I stayed there and cried—cried bitterly and inconsolably until the tears melted the chill. When I came back to my senses, it was quickly growing dark, and the arms of my watch pointed almost to nine. I jumped onto my bicycle and pedaled hard down the empty road, where I knew every dried-up puddle, speeding as if a coven of witches was on my heels. I dashed into the house, flipped on the lights and fell onto the couch. I thought for a moment, then gave the finger to the darkness beyond the window. I did not return to work after that, only went to get my pay. I bought vinegar at the store, some salt, matches, sugar and flour, some cheap candy; I spent all the money and went home, to Karmanovo, to winter.

· 9 ·

MARK GRIGORIYEVICH once recounted to me, from his mother's words, how she survived the siege.[17] His own memories of those years are vague: he remembers the wonderfully sweet latkes made with frostbitten potatoes; oilcake in large rounds that his mother chopped with an axe in a wooden tub; the gray pigeon broth, with delicious, bloody foam settling to the bottom. His Grandfather, with his long white beard and skullcap, sitting in a huge armchair; a thick book lies open on his knees, and he is muttering something, rocking back and forth as if he were using his dry beak of a nose to bore a hole in the book. His Grandmother kneeling before the small iron stove, stoking the fire with books from her library. She throws the books into the red maw of the stove and for some reason cries, covering her mouth with her hand. Both Grandmother and Grandfather later died; his Mom and older brother took one and then the other to the cemetery aboard the boys' sled.

"I wanted nothing. I spent the last six months lying flat under a blanket. Mom made me get up and exercise—it was torture. We lived for food, from one feeding to the next. Grandfather was a watchmaker and he must have had some gold pieces; Mom sold those, traded them for bread, but she never spoke of it. Right before the siege, her brother came to visit. He was a mechanic at an airfield, so as a present he brought us four bars of bitter Air Force chocolate. He got killed somewhere in Poland. The family's gold saved our lives, but we never got around to the chocolate. Mom was saving it for our final days. But how could you know which day would be your last? Her mother and father starved to death, my brother and I were on the brink of death, Mom was thin as a bed sheet, but the chocolate remained untouched. And then they opened the Road of Life—the Nazis retreated. Only then did she give each of us a small square of chocolate, but our stomachs could not take it. I had never been so sick in my life; it was as if my soul was begging to get out of my body. Mom took us to the rehabilitation center in a pram: at six, I weighed thirty-five pounds, and my nine-year-old brother, forty-seven. Soy milk—that's what saved us. Fifteen years ago, without telling Mom, I threw away the remaining one half and three whole chocolate bars. I found them in an old suitcase, at the very bottom, wrapped in an old newspaper. They were horrific to look at."

I look at Grandma Lisichanskaya's peaceful face, remember this story, and think that, had I managed to last that whole winter in Karmanovo, I would probably have saved and stretched each piece of hard candy the same way they did with that ill-fated chocolate. I was in no danger of starvation, of course, but I did purposefully isolate myself. I holed up in my cabin; Aunt Leyda visited me regularly, every morning and every evening, sat with me and talked. I listened, but I did not hear her. Day by day I was sinking deeper and deeper into a comatose slumber.

I have a complicated relationship with my age. Sometimes even now I feel younger than my forty-two years; more often, I feel a lot older. That winter, in the cabin in Karmanovo, I felt ancient, feeble. My needs were pared to a minimum. To boil some tea, to cook some potatoes, pasta or cereal, to stoke the stove. I often just lay there for long stretches of time, could not tell day from night, and watched for hours how the trees bent under the wind at the edge of the forest or how the October rain finished off the dying grasses. Even Mustang, whom I suspect Leyda intentionally sent grazing under my windows, could not lure me outside. The sun painted the woods with yellows and oranges; the wind tore off leaves. In the yard, Leyda pounded the chopper against a wooden tub: she was cutting cabbage to pickle for the winter; I did not go out to help.

As before, a jar of milk appeared on my table every day, and the basket of eggs appeared on Sundays. I barely touched my wonderful neighbor's gifts. Occasionally I would sip sour, clotted milk, but more often than not, on her regular visits Leyda just stubbornly replaced spoiled milk with a fresh jar, filled the same morning, confident that my apathy would pass and I would awaken to a new life.

"Get up, Vera-sweetheart, without work there is only death," she would greet me in the morning in her sing-song voice. I looked through her and squeezed out a smile, but had no desire to talk. I mean, I could speak, but did not want to. I kept my mouth shut on purpose, like an idiot. How sorry I was for myself during those three weeks! What tales I told myself when left alone! I'm ashamed to remember it.

Work! What work was this Estonian grandma talking about? Hacking at cabbage, mucking stalls—was that all I was born to do? Sloth enveloped me like frost encasing a fall flower. I lost weight. Dry and hollow, with no hope of anyone ever needing me again, I reached the extremes of despair and sanity.

One night I woke in the small hours. I was cold, having forgotten to stoke my stoves the evening before. Rain hammered on the roof; it had been pouring for three days—drizzling, cold and endless. Going outside to the woodpile seemed cruel and unnecessary, a torment. I opened the flues and stoked the fires with books.

I crouched and tore them into thinner sheaves, breaking spines with a crunch, then throwing them into the stoves, first into the big Russian stove, then into the one under the bed. Jack London, Mayne Reid, Emile Zola, Feuchtwanger, *The Captain's Daughter*, Dickens, *Dead Souls*, Nekrasov, Mayakovsky, textbooks with my Pavlik's scrawls in them, two misplaced grade books from sixth and seventh grade, with the fat signature of Faizullo Rakhmonov, the boys' literature teacher, next to each A.

At first, the books burned slowly; the pages only blackened around the edges and the thick sheaves did not catch fire. I jabbed at them inside the stove with the poker-*kukovka*, as it was called, and the flames overcame them, grew angrier, curled the cardboard into pigs' ears, leapt up the bricks, wailed in the chimney. The fire's orange flares danced around the walls of the cabin, chasing nervous, rag-tag shadows into the corners. I did not turn on the electric lights; the light of the open fire was enough for me. I tore, tossed, burned, tore, tossed, burned.

The cabin became hot, sweat beaded on my forehead; drops of perspiration or tears ran down my cheeks. Loose-haired, in a dirty, slept-in robe, I looked like a witch mixing a potent brew at midnight.

It is not easy to burn two hundred volumes in one go, but I almost did it. I worked my shift like a stoker on a steamship, tossed book after book, no longer tearing them, just opening them and feeding them, pages first, into the fire. The Collected Works of Balzac and of Chekhov, Russian fairy tales, Tajik fairy tales, Nils' travels with the wild geese,[18] Andersen. When we read *The Little Mermaid*, it made Pavlik weep. I remembered it and broke down sobbing: "Here's your "Tinderbox" and here's your "Thumbelina," and here's your "Tin Soldier"!

The bricks became too hot to touch; the sharp smell of burning mushrooms filled the air. I had forgotten about them. I had set four strings of my choicest porcini on the stove to dry and now I had set them on fire. But I noticed them in time, swept them into a dustpan and tossed them into the stove. The chimneys above my cabin spewed thick clouds of smoke. The Varyag's[19] stacks must have smoked the same way as it sped to its lethal rendezvous. The rain had stopped, the wind had parted the clouds. Stars dotted the skies. I opened the door to help vent the fumes from the mushrooms and stepped out onto the porch. A full moon hung over the near woods. Its light had thinned the darkness, casting everything around in an otherworldly color, seductive and ruthless. The wind had died down; the trees stood tense as bow-strings.

With a gulp of fresh air, I went back to my crematorium: the draft in the stoves was excellent, the chimneys hummed evenly, great words and crumbling letters silently grated against the brick and disappeared like something that cannot be returned, restored, rewritten. A word taken apart stops meaning anything; it turns into nothing. Like a body that after being dissected becomes less than a corpse.

I sat down on a stool in front of the Russian stove, rested on the poker and closed my eyes, but did not fall asleep. Rather, I entered a strange form of consciousness where dreams are not quite dreams, and yet reality is also not real: my thoughts became images and flickered in front of my eyes like movie stills, cut and pasted out of order. When I came back to my senses, night was in retreat, and Leyda's rooster was about to crow. Ashes still breathed in the stoves; their charred, deformed pages swayed, having died a martyr's death. It really is true, as Sirojiddin once told me, in the words of one of his sages, that one learns more in a single sleepless night than in a whole year of sleep!

I got up from the stool, lowered my face into the water bucket and felt my skin cool. I put on man's pants and boots, threw a padded coat over my shoulders, tossed into my knapsack potatoes, onions, a loaf of bread, matches and salt, a handful of candy, camping pot and a pocket knife. I stepped out onto the porch. Quietly, I crossed the clearing; Karay, Leyda's husky, came out of his doghouse, shook off his sleep, rocked a little on his front legs, and yawned, but didn't bark—we were friends. I walked across the empty, long-untilled field toward the woods. Where, why—those things did not matter. It was necessary to walk, and so I walked, put one foot in front of the other. Soon I was in the forest, reached the first and the second clearing, where I used to pick mushrooms, crossed the creek, thick with wild roses and odoriferous currant bushes. Taking the creek as my reference point, I set a course for its source. The ground rose. My feet sank in soft, wet moss; silently as a fish moving through water, I was putting distance between myself an Karmanovo, which had sheltered me and where I had my official *propiska*.[20]

. 10 .

FOR A WHOLE DAY, I walked. The creek soon ended—it was fed from a long marsh. I walked around it and intuitively turned right. Whenever I wanted, I stopped, found a dry spot, usually under a large fir tree with widely spread branches, and sat down to rest. Several times broods of partridge exploded from branches ahead of me. They made so much noise with their wings it was as if they were not small birds but flying elephants. Yet when a grouse suddenly lifted out of a blueberry patch off to my side, the racket made me fall to the ground in fright. He flew across the undergrowth, a shadow, and I calmed down and even laughed—he was a big bastard and I probably scared him more than he did me. If birds can give one chills, what about animals? I felt unsettled, but I was too ashamed to turn back; I couldn't imagine explaining my foolish actions to Aunt Leyda. I sighed heavily and set out again. At times, it was almost fun, as if I were just out on a stroll and not running away from point A to some point whose name I didn't even know.

The heavy rain that had been pouring down for days had stopped the night before; the weather front moved on, and the sun came out. As I crossed cut timber clearings I was almost hot. Then I would take off my padded coat and carry it in my hands. The forest around me was mixed—birch and aspen—the pine and fir trees were systematically and greedily destroyed by just about everyone, from peasants, the *kolkhoz* and the forest farm, to the main predators: roaming bandit brigades. These plundered wherever they wished, breaking a path with heavy machinery, cutting a temporary road, and then carving out the most valuable hundred-year-old mast trees, lopping off six-meter trunks at the root, sometimes even getting two standard lengths, then leaving the rest—branches, tops—strewn about, not even bothering to bulldoze it into piles. Of course, no one planted saplings on these plundered patches, and they became impassable dead spots. The criminals gave a cut to the authorities, so there was little chance of stopping their marauding. Kupryan, the main forest-killer, was said to be an aide to an important elected official; policemen on the road nearly bowed at the sight of his maroon Pajero SUV. In this plundered land, where factories and plants closed, farmland shrank, and tractors vanished without a trace, sawmills sprang up like mushrooms after a rain. The forest was the only thing that could provide some sustenance, and so it did. Monstrous trucks ground up already broken roads; day and night they pulled lumber to the asphalt, where it was loaded on second-hand Finnish "fiskras" and rushed to the St. Petersburg port to be shipped abroad. And yet the forest fed only a few; most people got by on potatoes washed down with hydrolytic alcohol[21] and, having forgotten how to work, stole whatever wasn't locked up.

One constantly felt the presence of people in these woods—dead-end roads patched over with new growth like the bedsore scars on Gennady's back; plastic cones for collecting *zhivitsa*—fir sap that was used to make stinging turpentine; cast iron skeletons of tractors peeking out of their mossy lairs, ready to hook and mangle a carelessly placed foot. You also stumbled across axe-hewn posts—block markers, an original forest compass. Their chemically penciled signs bled and faded, turning letters and numbers into forest spirit scrawls. After the sunset, the bubbling, guttural voice of the forest, filled with sobs and moans, rolled far and wide, mixing with the peat-aged, rich aromas of the marsh; it rose like a wind-blown scent, as if from nowhere, and fell without a trace—not even a secret language, but a broken line of call-and-response, a chorus of ancient forces that kept watch over the strangers who stole their ancient wealth. Holes pierced in the forest by human greed were overgrown with raspberries and small bushes and turned into winter pastures for the moose—they learned to walk over the fallen debris, biting off the juicy tops of brush and saplings.

I stuck to the edges of such clearings. Stumps stood festooned with over-ripe, lifeless honey agarics; morels poked through here and there—faded, washed out from cold rains like threadbare linens, colorless like globs of carpenters' glue. In the blueberry patches on the edges, there hung a few leftover berries, ones the grouse had missed; scarlet ash berries and elderberries, dangerous as small shot, burned in the bushes, and on the mossy marsh tussocks lay strings of cranberries, big and tough, like coral necklaces on the bosoms of elderly Turkmen women.

I liked walking in the forest: I had no purpose, didn't need to gather things, find things, or preserve them for the winter, as Aunt Leyda had always made me do. Here, in this half-decimated forest, one could feel a special strength, like in a wounded person who is quickly recovering. Quietly but steadily, the gaping sores were closing; trees, mushrooms, moss and grass, thorny raspberry bushes, birds, bumblebees, caterpillars and wood-borers did their job, lived for each other, eating and sustaining each other. I walked past this life, shared in its fragrant air, infused with heady aromas, and within me the feeling of raucous freedom overflowed like champagne spilling over the edge of a glass. Where was I going? Why did I turn first right, then left? Why did I cross the looping stream twice and then not a third time, instead climbing its tall bank and turning my back on it, cutting my path with a stick in the tall nettle? I realized I could not possibly become lost—there were twenty, at most thirty square kilometers of thick growth, no more; everywhere somebody was living, and eventually I just had to arrive someplace.

And yet I became lost.

I spent the night under a fir tree. I made a fire, boiled some tea, and slept fitfully through the darkness. Woke up with dawn and set out again, and again did not reach any human dwelling by nightfall. Even the old roads that I had stumbled across at first disappeared. I made the most unforgivable mistake: I began changing my course. It was as if the *leshy*, the forest trickster spirit, was spinning me around. Sometimes it would appear that I had already stood by this little marsh or that one, and hadn't crossed it. But then again, it could have been any other marsh and I found no human tracks, but plenty left by wild pigs.

On the third night, I distinctly heard their squealing and grunting; wild pigs were rumbling about in the marsh. Andrei Mamoshkin, who brought groups of hunters from Moscow to Karmanovo and always made sure to spend the night at Aunt Leyda's, told horror stories about those pigs. I kept telling myself that at least I hadn't wounded any of them, hadn't done them any harm, but every new squeal, every rustle and crack of a broken twig sent shivers down my spine. I stared into the night but could not see anything. The tops of the trees swayed in the wind, back and forth, and the breeze dangled brushes of leaves across the bushes; the owl screeched, but that seemed to be it. I fed the fire and drank more of my watery tea—I started saving my potatoes, and had already finished the bread.

The feelings of vigor and elation had left me a while ago, and I was tired. My body—so accustomed to the hollowed-out bed in the village and the spiking springs of its mattress, which I padded with rags—was not well adapted to lying on branches and cold ground. My skin itched with dirt and sweat; muscles went numb and hurt, and it did not matter how long I rested—I only became more tired.

On the fourth day, the rain began. I was immediately drenched and decided to return to my camp from the night before, which at least had a bed and a big tree that could shelter me from the rain. But the rain brought the wind with it; the air cooled off. I was chilled to the bone and started to cough. Soon there was sweat on my forehead—I managed to catch a cold and was running a fever. At that point, as soon as the night lightened to grey and the early birds raised their voices, I got up and set out. I walked straight, without turning; I swore to myself that I would walk until I dropped. On that day, I learned that "when bones hurt" was not an exaggeration.

After an hour or hour and a half of pushing myself forward, I came upon an old road, and in another half hour, weed-choked fields began to appear. The woods ended suddenly—the road took me to their edge and to an endless uncut field. Animal paths ran through its rain-beaten and wind-tussled grass; the road hadn't been traveled on for a long time, and its ruts were deep and almost everywhere full of water. I walked on the dense turf between the ruts and felt sure that I would get somewhere. And I did.

In the grey skies, thickly woven with clouds, there was movement; invisible bellows began pumping, tearing woolly shreds from looms of loose grey and blowing them away. It grew lighter. Far ahead, the underbellies of the clouds filled with purple. And then, like thunder, a thick, tragic sound spilled over the fields. Bom-m-m! I stood still, all ears. The hum poured over the earth like melted pewter, unhurried; it wrapped itself around things, like the rich aroma of a waking garden just before sunrise at home in Panjakent. Just when it seemed that I was hallucinating from exhaustion, when the last threads of this mournful voice thinned, tore, and were lost in the still, tense air, the sound came back. Bom-m-m! It reached out again, it called, it had such wonderful power that my eyes involuntarily filled with tears. Bom-m-m! It struck sooner, chasing and overtaking the previous wave as if it had lain itself down to smooth the way and was pulling the new sound after itself toward the light from an invisible source—just as a wolf tenderly pulls her first sighted pup out of her lair. Bom-m-m!—it spilled again, seeming sooner still, and stronger, happier. I did not doubt that somewhere, someone was sounding a bell, not to call for help, but in measured, mighty strokes, as if tuning the new day to its sound. Bom-m-m! Bom-m-m! Bom-m-m! A new rhythm appeared. It was still unhurried, not the quick canticle like in a Dushanbe church at Easter, where I had once gone with the kids to see the procession, mostly to spite Gennady. Still the bell grew stronger, drawn by an experienced hand that swung it with certain amplitude, making the tongue hit the dome every time a bit sooner, a bit stronger: one-two-three, one and one, and one-and-two, and one, and one-two-three. I came back to my senses and ran towards the sound. This was not a coincidence—someone was letting me know that rescue was at hand; bells had served as beacons to lost travelers since the beginning of time.

The field rolled down to a river. On its far shore, uphill, stood dark shapes of buildings—barns, a house—the wind carried the dogs' barking. Another half an hour straight, then across the river, on the stones. I mis-stepped and fell waist-deep into the icy, burning water, but I did not fear any more. The bell kept ringing, urging me on. I walked up the hill—on this side, someone had cut the grass. Here was the house, the *banya*, two barns, and an orchard—a homestead, like Leyda Yanovna's. Behind the house were the woods severed by the road that had saved me. Then the sound stopped, as if it had never been, and only its echoes rang in my head for a little longer.

Straight ahead the sun was rising from behind the forest. It took my breath away; I stood still and finally noticed that, next to the house, be-side a simple bell-tower—a crossbar on tall posts with a shingled roof to protect the bell from the weather—stood a tall old man in a quilted jacket, his back to me, his face to the sun. He raised his hands as if in greeting, as I used to do on the remains of the Panjakent fortress, not paying atten-tion to the dog who was barking madly, lunging after me on its chain. I couldn't help it anymore; I hollered, "Ogo-go-go!" and ran towards him.

Finally the old man turned and saw me, but did not move. Tall, strong, with a long grey beard, he was looking at me, holding a hand to his fore-head as if he had a pair of binoculars. I tripped suddenly; the ground spun away from my feet, rose up to my face.

I came to inside the house. Somehow, the old man had managed to drag me inside. I was lying on a bed. Next to me a stove was burning, a radio burbled, and the old man was sitting on a chair just as I had sat so many times next to an ill person, waiting for their eyes to open. I opened my eyes. The old man had a kind face. I smiled at him and closed my eyes again, falling into blissful sleep. I was growing feverish—it hurt to look at the light. My body felt like it was on fire, and it seemed to me that the fire from the books in Karmanovo had leapt onto me from the stove and was branding its revenge into my face, arms, shoulders and chest. I was breathing fast but not getting any air, and again I lost consciousness.

. 11 .

A SHARP SMELL brought me back to consciousness; I raised my head and looked around, but could not get up. I was lying naked on an old blanket, swaddled in a wet, acrid-smelling sheet.

"Vinnegaar will pull oout the heat, you're on fire."

The old man elongated his words, pronouncing them with a strong Estonian accent. A towel soaked in the same sharply-smelling fluid rested on my forehead. It would have been a pleasant feeling if not for the heavy, aggressive smell. Soon, however, I got used to it. My white-hot body clung to the wet fabric, it felt good and then cold; I had the chills. The old man rubbed me with a towel, thoroughly massaging every bone, and then covered me with a fresh, dry sheet and a warm down comforter. Then he made me drink some bitter herbal brew. I had a strong headache; fiery gnats danced before my eyes.

"Get stronger, sleep, we'll talk later."

He put his heavy, knotty hand on my forehead and started massaging my temple, very lightly, with the tips of his fingers. The miserable ache soon retreated, and the gnats disappeared.

His caring fingers, rough as sandpaper, stroked and tickled my temples, brushed against my eyebrows. My Pavlik used to stroke my head this way. I thought of him, but strangely I felt neither bitterness, nor pain or fatigue. I felt nothing but these hands, which had begun to command me with their tender rhythm. My mind quieted. My fever dropped significantly. My body no longer burned. I felt peaceful atop the thick linen sheet. I warmed up and fell asleep, and when I woke up the old man was right there, sitting on a stool in the head of my bed. He was not sleeping. A small lamp burned dimly next to his bed in the other corner of the cabin. It was dark outside the window. I had slept all day.

"Do your business, don't be shy, I won't look," he held out a chamber-pot for me.

How many times had I put a bedpan under a patient, how many times had I held out a chamber pot—the very sick were never embarrassed, and I even helped them with words of encouragement. Judging by the fact that I felt not a drop of shame in front of this strange old man, I concluded that I was seriously ill. I went into the pot, he took it out, and I sank again into the soft bed, pulling the multicolored, patched comforter up to my chin. My chest hurt, my throat was raw, it was painful to cough—it had to be my lungs. The old man came back from the yard, poured tepid broth into a cup and had me drink it, then made me drink a still bitterer brew. I felt better, but it was only the beginning.

The old man was always at hand—chopping firewood in the yard, fixing a harness in the stable, replacing a rotten board on his sleigh. And he would interrupt his work to check on me every hour or two. When he came, he told me what he was doing. He talked, and I listened silently. He even skipped his regular trip to Konakovo to buy bread. Once a week, a truck came there from the factory bakery. So instead, the old man made his own dough, baked bread, some buns and Danishes. He had two cows—a heifer, and a calf—and more milk than he could possibly use himself.

The only hour when he abandoned his watch over me was in the morning, before dawn. I would wake up to the peals of his bell and listen to its fine report. Its anxiously-triumphant song outside my window marked the day that had passed and the new one that was beginning. I got used to the sound of the bell and waited for it. The first drawn-out "Bom-m-m" spread through me like sweet wine and then, for a very long minute, I waited, impatiently, for the second, and then the third peal to follow. The voice of the Estonian bell stirred my strength, which, I have to confess, I was very short of.

I spent a week, and then another, and a third in bed—the old man prohibited me from getting up. I alternated between being awash in sweat and shaking with chills. Vinegar, herbs, rubs, broth, *gogl-mogl,*[22] cottage-cheese soaked in milk, and constant care and attention the like of which I had never known. Honey. Weak tea. Cranberry *mors.*[23] Those were the medicines. And the living bell ringing before dawn.

"You should get antibiotics and call for a doctor."

"Lie quiet. I'm in charge of you. I've cured worse."

I believed him immediately. What other choice did I have?

At the end of the third week I got up—skinny and weak—shuffled to the kitchen table and ate some mashed potatoes with a glass of sour milk. My illness retreated. The cough clawed at me for another week or two, but the pain in my chest was gone—old Yuku Manizer had cured me.

Like Leyda Kyart, he lived in the only house that was left in his small village—Kukovkino. By himself. The last Estonian in Nurmekundia. The colonists' lands ended behind the river and the uncut hay-field that I had crossed on my way here.

They were brought there at the end of the 1920s—the Manizers, Tokmans, Hurts, Loiks and Melzers. The Manizers' homestead was just at the edge of the field where I heard the first peals of the bell. Yuku promised to show me the stone that marked the boundary between his land and his neighbors', the Tokmans, but he did not have time. When I finally stepped outside the earth was covered with snow. Winter had come.

. 12 .

YUKU MANIZER HAD BEEN living alone for a very long time. He was born in 1899, which means that he was ninety-six the year I met him, but I've never met even a seventy-year-old who was stronger. He wouldn't think twice about, say, fetching a sack of flour from the pantry—Yuku would carry it in his arms like a baby, grinning. Surprisingly, he had kept all his front teeth and even a few molars; his cheeks did not look hollow, as often happens to old people. True, his lush beard, which cascaded down onto his chest, hid his cheekbones. And were it not for his naturally slim, sinewy build, Yuku would have thoroughly resembled Santa Claus, or, rather *Jõuluvana*—"The Christmas Man," as the Estonians call him.

Pure white hair; large bald spots on his forehead, etched with wrinkles; nose like a potato; round eyes that had been bright-blue in his youth and were now bleached as if from repeated washing. He only wore glasses for short-sightedness; he put them on when he worked on small details or read the local rag, *Firov Truth*, which he picked up in Konakovo when he went there each week to buy bread.

The old man identified me as soon as he found me, even as I lay that first day raving in fever and could not speak. When Leyda saw that I had disappeared, she sent the news around the district with the mailman. People did not go looking for me, exactly, but knew that I might turn up somewhere. As soon as he realized I was the missing Vera from Karmanovo, Yuku hitched up his horse and made a quick trip to Konakovo to let people know that the escapee had been found. The message went down the line to Leyda and she stopped worrying. It only took a day or two—an incredibly short time given the absence of telephones. The oral editions of the "Nurmekundia Daily" must have discussed my escape and miraculous rescue for weeks.

When I came around and could move again, the first thing Yuku said to me was: "Get your things together, I'll take you back to Karmanovo. Leyda's waiting for you and is keeping your house warm. But, if you're not in a hurry, stay with me a while, I've gotten used to you."

Somehow, it immediately made sense for me to stay. I delighted him. The old man even started dressing in clean shirts: first I noticed it myself, and later he shyly confirmed it, not looking me in the eye. When I felt like myself again, I took up housekeeping: I washed and scrubbed every log with a wire brush dipped in baking soda, swept out century-old dirt, painted window frames, doors and the floor. I had everything I needed—Manizer's fortress was as ready for a long siege as the Kyart homestead, but Yuku could not manage such large-scale cleaning on his own. He meant to every year, but just never got around to it. He already had his hands full with the chores: he woke before dawn, drank tea with a bun and his homemade butter, and went to the bell-tower. After he rang the bell and welcomed the sun, he attended to the immediate needs of his farm, and did not come back inside until I called him to breakfast at nine. If he ran out of work, he found new tasks—sharpening knives, axes, or saws, fixing his tools, or hemming the horse blanket (which hadn't been on a horse in years). He didn't know how to be idle.

"I was a jack-of-all-trades in the labor camp, too: sewing, tuning, weaving, soldering, sharpening, putting a thread on a bolt, anything. I even made a guitar and they played it for a long time there. I was a master at working steel and I even made money behind those barbed wire fences."

They picked him up in January of 1937 as an enemy of collective farming. Yuku had tried to protect the Manizers' and Loiks' hay meadows, but the *kolkhoz* plowed them under but could never grow anything, since only native grasses thrived in the marshy soils. He, as was the custom, was blamed for the mistake. He returned home from the Rechlag near Taishet[24] in '55, back to his Tver woods from the taiga beyond Lake Baikal. His wife Ilsa was not there to meet him; she had died, either of grief or starvation. His only son Jacob had also died three years earlier, of peritonitis; they couldn't get him to a hospital in time.

Yuku came to Kukovkino, which was desolate after the war ("there were only three houses standing"), built himself a log cabin (the old one had burned down) and went to work for the *kolkhoz*. He did not remarry, lived alone, made hay and dried it on raised platforms the same way Kharabali fishermen dry their nets.

"Estonians always dry hay raised off the ground—the wind blows through it and makes better hay."

By himself he mowed as much as a brigade. In the last years of Soviet rule, the authorities recognized his work with diplomas. Yuku burned them in the stove.

"After Rechlag, we parted ways."

He thought for a minute and added, "And even before that, we weren't going in the same direction. My father bought this land from Brandt with his own money, pulled tree stumps with his own hands, plowed and planted it. When I was a boy, I pulled the last stumps from the ground. Money, it's not so easy to come by. I don't live on my pension alone, even now. I mow hay, dry it and sell it. The whole district comes to me, as if their own hands have dried up. Work, don't be lazy, and you'll have it. There is one day to rest in a week: Sunday. As a boy, I ran to the *kirche* on Sundays, to help the bell ringer. Ten miles one way, to Pochinok, where the Nurmekundian cemetery is, and ten back."

He managed to hide the bell in the woods in 1932, when a Komsomol squad burned down the *kirche*. When he came back from the camp, he found it, cleaned it and kept it. He rang it for the first time in '91. Now he rang every day, not to signal the end of the service, like at church, but to welcome every new day.

"They laugh at me in Konakovo—when the wind is right, it carries the sound all the way to them. But I don't care. I made a pact in the camp: if I survived I would ring. I had a dream about it."

The bell was not large—two *poods*[25]—and simple; it was covered with a green patina, just like the ancient pots in the Panjakent museum. Inside, its entire surface was covered with Estonian writing, carved by Yuku with his knife. He read the inscribed family names to me, and often repeated the list, so I memorized everyone: Yansens, Hurts, Mills, Myags, Tokmans, Kyarts, Riysmans, Loiks, Treumans, Lunds, Tarvases, Pialsons,

Kumms, Tinners, Manizers, Nellises, Melzers, Adamsons, Vagas, Austers, Poldmans, Haabmans, Sulgmans, Kivimaimans.

"I wrote everyone I knew. Let the bell ring the names."

On the top, around the crown, two lines of letters—Russian and Estonian—circled the bell.

"These are the alphabets. I thought: I couldn't tell it all, the bell will tell. In Haapsalu, where our pastor came from, they always wrote names on the bells, so it's not my idea. I just added the alphabets, the Russian and the Estonian, just in case, you see?"

I nodded my head. He smiled at something.

"Yuku, what are you smiling at?"

"What do I have to be sad about? Now I have you—I can leave you this house, would you like to live here?"

"I don't know. I really don't know."

"That's okay. It's not yours, so you don't want it—that's alright. A man has to live off the work he loves. I can't leave here; this is my land, the Manizers' land. I know it."

"How is it yours? It is part of the *kolkhoz*."

"*Kolkhoz* or not, it's mine. The filthy thing is, *pari-blyamba*, that they took the land, tortured it, and then left. If people had their own land, who would abandon it? They would sell, maybe, but that's different, it would still have an owner. That's why they drink—because they have nothing to die for. Estonians came for the land, got it and lost it, and…"

"But they all left, almost all of you."

"When you don't have land, your language becomes your home, so they followed it. They were right to leave. Loik Nele left for Estonia in '91, with the last Nurmekundians. She begged me to come with her—but I didn't. I was born here and I am needed here. Now my bell is the only one here who understands Estonian. Like now: I'm talking to you, but I'm thinking in my own language."

"Yuku, you speak correctly and beautifully!"

"Eh… I'm not sure. Speaking in another language is like writing a love letter with a dictionary. I tried to write to Ilse from Rechlag, but gave up, it was a waste of time: they did not allow writing in Estonian. And you say I speak beautifully—you must want to deceive me?"

"Never, Yuku. I wouldn't think of it."

"Alright, I'll believe you. It's always better to believe than not to believe."

We were soul-mates. I was happy with Leyda, but with Yuku I had something special, and I came to love him.

We, Russians from the Kosmodemyanskaya Street, nomad Tatars that had washed up in Panjakent on a random wave of Soviet history, always envied the Tajiks. People said, "They have land." Tajikistan, like everywhere else, had collective farms, but every Tajik knew where his fathers' lands were, spoke of them proudly and kept an eye on them as one cares for a cemetery plot. Directors of state-owned stores, barber shops, kiosks and bakeries always proudly called them "My establishment," and regularly paid bribes to the higher authorities so it was impossible to transfer them any place else—such positions were bought and sold, and no court would dare take them away. I did not understand what it was that our people envied when I was little. Yuku opened my eyes; he remembered.

Here, in the forest-edged fields, stood his property: his barn and his stable, the hen house, the pigsty, hayloft, bathhouse and the cabin where he lived. It was quiet and peaceful here; I took care of Yuku and he took care of me. Sometimes, a blasphemous idea would occur to me: were he forty years younger, I would gladly marry a man like Yuku.

I did not think much about the future; I let my own family in Volochok and Kharabali slip from my mind and I rarely remembered them. But I promised myself: when the winter is over, I will make a decision. I cleared narrow paths around the house with a wooden shovel, looked around and knew—these drifts are not like my yard in the city, a lifetime would not be enough to clear them all.

That winter was particularly snowy; often blizzards lasted for days, the wind tore the wires and we spent weeks without electricity. We lit kerosene lamps. I learned to spin wool. The old man sheared the sheep and collected the fleece into big sacks. I washed the dirty, matted wool, picked it over, cutting out clumps, and dried it on a line above the stove. Then I combed it, first with a thin-toothed comb and then with a thicker one. When I could get a handful of clean, light hair, I pinned it with an antique cast-iron pin to the head of the old spinner. At night I sat spinning, pinching loose locks, teasing them out, stretching, spinning the thread. After some practice, my thread became even. Yuku even praised me. Actually, I never heard a cross word from him, not once. When something wasn't working the way he wanted and he lost his temper, he only exhaled, "Oi, *pari-blyamba!*"

"You have a funny way of cussing, Yuku."

"Russian Old Believers from Skomorokhovo taught me this: you shouldn't defile your mouth with cursing or God might snip your tongue out."

I rolled the woolen thread into balls and knit warm socks with it, for Yuku and for myself. He found some vintage ladies' underwear in his pantry—people had kept Ilsa's trunk waiting for his return—and I sported lacy silk pantaloons and slips that were perhaps not the most common fashion of the day, but very elegant; Ilsa's mother herself had placed the orders with the clothing store. The women's blouses resembled hospital robes with their large openings and standing collars, embroidered with cross-stitch patterns. They were meant to be put on over one's head; in Dushanbe, we called this cut "Somebody, help!" The blouses were warm and comfortable. I wore the calico and plaid skirts, too, and with great style—after I washed out the mothballs and aired them outside. In the house we wore ankle-cut *valenki*[26] or *porshni*, soft moccasins that Yuku crafted from a single piece of thick leather, held in place with a lace around the ankle.

"In the camp, I was the premier *porshni*-maker," he said proudly handing me a pair of the comfortable footwear.

In the evenings we sat opposite each other, each working on his or her task. Yuku told stories. In this life, aside from regular work, there had also been impossible, back-breaking work, and, in the rare minutes of leisure, there had been songs and the happy, bouncy music of the brass band, and moonshine within reason, or sometimes without, but not so much as to knock you down, just enough to urge you on to new work.

"We had fun celebrating holidays, but we didn't get bored working either. Work is always interesting, you can see for yourself."

A group of big, mustachioed men in long dress coats stared out at me from an old picture on the wall: Nurmekundia's brass band. Yuku's father, Martin Manizer, sat in the front row holding a great big trumpet to his chest. Next to him was his best buddy, Paul Tokman, Ilsa's father, with a French horn. He wore a better coat, and had a watch chain, studded with pendants, stuck into a special pocket. Tokman was a miller, of the same fortune that provided for the silk underwear which, as best I could tell, I was the first to wear—it had been reserved for a special occasion. The photograph was faded with time, like Yuku's eyes. It was hard to imagine these finely-dressed, serious people working until dark in the fields or in the woods. I had only seen such courage and dignity in the eyes of the

Pamir tribesmen who sometimes came to market in Panjakent. But those people are Asian highlanders; they have complicated relationships with Tajiks and Uzbeks, from whom they had always remained separate, and when I was little I thought that's why they acted so noble. Yuku wasn't lying, however: the settlers in the picture worked long and hard, but they still found time to run their callused fingers tenderly over an accordion's keys, to speed up and down the notes of a piano or to cuddle a flute. This was my kind of life.

By the beginning of April, the snow had almost all melted, and I could drive the cart to Karmanovo. I didn't want to spend any longer than necessary in that drunken village. The people who lived there were dirty, unkempt, their eyes swollen from constant drinking, and the cursed without end. I bought bread, collected Yuku's pension and went back, three and a half miles through fields, then through a forest and across a field to Manizer's home, as familiar as if I had grown up there.

On April 12, I returned home with the bread, drove up to the door, but Yuku did not come out to greet me. Sensing trouble, I ran into the house without unhitching the horse. He lay on his bed, face to the wall.

"Yuku!"

He turned to look at me—his face was grief-stricken, I had never seen him like this.

"What happened?"

"The bell!"

That morning Yuku had rung as usual, with no premonition of doom. After he finished, he went to the stable, and when he came out again, he saw that the space under the wooden beam was empty. The movement of the bell had gradually loosened the metal bracket that held it. The bell fell, and even worse—hit the anvil that Yuku had dragged there about two weeks ago and forgot about. A crack split the bell along its entire length. The old man hung the bell back up, but it had lost its voice, sounded false and fell silent, didn't carry on the wind.

"It's my woe, Vera. Old fool—I've only got myself to blame."

For the first time, I saw him cry. Tears ran down his cheeks, trickled into his beard; he was not ashamed, but somehow had shriveled, became smaller, as if he had lost his entire fortress.

I spent a long time comforting him, sat by his side, rocked him like a baby, stroked his great gray head, and the warmth of my hand finally soothed him. He got up, washed his face and went outside, to work.

At night, we talked for another half-hour, lying in our beds already. Yuku listed things that needed to be done the next day, then suddenly remembered that he hadn't put the fresh batch of cottage-cheese into the cheese-cloth, got up and did it himself, didn't let me do it.

In the morning he looked out of sorts, took a while getting ready, walking from one corner to another to postpone going outside, but finally went. I watched him through the kitchen window. The old man stood by his bell-tower for a long time, arms at his sides as if at a freshly dug grave, and then he took a step, his legs folded awkwardly under him and he fell face down into the wet April mud.

I rushed to him: the old man's face was purple, his lips blue, he was no longer breathing. He died instantly of a stroke, as holy people die—without suffering or torment, probably without even noticing. I dragged him to the house, washed his body, dressed him in clean clothes, laid him out on boards propped by two stools, tied up his jaw with a towel.

By midday I was in Konakovo. Fortunately, the only telephone in the village was working that day. I called Zhukovo and then the *kolkhoz*. They sent a coffin. On the third day, we buried him in Pochinok, in the old cemetery. Many people came to say goodbye to old Yuku Manizer. Leyda came up to me, "Vera, are you thinking of coming home?"

"Yes, Aunt Leyda, let me just sell the cattle, close up the homestead, and then I'll come."

That's what I did. Two cows—a calf and a heifer, a piglet, a horse, eight sheep. The *kolkhoz* helped me sell them all for what felt like unimaginable wealth. When I exchanged the rubles for dollars in Firov's bank, as that's how Moscow hunters had advised Leyda to keep her money, it came out to thirteen hundred and fifty dollars. More cash was squirreled away in Yuku's hiding place, which he had shown me, saying, "You'll have something to bury me with. If that's not enough, I'll make some more hay in summer, and you'll have more. One can make a buck here and there, just keep moving. The Konakovo people are lazy, they'll be all done for soon, and I'll live to see the other side of a hundred, right?"

And he would have, if not for his bell.

I can just imagine the field-day "Nurmekundia's Daily" had with my newfound wealth, but I did not care. The *kolkhoz* brick-layer Lenya Kustov made the grave marker: I asked him to set Nurmekundia's bell in the concrete base that ran around the grave, leaving space for flowers in the middle. I hope it stands there for a long time, although I'm afraid that the locals will dig it out and sell the metal for scrap.

I returned to Karmanovo. Leyda, always tactful, did not speak a word of my hysterical flight. Like clockwork, she had fired the stoves in my house once a day this entire time, and watched over the potatoes stored in the basement. We picked up where we left off, living like a team, as if we had never parted; I told her about Yuku Manizer, and she listened, commenting laconically, "He was a hard-working man, a real farmer. You don't see people like him around here anymore. My Peter had great respect for him."

A week after the funeral, I hitched up Mustang and drove to the cemetery. I tidied up the grave, planted some small marsh flowers and snowdrops. The bell still stood; on its bronze surface, rain had drawn its first malachite paths.

. 13 .

THE MONEY I INHERITED from Yuku offered the hope of escape. His death put an end to my self-imposed hermitage. One had to be born here to submit to this kind of life naturally, without complaint, even joyfully, like Yuku and Leyda. I was in no danger of drinking myself to death like other locals, but neither did I want to work for nothing or to live off someone else. Of course, I did not have much, not enough to buy a place to live in the city, but I kept thinking of my family that had remained in Kharabali: they had even less, and yet they made it. I realized suddenly that I missed hospitals and patients, the smell of chlorine, the night shifts. Yuku needed my care, but Leyda did not. It was clear that it was time to find my way out. The only question was where and how.

At the end of April, out of the blue, Valerka rolled in: they ran out of potatoes. I had my basement full of them, and I was happy that I could help the city-dwellers—I, who hadn't earned a penny. I filled two sacks for them: one for my mother-in-law and Petrovich, for letting us stay with them, and the other for Valerka and Sveta, to hold them over until the harvest. In the basement, I showed him what I had saved for seed.

"For the holidays[27] I don't care how you do it, but you come and plant them yourselves—I'm not going to play *kolkhoz* anymore."

We sat down, talked it over. Valerka promised to look for a job for me at the hospital. He felt at home in Volochok and had earned a good reputation; almost everybody had him fixing their cars. The Head of the Central Hospital, Belyayev, was also among his clients.

"I'll come back for you as soon as I figure it out," my son said, then gave me a peck on the cheek and rode off.

Leyda and I had agreed not to tell him anything about my winter saga. He did not come to visit at New Year, so there was no reason for him to know of my life with Yuku Manizer. I was a bit irked by my son's behavior then, but remembered the old man's words, "Rely on yourself, help without expectation, don't ask for help." His whole lonesome life and labor camp experience were encapsulated in that formula. Yuku never took offense with other people.

"Why should I? Let them pout at me, it's easier not to notice. It's all nothing."

I did not hold a grudge against Valerka; he couldn't have made it here even if he had wanted to: the five miles of the road from Konakovo were a single snowdrift with the tracks of Manizer's sleigh barely visible on top of it. Yuku told me that, traditionally, Estonians celebrated Christmas, not the New Year, so I prepared to give him a present on the night of January 6.[28] I was so delighted when he returned from Konakovo on December 30 and put a bottle of champagne on the table.

"It's Uus Aastat—New Year's Eve—tomorrow, come on, Vera—whip up your dough, we'll celebrate!"

I baked pies, made cutlets, and put head cheese to set in the cold mudroom. I had noticed that Yuku was up to something; for the last week, he camped out in the shed where he kept his tools, fussed with the soldering iron, and answered my questions evasively. For my part, I was secretly knitting him a high-necked sweater. On the front, I embroidered "Nurmekundia" in white wool, and on the back I put "Yuku Manizer" and a big number 1, like on a soccer-player's jersey. We sat down to the table at eleven, drank a shot of homemade cranberry-infused vodka and ate a bit to say goodbye to the old year. At about ten to midnight, Yuku stepped out into the mudroom. At midnight sharp, there were three loud knocks on the door.

"Who is it? Come in!" I said ceremoniously.

Yuku came in wearing Jõuluvana's costume: ballooning red pants and a red cloak, he didn't have it in him to make a tailored coat. He had fashioned the outfit from an old Soviet flag, and the cloak still showed a faded hammer and sickle painted in bronze.

"*Head uut aastat!*" the Kukovkino Jõuluvana greeted me.

"*Head uut aastat!* Happy New Year!"

I hugged him and kissed him, thrice.

Yuku pulled a small birchbark box from his pocket. It held a golden cross on a leather string.

"*Aitah*, Yuku!"

"You're welcome, Vera!"

I still wear this Lutheran cross—Yuku had one exactly like it, only copper. He used his cross to take the measurements, carved a mold out of stone, melted an old coin with his soldering iron and cast my present for the holiday. The old labor camp smithy made a wonderful little cross, giving it such a high polish that it shines to this day. The old man had found the coin when he cleared the remains of his parents' burned out home. The builders, by ancient custom, had placed a gold piece, for luck, under the front right corner of the foundation.[29]

I thanked the old man, but kept my present for later. I laid out the sweater next to his bed on Christmas night, and when he woke up, he appreciated the answer I had given him: traditionally, Estonians celebrated Christmas, not New Year. So I held no grudge against my son; I'd be ashamed to admit it, but I was happy to spend that night with Yuku Manizer in Kukovkino.

Now I resolved to trust Valerka, to wait for a month, to help him plant the potatoes, and maybe then... I did not make any plans, just prayed silently while superstitiously holding on to my little golden cross.

On the first of May, Andrei Mamoshkin drove in, with three other hunters in his large American SUV. The hunters came after wood-grouse; there were four different mating grounds around Karmanovo. They put up two blinds in the fields: two men hunted heath-cock and the third went after grouse, under Andrei's guidance. The following day, they switched sites; everyone was happy, everyone had his kill. They slept during the day; at night they'd go down to the stream, to shoot woodcock in the clearings. Andrei would not let them hunt hazel-hen in the spring: hazel-hens mate for life, if you kill a male, the female won't choose another. I liked this thoughtful approach, and Leyda simply adored Andrei. He had been coming there for years and had been friends with her Peter, who respected real hunters but never took a rifle into the woods himself, as he pitied all living things.

The main hunter, an entrepreneur, stayed with Andrei at Leyda's and I took the other two. They paid five dollars a night for the room, fed me out of their provisions and entertained me as best they could. With them in Karmanovo, we had fun—roasted *shashlyk*, sang songs, and drank very little vodka: being real hunters, they saved their energy for the hunt.

Igor and Ilya, my guests, were surgeons from Moscow. Once they learned that I was a nurse and heard my saga, they wanted to take me back to the city: there were plenty of vacant nursing positions, since they paid very little, like everywhere. The men worked in the Bakulev Institute. I plucked up my courage, and asked, "Do you know Vitya Bzhania?"

"Vitka? How do you know him?"

It turned out their units were next to each other. How could I not believe in miracles after this? We decided that I would write a letter to Viktor and they would give it to him as soon as they got back. Together, they would figure something out for me.

When it came time to part, we hugged as if we were family. Igor said, "Set your clocks: you won't spend more than a month here. We'll get you out!"

They left on the tenth, right after Victory Day. On the holiday, we planted potatoes—Valerka, Petrovich, and I; Lyonka Kustov from Zhukovo helped with a tractor this time. I walked around Karmanovo counting the days, dreaming, dreading. To work in a hospital in the capital, with modern drugs and state-of-the-art machines… and yet I knew I could do it, I was prepared to learn and work like a horse.

Ten days after the hunters left, in the evening, a humble Zhiguli drove up to my house.

four

. 1 .

VIKTOR ARRIVED WITH his wife, Lyuda, a radiologist who also worked at the Bakulev Institute; they had met there. Their four-year-old daughter Natasha stayed behind in Moscow, entrusted to Lyuda's mother. It looked like Vitya had found his happiness: Lyuda loved him and he was irreplaceable at work (as I later found out, it was not at all easy for them to take three days to go to Volochok). His wife was the right woman for him: easygoing, kind, quick to defer to him in public. The way she readily went to make the beds, swept their room and joined me in making dinner convinced me that Viktor was in good hands. Bzhania sat in the kitchen, listening to our chit-chat, and gradually opened up: we reminisced about Dushanbe and our Head Doctor Karimov. Some young, worthless surgeon did push him into retirement after all, and Karimov and his wife lived in poverty, although so did just about everyone in Tajikistan. Karimov and Viktor maintained correspondence for many years, but about six months ago the letters had stopped. We decided to write to the old man together. I, who could barely be made to write even to Kharabali, agreed surprisingly quickly.

Vitya chastised me for not writing to him from Dushanbe; he felt confident in his position now, and, had I written to him before we left Tajikistan, I believe he would have moved mountains to get us all to Moscow. He acted as if he had never said anything about his love for me, as if he had never been the one trying to conceal his anxiety in a café, when his fingers mechanically shredded a paper napkin. There could be no doubt: Viktor loved his wife. My soul rejoiced for him. Viktor Bzhania was solid as a rock.

We finished dinner. At tea, I finally asked the question that had been nagging at me all this time: where and what would I do for a living? The answer was not what I had expected:

"A nursing job, plus side jobs—doing injections, massages, and, if you take a special course, other home-care procedures. You can live on that, but it won't solve your housing problem. Housing in Moscow is expensive. The guys—the ones who came here to hunt—and I have found a different option, at least to start. There is an old lady, a stroke patient, in a difficult condition, and her son is willing to pay five hundred dollars a month for live-in care, plus five hundred more for food and drugs."

"Many nurses now leave to take up private home care. There's a colossal difference in pay," Lyuda added.

I couldn't have imagined this kind of money in my wildest dreams. As far as the work was concerned, beggars can't be choosers—it was more important to get a start in the city.

After dinner, I put them to bed and began to collect my things until I suddenly realized that I could not possibly appear in Moscow dressed in the clothes I wore in Karmanovo. A few of Ilsa's shirts, a sweater, the socks I knitted at Yuku's, three skirts I had brought all the way from Dushanbe, and a dress. I didn't have a fur coat or even a lined raincoat; I would have to buy everything in Moscow.

The next evening, I said my goodbyes to Leyda. We ate pies, Viktor roasted *shashlyk*. Leyda was happy for me and chatted as gaily as always; I just sat there quietly looking at her, as if trying to fix her in my memory. Early in the morning, while the Bzhanias were still asleep, I visited "the chickens," "the doggy" and "the little cow," saying goodbye to them all, and then went to see Mustang. I stood, pressed against him, and watched his mighty pulse throb in the vein of his neck, breathed in his spicy smell. Fear came out of nowhere. Frost covered my cheeks, my face instantly lost all feeling, and if it weren't for good old Mustang, who warmed me with the heat of his body, I wouldn't have held it together. A tear rolled down the horse's eye—I scooped it into my palm and rubbed it on my face, like night cream. Mustang nodded his head in affirmation, as if putting an unbreakable seal on our pact of friendship.

The following day Viktor and Lyuda asked me to take them to Kukovkino. I had told them so much about Yuku's homestead the night before that they wanted to see it with their own eyes. We drove their Zhiguli as far as Konakovo and parked the car at the unfinished bridge. In Soviet times, this was supposed to be part of a road to the neighboring Kuvshinovsky district, to a military testing track, but the construction had been abandoned. Either the money ran out, or the track was no longer

needed, or the idea had proved unpromising. The few residents of Konakovo, when they spotted us, turned away and hurried into their homes.
Since I had hardly spoken a word to anyone here, I could not possibly
care less about their envy and hostility. We forded a shallow little river
and walked the three and a half miles through the woods and across the
fields dotted with low bushes and volunteer saplings.

The picture we saw next remains branded on my mind. Not even a
month had passed since Yuku Manizer's death; I, the lawful heir, had
not yet left for Moscow, yet the hungry scavengers from Konakovo had
already had their fun with Kukovkino. Everyone knew that I had no
official papers for the homestead, which meant that the police could
be ignored.

The house still stood, but someone had knocked the door off its
hinges and threw it into the grass. They ripped out and carried off the
window panes, demolished the stove. The brick that could still be used
was stacked into several piles, ready for evacuation. Yuku's bed was gone;
the couch I used to sleep on had been broken. They had already yanked
out several floor boards, pulled them through the window and stacked
them neatly into a pile outside. Strewn everywhere were broken plates,
dirty glasses, cigarette butts and empty bottles left from the demonic
wake the locals gave to Nurmekundia's last Estonian.

The workshop had been pillaged even worse than the house: all the
shelves were collapsed, and the tools were gone; a horde of wild Mongols,
had it run over this place, would not have produced such thorough dev-
astation. All that was left was a house ripped wide open and gutted; the
wind whirled freely over the trampled orchard, through the defenseless
remains of the home. With Yuku, even the wind here had howled in a
peculiar way, singing on stormy nights—wild and fierce songs in endless
blizzards that somehow seemed organic to the place. Manizer's fortress
received their assault gamely, playfully, with a vigor appropriate for a duel
with an enemy of equal spirit. Now the wind slipped mutely through the
empty eye-sockets of the windows. It cared more for the grass and the
overgrown weeds, stroking them far more gently than the abandoned and
defiled home, a home that had been tormented expertly and ingeniously,
left with a broken spine and cracked ribs. Only *partizans* are this good at
crippling someone, and they only do it to one of their own, someone who
had been caught or suspected of treason. The sound that used to inhabit
this place had already left; the earth prepared to swallow the ruins. A

cloud floating in the sky looked like a monstrous fledgling of an unknown bird, its bottomless maw open wide, showing the abyss of its gut.

Grief and destruction penetrated me. My stomach hurt, my pulse slowed, I leaned against the single standing pillar of the bell tower and watched Viktor and Lyuda wander around the homestead. Lyuda found an old copper ladle.

"Vera, take it with you, as a memory."

I shook my head and gestured that she could keep it for herself. Viktor appeared from around the corner of the house, carrying a large, German-made padlock. They could not break it and tore it out together with its brackets.

"My god, what bastards, they threw it into the weeds."

I reached into a crack between the logs of the workshop and felt the key. Viktor opened the lock and freed it from the mangled, busted piece of iron that a pickaxe had left.

"It works! It must be a hundred years old, and it works!"

"Everything used to work here. Let's go back."

They nodded in agreement, and we walked away. At first we were silent, but soon Viktor's anger spilled out and he began upbraiding the locals.

I cut him short, "They have nothing, you can't blame them."

He had nothing with which to counter that, and proposed that the past had to leave, to die, in order for a new life to be born. It was unclear, however, what kind of new life it was and how it would manage to be born here.

On our way back, we stopped at Pochinok cemetery; they hadn't stolen the bell yet. We stood at the grave. Yuku knew how to go on living in unlivable conditions, so I would survive, too. You can always make money, just don't be lazy, as he liked to say.

On Viktor's last day off, after a hurried goodbye to Leyda, we left for Volochok. At the cemetery, at Pavlik's grave, Viktor and Lyuda left me alone. I tidied up, fixed the sagging mound of dirt and packed it tighter by patting it all around with a spade I borrowed at the office. I weeded the plot. Then I ordered a flower bed and a simple monument with an inscription. Endless rows of graves, open holes even along the paths—the cemetery could no longer hold the new dead—random trees struggling to survive on sandy soil, plastic flowers, and bronze cemetery paint. I did everything that was supposed to be done and knew that I could not come here again.

Valerka and his wife gave us a warm welcome. While Sveta made dinner, Valerka gave Viktor's Zhiguli a thorough inspection in his garage: Vitya complained that he never had time to service the car in Moscow. "Bring it here—I'll fix it for the price of the parts!"

Valerka had always respected Uncle Vitya, and now it was Viktor's turn to respect my son. In the year that I had been gone from Volochok, Valerka had acquired a tire business, took out a loan, and, while working to pay it off, dreamed of adding a facility with lifts to his small metal building. And then he did just that: Tajik's Service Garage with three bays. He's in debt up to his ears, they never have any money, but he looks confidently into the future. He is the pioneer who cleared the virgin land, raised his barns and will be fine as long as collectivization doesn't strike again.

. 2 .

I'M NOT NEW to urban living, but it turned out I had good reason to feel apprehensive: Moscow is not Dushanbe; everything here is different. In Dushanbe, I avoided people on purpose, I didn't need them—I hardly had time for my own family. But at the same time I knew more people than just my immediate neighbors; the whole apartment building was as open as an unfolded palm: there were the Politonovs, the Babichi, the Khazins, the Krimcheyevs, the Gafurovs, the Rovinskys, the Asafovs, the Vzvodovs, the Katzes, the Arkhangelskys, and the Karins. They belonged to the hospital, the police, the school and the meat packing plant. Only in Moscow did I realize that in Tajikistan I lived in the thick of a real crowd, all of us melding together in the giant Dushanbe pot. It's just like cooking our famous *plov*. Every one of its big and small ingredients has its proper role and place, whether it's a grain of salt, a crack of fiery pepper, a dried tomato, a slice of carrot, a cumin seed, a dried barberry, a choice cut of lamb from the shank or the shoulder, a translucent piece of sheep fat, a sweet, round-bellied head of garlic or the thrice-washed rice, hard as scatter-shot, that is the foundation of this celebratory dish that brought all the peoples of our southern city to one table. Without well-chosen rice, *plov* is nothing; all its precious elements become no more than sides for the fried meat, and the whole dish has none of its exulted culinary meaning.

The Moscow stew is not cooked like this at all; there is no single, named main dish. Instead of the lively *bazaar*, stores and supermarkets rule the kitchen. Bread alone comes in so many varieties, you can't even remember them all: spongy white, rye, poppy-seed *halas*, *man-takash*,[1] sandwich baguette, Capital baguette, hulled-wheat, mustard-seed, French baguette, matzo, croissants, Armenian *lavosh* in sheets, Georgian lavosh in scoops, tortillas, Tajik and Uzbek flatbreads (not nearly as tasty, of course, as those made in a Panjakent *tandyr*), Finnish bagel chips, diet waffles and German bran loaves, Borodino[2] with caraway seeds, tofu bread, Viennese buns, rolls, and pretzels. Perhaps the only kind of bread that is commonly available and equally loved by all is the liquid variety: vodka. It is always referred to diminutively, as "vodochka." It unites, cheers up, heals, accompanies weddings and funerals, fills life's empty pauses.

The capital shuffles people like cards in a deck dealing each one to a new place—Zhulebino, Mitino, Sviblovo, Strogino, Kapotnya, Varshavka, to the Red Dawns street, Kuusinen Avenue, Lower Zhuravlev Alley, to Bolotnikovskaya, to Liza Chaikina Street, to Carriage Yard, to Academician Lifshits, or Standard Street. The newcomers try to stack together into their own decks and line up as best they can, from two to ace, in begged-for, paid-for, fought-for or just shamelessly stolen slots. Each to its own suit, but there are only four suits in a deck and as many decks as stars in the sky. Some disappear, some ignite: love, death, betrayal, law, chance, luck and sloth... An invisible hand keeps shuffling the deck, keeps tossing them out, one by one, to fly, like the Milky Way, ahead into the unknown, where each is doomed to live his allotted time. This constant moving of people from here to there creates a frantic energy in Moscow's guts: theirs is the heat that melts any snow that comes to the city, theirs is the strange, insufferable microclimate in which winters are not cold and summers are not warm, and only springs and autumns retain a degree of normalcy.

After the silence of Kukovkino, Moscow crushed me with its roar, but within a week I began to get used it. I stopped shying away from cars and people and realized that the city's comforts, conveniences, planning and abundance generously make up for its noise. Greedy for new experiences,

I began to study local life as soon as I dove into it, but it took me a while to really understand it.

For the first two days I stayed with the Bzhanias. They gave me a key and wrote their address on a slip of paper, just in case. I walked around, window-shopping stores filled with food and attractive goods. The prices, I noted, were at least fifty percent higher than in Volochok. I went down into the subway, rode for three stops and turned back—I hadn't seen so many people in my entire life. I found the way home all by myself. There, I made dinner, tidied up, although the apartment was already pretty clean, did a load of laundry and hung it out to dry. Thank goodness, my hosts accepted my help graciously, understanding that I was trying to compensate them for their kindness.

At night, when the conversation turned to Moscow, I could barely conceal my anxiety and awe.

"Moscow melds everyone to its mold. You'll get used to it soon," Viktor said.

Lyuda was a native; three generations of her family had lived here and she was proud of it. Before the revolution, her forefathers came to work seasonal jobs in Moscow, and spent more time in the city than in their native villages. They returned home to visit, to pay taxes, to give money to their families and breed the next generation. Lyuda's ancestors came from Tula and Kineshma. But Kolomna, Tver, Sergiyev Posad, Kostroma, Volokolamsk and many other towns and provinces also sent a steady stream of labor to the city. Gradually, the men would pull their families to join them, teach their craft to their children, and keep at it—scheme, take chances, and pursue better-paying, cleaner jobs. The Revolution, then the Civil, Finnish and the Great Patriotic Wars and Stalin's terror shredded and vanquished Moscow's own. Before the Great War, there were a million and a half people here; after it—eight hundred thousand. Those who survived had developed vast networks of connections, raised and educated their children. They would not take a factory job or sweep streets anymore; that was out of the question. Lyuda's grandfather was a humble nurse's assistant, but her father was a professor of urology.

With the passportization of villages, a new wave of "quota" hires flowed into Moscow. For them, hard, base labor guaranteed a place to live. By the time I got here, the worst jobs had been left for us, the Empire's broken-off shards, refugees, migrant souls. Moscow always needs workers, and she takes them all–Moldovans, Belarussians, Ukrainians, Uzbeks, Tajiks and even smuggled in Vietnamese and Chinese.

This new great migration has flooded Moscow with strange, never-before seen people who barely speak Russian. Many of them, of course, will perish on their way to a better future, or will move on, into Russia's limitless spaces, where they will live out their lives, born of warm sun and sweet fruit, in some mosquito-infested marsh, with a plate of potatoes and a jar of pickles. But those who survive will be Muscovites.

Right away, I fit in and blended into the crowd; everyone thought I was a native. Except for the Bzhanias, no one cared what happened to me, and I was very happy with that. On the third day, Viktor took me to Racing Street, to the apartment building where I was to live with the paralyzed Grandma Lisichanskaya.

· 3 ·

VIKTOR HAD DESCRIBED the case to me: an old woman, a bad stroke, her speech and movement essentially gone. Her son, a famous pianist, lives in Italy; he cannot bring his mother to live with him, and it's pointless, anyway–Mark Grigoriyevich believes she should die in her own home.

"There are also some distant relatives, but he does not let them close to his Mother. It's the usual family stuff, you know: you'll have to play the guard dog, too."

I did not have a long run in the role of guard dog. As soon as I complained about the relatives, the two old ladies evaporated. Mark Grigoriyevich strictly prohibited them from visiting his mother. He received us in the kitchen that first time–an eccentric-looking fifty-year-old man, not tall, with a head of curly gray hair, wearing thick glasses, a dark suit, and shined black shoes–ready for the stage. He made us coffee and chatted non-stop, but I noticed that his coffee was delicious and strong, his stories were not dirty, and his kitchen glistened as if scrubbed and scoured with sand. He caught my eye.

"Before you, Verochka, I had this woman who cleaned pretty well, but I couldn't get along with her. Can you imagine, she turned out to be a born-again psycho who had taken a vow to help the sick and the helpless, but for money, mind you. She named her price before she'd barely gotten through the door. She came in, all eyes, and she had these ribbons in her hair, with the prayers that you put on dead people's foreheads. She is cleaning and muttering the liturgy for the repose of the soul. 'You are already sending my Mother to her maker,' I say. She—bam!—falls to her knees, 'I'm sorry, dear, it's just in case.' 'Quit it,' I say. 'You don't pray like that for people who're still alive, you silly goose.' She looked at me with respect at first, and was quiet for some time. And then suddenly she comes up to me, like she's spoiling for a fight, and asks, 'Is your apartment blessed?' I must tell you, I was totally stumped. Was it supposed to be? Mom came from an atheist generation, and on top of that, what business is that of hers?—I hired her to clean, not to make rules. So, long story short, she tidied the place and I sent her on her way, bless her heart. I can't stand those Bible-thumpers."

He was a natural talker and could not keep it in when his emotions overflowed.

We finished our coffee. Mark Grigoriyevich sort of faded and said, almost in a whisper, "Let's go; she was asleep half an hour ago."

We entered the bedroom. The Grandma was lying on her back: a white face with a little bird-like nose, her eyes closed, a waxy hand on top of the comforter. Mark Grigoriyevich sat down on a stool and gently stroked his mother's hair.

"Mom, I brought Vera to meet you."

The air in the room was stale. I began by pulling back the curtains, then opened the window. A cool breeze entered the room; the Grandma opened her eyes. I came up to her, took her hand and began stroking her fingers as I've done so many times. She had the hands of a very sick person: cold and anemic, but I was already warming one of them in my palms, making the stagnant blood flow again.

"Hello, Grandma. I am Vera."

"Vera-Vera," her eyes dashed anxiously from side to side as if she was desperately trying to fix my name in her mind.

Bookshelves lining the walls, a baby grand in the next room, the sensitive Mark Grigoriyevich tearing up—everything about this place was warm, and, like a stray dog who finally finds a home, I understood in a flash that my place was here.

"Viktor, she welcomed her, even said her name. Perhaps she is improving?"

Vitya tactfully evaded the question. Mark Grigoriyevich switched gears and steered the conversation to business matters. He confirmed the conditions of my stay and we agreed that the next day we'd open a new account at the neighborhood bank where he could transfer the money.

"Well, that's that, you can move in as soon as tomorrow. Come around two, I have to teach in the morning."

And when he said that, for some reason, he turned a deep red.

I moved the next day. Mark Grigoriyevich handed me the keys and dashed out; he came back late, close to midnight. Grandma and I read or, more accurately, I read *Dead Souls* to her. When I began to read, the wrinkles on her face stirred and formed into a serious and thoughtful expression with which she followed my fingers as they turned the pages. I sensed it: Grandma could hear me and enjoyed the reading. In those first days, she remained in excellent spirits. I changed her linens, gave her a sponge bath and rubbed her entire body with a fluffy towel. Grandma dined on pureed chicken with mashed vegetables, drank half a glass of carrot juice and lay on her clean sheets gleaming, lively-eyed and puffing her nostrils slightly like a thoroughbred who'd just won a race.

"She's welcomed you, Verochka, I swear to God, she has," Mark Grigoriyevich rhapsodized in the kitchen. "It's a load off my soul, you can't imagine how much I love her."

We drank tea; behind our window the restless street hummed, refusing to turn in for the night. Mark Grigoriyevich took off his suit coat, undid the top two buttons of his shirt and complained about the difficulties of living abroad: one had to get used to everything anew, to start from the bottom. I nodded—I understood him better than anyone else, except he didn't know that I understood him, which was a bit funny. At some point, I interrupted his drawn-out confession to take a minute to check on the Grandma: she was snoring quietly, asleep, like a good girl, with her hands crossed on her chest. It was as if she were chiseled from stone. When I returned to the kitchen, Mark Grigoriyevich was asleep. Unfinished tea steamed from his cup. I roused him and led him to his room; he did not apologize, but followed me obediently, like a calf, fell onto his bed, and muttered as I left, "Good night, Verochka."

The night, indeed, was good and quiet, and so was the next one. For the five days that Mark Grigoriyevich stayed with us, Grandma was on her best behavior. But as soon as he left, she began pulling tricks. Grandma missed the son who had abandoned her, went on hunger strikes and refused to keep her monstrously high blood pressure down. So began our process of getting used to each other. Only with tenderness did I slowly and carefully finally gain her real trust. After that, our life together began.

· 4 ·

I RARELY SAW the Bzhanias now. Vitya made sure I got the job with the Lisichanskys and then disappeared for a long time. I didn't want to call him first: they had their hands full already, and then there was Vitya's work, which sometimes kept him in his unit overnight. Nonetheless, I was invited to his birthday party, and not without a hidden agenda: Lyuda seated me next to a likeable, shy surgeon named Naum Yakovlevich, a fifty-something bachelor. We talked the entire evening, but things didn't go any further; he, like myself, must have resisted being set up.

I could not say I suffered from loneliness. Grandma, while we were getting used to each other, demanded constant attention; in this respect, she was no different from, say, Mustang. Every living creature needs attention and trust. But touch is essential for more intimate contact. When I take a patient's hand, or place my hand on his head or chest, I am mysteriously transformed, as if I had never before seen clearly and then put on glasses for the first time. I begin to think with my heart, to see the patient the way he or she could have been if fate hadn't chosen otherwise. I do not hide, I don't put up a shield of words, everything happens in perfect silence and that may be why I feel that a part of my soul is revealed to the patient too—that part that is inborn and intact and isn't scarred by the constant battles we all wage with our reason or conscience.

I have known many doctors, but only those who engender trust in their patients were good. Some people can do this easily, without thinking about it, but others do not have this gift at all. A doctor who has the gift of persuasion knows how to fight off The Reaper. He alone, guided by his inborn compass, can find those anchors that still hold a gravely ill person in the world of the living.

Life held on in Grandmother Lisichanskaya due to her incredible will power and that alone. When I gathered her fingers into my hand, when I began massaging them, when my warmth reached her, her nostrils flared and she inhaled deeply, studying my smell; when she believed, in that instant, that she could trust me, she reached out towards me gladly. Later, her willfulness took over, and her whims followed—a series of tests, really—

she needed to know if she could count on me when she was desperate. Only kindness and care allowed me—not quite to win—but to ensure my position as someone who guides her, something she could no longer do herself. I had no chance to get bored: a massage therapist came every morning, and twice a week her physician visited, a responsible and attentive doctor who listened to my observations, examined Grandma and was prepared for any trick she might try. He and I got along great. Then there was the ironing and the cooking; I couldn't keep up at first, but after two or three weeks things found a certain rhythm—only rarely broken by unpredictable crises.

In the mornings, after an early massage, Grandma would doze off and sleep until two or three in the afternoon. After that, we had all-body rubs and our ongoing battle with bedsores that were healing, thanks to trusty buckthorn oil. Then lunch and the afternoon nap until five or six. Evening reading, juice, vegetable puree, sleep. From ten till two and from nine p.m. till the morning, if everything went according to the plan, I was free. In the mornings I did shopping or went to the pharmacy, cooked, washed and ironed, and in the evenings, after nine, I had my personal time.

I decided not to spend the five hundred dollars that Mark Grigoriyevich paid me, so that, within two or three years, I could save up for an apartment in Volochok. I knew, of course, that I couldn't count on this job to last that long, but I had no other plans; I had to become independent, and that meant I had to save. We had enough money for food, and I did not spend a penny of it on myself; I collected all the receipts and taped them into a big notebook to report to Mark Grigoriyevich. When he came to visit and saw my giant ledger, he just said:

"If it's easier for you this way, waste your time, write all you like. But I don't need your reports; all I care about is that Mom is alright."

I did not stop my accounting—who knows what might happen, and life had taught me to be practical—but I didn't show him the notebook any more. As I said, I had no chance to get bored, and, on the other hand, easily found little odd jobs. The apartment building where I lived was a residential cooperative and it was originally inhabited by musicians, artists and professors from the Pedagogical Institute. Of course now it was all mixed up: some of the old people had died, others went to live abroad, and still others sold their apartments and left, never to be heard from again. The Lisichanskys, by the way, were among the founders, a fact which, for some reason, made Mark Grigoriyevich extraordinarily proud. The building fed itself, hired its own staff and repairmen, and its news, as had always been the custom in such buildings, accumulated in the con- cierges' tiny room on the ground floor next to the elevators.

Our concierge was Polina Petrovna, a skinny, arthritis-bent old woman who had seen her share of life. She had thin, silvery hair held in a ponytail by a black rubber band of the sort pharmacists use to hold down paper caps on pill bottles. She had a narrow forehead scored by wrinkles, no eyebrows whatsoever, tiny black eyes that never blinked, a long beaky nose and, under it, a narrow slit of a mouth that revealed a row of small, sharp teeth, like a ferret. Her tiny chin rested on folds of dry skin, and she always smelled of whatever she happened to be cooking on her electric plate. Her defining characteristic was an incredible resilience; she would have survived a nuclear holocaust, like a cricket—she'd find a warm place, nestle into it and start chirping about whatever caught her sharp little eye. She worked all her life at the Vagankov market. When that was torn down, she moved to our building, to live out her remaining watchful years. Her tiny cell of a room had a couch, a table, a telephone stand and an old TV. Petrovna went to bed at half past eleven and got up at half past five. Her daughter, as she told me plainly and without embarrassment, was a prostitute by calling, and when she could no longer walk the streets she started drinking, so Petrovna's home life wasn't much to brag about. Without anyone really noticing, the old woman started to work double shifts, which meant that she basically moved into her little cell, forcing out the woman who used to cover the other shift. On Saturdays, she washed in the basement where we had two shower stalls for repairmen. Sometimes her grandson came to visit, a young man of about twenty-five, of whom Petrovna was very proud. He always brought her a cake, and in exchange, she gave him cash. She lived simply and saved, knowing the price of money and taking any small job she could still do.

Our building also had Volodya the electrician, a thirty-year-old man. He did not see much fresh air: he was either in his workshop soldering something, or on a call to one of the apartments. Volodya came from somewhere around Penza, and that was the only thing I knew about him, but he was a good worker and never turned down a side job. He lived in a basement room without a window, didn't bring girls around, spent his evenings with beer and TV and despised stronger drink. For these reasons, he became part of the building, was thought of as irreplaceable, and in his three years here had taught himself plumbing and "European-style" tiling. Clearly, he was also saving; the electrician had his paperwork in order and the police didn't bother him.

In the other wing of the building, also in the basement, lived a Bashkir, the groundskeeper Fedya. He had come a year before me, by himself, and took over the former Red Corner,[3] with a toilet and a shower next to his room. I lived in a similar basement in Volochok, so I knew very well what it was like. Fedya was soon joined by his son, a boy of about fifteen, quiet and diligent; I never heard anything but "Hullo" from him. Later, when they were already established, came Fedya's wife, a woman without a name. She only came out after massive snow storms, to help her family clear the yard.

Clearly, I belonged to the same class of residents as the Bashkir groundskeeper and the electrician. Petrovna welcomed me as one of her own and stopped me occasionally to tell me the news: who, where, with whom and for what. I was forced to listen: the old woman took her job very seriously and considered information gathering an essential duty. She saw and knew everything, but discipline learned at the market had taught her to keep her mouth shut, and she only indulged in talk with people of her own standing. I was still a newbie, and although I realized it was unlikely that someone would want to run me out of a terminal patient's apartment, I listened dutifully. Petrovna, should she be offended, could show her claws.

At first I listened to her out of necessity, but then I got hooked. Life in the apartment building was so interesting that the soap opera *Santa Barbara* paled in comparison to the saga unfolding under my nose. However, after a month or two, after I had earned Polina Petrovna's trust, I stopped visiting her in the evening. I had a new reason not to, and, to tell the truth, I grew tired of her stories. It was the same gossip as at the linen factory, only set in Moscow. The Nozhkins had their dacha broken into, but they are rich, it's like buckshot to an elephant. Bessonov, the retired pilot, drank himself to delirium tremens and his wife shipped him off to a lunatic asylum. The young Kamarin made a ton of money on his paintings in Holland and bought his daddy, a People's Artist of the USSR, a Japanese SUV. Daddy went to the dacha in Abramtsevo, but lost control of the thing, flew into a ditch, and is now in the Botkin hospital with multiple fractures. There were two Hari Krishnas in the building: the quiet one—the Armenian Pogosov, and the crazy one—the Jew Gorelik, who chased his mother around the apartment with an axe each time she secretly ate a cutlet. He put the poor old woman on a vegetarian diet and made her recite an incomprehensible prayer in a foreign language every night before bed. There was a show-business lesbian—"She's got an expensive car, and all her girls are no older than twenty, but she's nice, always brings me chocolates!" There were fags, epileptics, diabetics, a retarded kid, a grandpa who hooted at night like an owl, a circus acrobat who despised the internet but crouched nightly by his radio and was crazy about Morse code, and the Gypsy Syova from the Romen Theater, a lover/hero who often suffered the consequences of his own debauchery. In the middle of the night strange-looking couriers brought him cocaine. Syova was repeatedly robbed by the whores whom he sometimes beat mercilessly and at other times showered with flowers, as he did with Petrovna, to whom he presented the roses he received after his concerts. The police visited Syova regularly on the subject of his debauchery, but he always bought them off, and on more than one occasion the cops barely crawled out of his Gypsy lair. Generous with vodka, Syova could drink anyone halfway dead. There were also remains of the old *intelligentsia,* quiet people living hand-to-mouth, and people who still could not get used to the new order: former professors, Distinguished Artists and People's Painters who were no longer commissioned to portray heroic pioneers. These sighed heavily at the elevators and complained to Petrovna about their lives, and she winked at them conspiratorially, as if to say, patience, everything is possible, just watch and wait until these democrats drown themselves in their own bullshit. Such camaraderie and affected rudeness were pleasing to these leftovers from the past—they felt at one with the people, lifted their chins and stepped into the elevator like Gagarin into his rocket. Petrovna was always good for a shoulder to cry on; she was the one people asked what to feed a sick dog or how to treat their daughter who had just aborted a child of the husband who loved her to death. There were foreigners in the building, too: they rented apartments for a month or up to a year. Mostly they were the politely smiling American students and the Indian businessmen whose white turbans, for some reason, instilled in Petrovna sacred trepidation. Once a real Swede appeared and then disappeared, with a pipe that exuded a divine aroma. Petrovna assured me that sometimes, right before she fell asleep, she could still catch a whiff of that tobacco, even though he'd been gone for three months. There was a Japanese cello player, a fifth-year conservatory student. She managed to flood, at three in the morning, the loony designer Tamara, who threatened to go to court but settled for two thousand dollars, although there couldn't have been more than five hundred in damages. The Japanese girl had fallen asleep in the bathtub, where she lay meditating to rid herself of the strains of a Shostakovich string concerto that were haunting her. Petrovna collected the news, ranked it, sorted it, and apportioned it depending on the trust she had in her listener: the fresher and more scandalous for some, and completely outdated for others. One real good did come out of it, though: she offered me the job of washing the stairs.

"You're not a princess, you can spend an hour or two mopping, and pocket three and a half grand. I used to do it myself, but I don't have it in me anymore."

I agreed on the spot.

In the evenings, I went out with a bucket, rags and mops, and washed the staircase and the landings. I didn't have to work especially hard: the residents were all decent people; all I had to do was give the place one good scrub and then just maintain things. The residents got used to me, greeted me first, and several times asked me to tidy up their apartments after parties. Five or six hundred rubles was a solid extra, and it was a rare month when I didn't add to my straight five hundred dollars another hundred or hundred and fifty. I had no trouble sleeping, of course, and fell asleep quickly. Mark Grigoriyevich bought a baby monitor for us. One transmitter, always on, stood next to Grandma's bed. I sleep lightly, and if I heard anything awry, I got up and dashed to my charge.

Things would have continued in this fashion and I would have lived with the Grandma for as long as she had left, but then something happened I had not in the least expected.

· 5 ·

AT THE END of our hallway was the door to apartment 84. Clearly unusual, it advertised its owner: its faux leather cover was torn and cotton padding hung from the rips, the glass number was broken, twisted upside down and held by a single screw. They must have changed the locks more than once; the holes left by the old locks were filled with construction foam—in the dark hallway the orange blobs attracted your eye like flashlights in a cave. There was no sign of a handle; they must have opened the door by pulling on the loose bits of faux leather. Everything about it indicated that the apartment owners were alcoholics. Imagine my surprise when one night while washing the floors I first ran into the girl—a flaming redhead, slim and tall, wearing fashionable red tennis shoes, jeans that showed off her toned legs, a dazzling white blouse and a leather tote over her shoulder. She exited the elevator, greeted me happily and walked lightly and noiselessly towards the unfortunate apartment at the end of the hallway.

I couldn't help peeking at her: she pulled out her keys, a whole heavy ring of them, opened the door and shouted into the apartment, "Toshka!" Then the door closed. Clearly, the girl lived here.

Another time I saw her in the street: she was getting out of a small, red Volkswagen. In the passenger seat sat a young man who could be described as attractive—slim and tall, but wearing a dirty t-shirt, a rumpled pair of dirty jeans and a strange, out-of-season fur cap that he had pulled down over his eyes and ears. I remember I thought that the girl was too lazy to do his laundry. The boy was clearly sick, either nursing broken ribs or an upset stomach: he climbed out of the car slowly, hugging his midsection, and shuffled along behind his very fit girlfriend. He walked bent over, turning his head from side to side as if to see if he were being followed; a pair of murky eyes appraised me from under the cap. The girl grabbed him by the elbow and began to tell him something, laughing, but he was not listening. He was completely focused on the pain inside him and obviously wanted nothing more than to get to his bed. They were both in their early 20s. The girl said hello to me, and I smiled back.

On the same day, when I took out the trash, I noticed their window: it was about three feet above the overhang that shielded the back door to the building. A downspout ran next to the overhang. A dirty bed sheet that somebody had tied into knots hung from the window. Fedya the groundskeeper was sweeping the yard with his taciturn son. When he noticed that I was looking at the window he came up to me.

"Druggies live there. You didn't know?"

"How would I know?"

"Their whole life is an adventure, isn't it, son?"

The boy nodded silently and turned away.

The Bashkir shook his head.

"I pulled mine out, brought him here. I thought, it's the capital, we can hide, and still I'm sweeping up syringes every day. If I don't watch out, dummy here will get into it again. What'd you say, son?"

"I won't, you know that," the boy muttered through his teeth.

"You watch out, or you'll turn into some kind of ape that no zoo would want," Fedya smirked ruefully. "You see now who your neighbors are?"

"And the girl, too?"

"Oi-vey, you should have seen her when she came here—she'd be prettier if she'd fallen out of a dumpster. She had no clue whatsoever: 'Anton, where's Anton?'" He mimicked and added proudly, "I led her to him by the hand and right at the door he—wham!—gave her one in the eye, pulled her inside, and slammed the door. Never thanked me or nothing. His Dad took charge later and brought them around, more or less; they spent two months in a hospital, and now, you see, they're at it again. He's knotted himself a ladder and eloped; must be on the needle again."

"How so?"

"Kolka, is he on the needle again?"

But Kolka pretended he did not hear and kept sweeping ferociously.

"You're better off not knowing these things. My wife and I have been through it all. I didn't take mine to the hospital—brought him here. I'm hiding him from the army: if they roll him in, he'll start using again, and that's it, the end, Mom and Dad can't help him there."

After that day, I looked at Fedya and his son with new eyes. He, too, having opened up to me, seemed to treat me kinder, and only the boy kept his distance, as he did from the rest of the world in which he lived, gloomy and unfriendly, like a robot whose life had ended before it had the chance to start. Petrovna, of course, eagerly supplied me with information: Anton Kolchin has lived on the second floor for about two years; his father, a photographer, had bought the apartment for him.

"You know him, he is that sharp man, like retired military, who lives on the ninth floor. As soon as Anton messes up, his Dad dumps him in the hospital; he makes short work of it. The boy is a confirmed addict and his mother won't touch him, I've only seen her once. She seemed like a cultured woman, but she walked past me without saying hello. That was when they took Anton away the last time. The boy does have a heart of gold, always tried to help me when I was washing the floors—carry a bucket, say, or let me fill it in his apartment so that I wouldn't have to go all the way down to the basement. I don't know why he wants to destroy himself."

"And the girl?"

"Yulka? If it wasn't for her, Antoshka would have been done for. She nurses him like his own momma, because first he nursed her. Her Dad is some big general, but she does not live with him. Now they take turns getting high."

I told her about the knotted sheet.

"I know, but what can you do—he's paranoid, has nightmares. Maybe he'll sneak back at night, or else he'll be out there hiding until the police catch him."

After this tale, I didn't feel like coming back out to wash the floors that night. I put Grandma to bed and decided that I would wash everything tomorrow. I sat down in the armchair next to my patient, where it was warm in the glow of the lamp. A wave of sadness washed over me: I thought of Pavlik, Valerka, my family in Kharabali... the last letter I received from them came three months ago to Volochok; they did not know my woodland address. Grandma slept quietly, and I nodded off to sleep myself. Immediately I was plunged into an endless nightmare: somebody terrifying and faceless was after me, was breaking through a wall, screaming and beating on it with his fists. I came to my senses covered in a cold sweat, but the nightmare went on: someone was screaming outside the door and hammering on it in desperation. I ran to the door. It was the neighbor girl screaming; I recognized her voice.

"Open, for God's sake, open, Vera! You must help me, you're a nurse, aren't you?"

I opened the door. She fell into my arms, gripping my robe. Her eyes were wide with fear and her nightgown was splattered with blood.

"Please help!"

"What happened?"

I did my best to say this calmly and coldly.

"Antoshka opened himself up, let's run, do you have bandages and stuff?"

She instantly switched to the familiar "you" and all at once I realized that she was not just alarmed but also high, which aggravated her panic.

"All right, let's go!"

I grabbed the nurse's bag that I took everywhere and walked to apartment 84 as calmly as I could. Yulka instantly obeyed, feeling a bit calmer in the aura of my confidence.

. 6 .

WE FOUND ANTON in the bathroom. He was standing upright, completely naked, and everything around him was splattered with blood. In the bathtub lay the scalpel that he had used to cut his left wrist several times. Anton was deep in the throes of his psychosis: with the fingers of his right hand he was methodically squeezing blood from his cuts like a teen squeezing pimples. The process enraptured him and he moaned with pleasure rather than pain as he watched his blood trickle down his wrist and palm. Every so often he washed off the blood with the hot water from the tap, then squeezed again and moaned again. When he heard our steps behind his back he didn't even turn around, thinking it was only Yulka.

"It's coming, it's coming out, bitch, I'd have burst if I hadn't cut it," he muttered under his breath.

"Tosha, I brought a doctor."

He jerked around and shot me a wild look.

"Who are you?"

"Vera, your neighbor. Come on, let me see what you've got there," I tried to speak calmly, as if I had seen all this a thousand times.

"You in?"

"Sure, I'm in. By the way, the human body contains seven liters of blood. How much have you drained already, Mr. Donor-Wanna-Be? Are you nauseous? Dry mouth? Stomach pain?"

I peppered him with symptoms as fast as I could think of them; I had to distract him from his mangled hand, scare him, make him latch onto something else.

"The pain!" he shouted. He forgot about the hand; the odds were stacking up in my favor. "I'm about to burst here! Do you even know what it's like?"

"You're filled with gas, like a balloon. And you think it'll come out with the blood? F for effort, pal, only given how long you've been at this, you should know better. Is your head spinning?"

Yulka had time to tell me that Anton was shooting meth, which made him feel like the drugs were about to make his insides explode–this is why addicts slash their wrists, to release the tension. It was about time he started to feel lightheaded; he had lost quite a bit of blood.

"Seven liters?" His eyes darted around the bathroom. "It is spinning… does this mean I am dying?"

He suddenly shook with chills, dropped his arms and howled like a little child who had driven a splinter into his toe.

"Almost. Let me see!"

He extended his arms to me; his teeth were clattering and large tears rolled out of his eyes. He looked at me like a loyal dog.

"Good! Sit on the hamper!"

He obediently lowered himself onto the laundry hamper. The cuts were not deep and, thank God, not across the wrist arteries but spread all over: he had slashed skin and the fat underneath but missed the main blood vessels. He made multiple cuts—I counted forty-two. On top of that, he had messed with his arm trying to squeeze out the bottled up tension, as he called it. Naturally, the hot water he kept running over the wounds did not promote coagulation.

"This is going to hurt," I warned him, breaking open a capsule of iodine.

"What is that?"

"Iodine."

"The fuck for? It's all sterile. No!"

"Sure, let's play doctor now, like in kindergarten. Would you like it to go septic? The clock is ticking and the blood is running. Do you know what septic means?"

He did, and was scared enough to obey.

"Deal with it!"

I generously poured iodine over the cuts, padded them and put a tight bandage on top. He didn't even seem to notice—he was already obsessing about something else.

"Do you have it?"

"Have what?"

"You know what—Demerol. The pressure is terrible—my bones are cracking open. I need something to get it out."

"Follow me," I took him to the bedroom and made him get in bed. Yulka trailed behind, watching with interest, but, thank God, not offering advice. When I asked her, she brought me a chair from the kitchen and I used its back to rig an IV drip with haemodesum. He let me put a tourniquet on his arm and without further instructions made a fist, as he was used to doing to make the veins come up.

"Haven't shot up for ages!"

He loosened up and was now smiling with anticipation. But his moods changed instantly, and the next moment his teeth were clattering again, goose bumps ran all over his skin and a new wave of fear washed over him. He whispered in a tragic, theatrical voice:

"Doctor, hurry, I beg you. I am dying, my feet are cold."

I cracked four ampoules of relanium: it would take a horse's dose to knock him out. Anton was now overexcited and anxious, chattered in a constant stream, but then would cut himself mid-word, bite his lip dramatically and watch my preparations with tear-filled eyes, then let loose again, ask one question after another, roll his head back and moan. The fear lodged firmly inside of him and did not budge.

Finally I caught the vein and connected the drip.

"What is it? Tell me!"

He watched the bubbles in the pouch fearfully.

"Right, I got nothing better to do but educate you here. Lie still, keep your strength, you'll get warm now."

I put my hand on his forehead, which had instantly broken out in a sweat, and began to rub his temples. He pulled his knees to his stomach, stretched out both arms and fixated on the bubbles.

"Are you warmer now?"

"This… what a kick, yeah! What'd you give me, you witch?"

"Quiet now. You almost got us driving you to the cemetery. Lie still, be quiet, it's ok now, everything's over now."

He relaxed right then, the muscles of his face unclenched and he closed his eyes, believing that I gave him a dose. He fell asleep even before the relanium started working. I made sure he got 400 milliliters of haemodesum and only then noticed the fierce draft blowing through the apartment: the window in the kitchen was wide open and no one had bothered to close the door. Yulka had sat all this time, as if under a spell, on the floor, with her back to the wall and with ear buds in her ears. I shook her awake, turned off her player, shut the window and closed the door.

"He has to sleep through the night, and in the morning he'll need another drip. He will sleep for a long time now. I suggest you call a doctor. Who is his attending?"

"There is this one pill-pusher, but he wouldn't have made it here in time. I panicked, he was all worked up, sliced his veins, it looked deep to me, blood sprayed everywhere!"

"What do you mean, worked up?"

"The fear. It comes after you've been clean for a week. It seems everything's good, fun, cool, and then suddenly you have this little worm inside. At first, you don't even know what you're afraid of. It's just this fear, all by itself. It comes from inside, like in waves, now it's huge, and then it's gone. And every time it rolls over you, it's stronger, as if it were growing there inside you. And it gets bigger and bigger until you get this mania. You think someone is out to get you. This time, Toshka just raped me, at least he didn't try to strangle me."

"How?"

"Simply. He just grabbed me and fucked me, hard. When he's high, he's strong as a bull. Actually, I like him like that, but this was over the top, and I figured he'd lost it. He didn't recognize me, called me Svetka—that's his wife, she'd left him. I started to scream, thinking maybe he'll come around. He did, said he was sorry. And then his fears came back. He had it in his head that the pigeons were watching him. And he's the one that lured them here; he feeds them with crumbs he throws onto that overhang. He ran away, hid somewhere, then crawled back at night—the birds don't fly at night, you see. Then he took a dose and went off the rails."

"That's when he started to cut himself?"

"I've seen folks chop half an arm right off: there's no pain, just the fear of bursting and the relief when the blood flows. I've never done it myself, but I've seen it. And the other thing—roaches. They live under your skin and they stink like pus or shit, and eat you from inside, and breed there. Last time he pricked his feet to get rid of them. He stood in the bathtub for three hours straight waiting for them to fall down and crawl out through the holes. Pure comedy!"

She suddenly laughed.

"That's how it goes... you didn't know?"

"I've no desire to know. Hand him off to his doctor. Better still, get him admitted, he's on the edge, trust me."

"No, not yet," she sighed. "Can't take him to the clinic, they'll reel him in for good. He'll come out of this; he'll be like a rag tomorrow. You come, keep him on the drip for another day or two, so he'll sleep and not get up. You keep him on the drip, I'll give you money."

"I'm not a doctor. I can't take that responsibility."

"Well, that's alright, thanks for what you've done already. I'll have to ask Skull, he'll call the right doctor."

"What about you?"

"I smoked a bit; I have to keep it on the straight and narrow now. When he's got the shakes, I have to be like the heroic pioneer Valya Kotik,[4] always ready."

She was falling asleep right in front of me; her speech became incoherent, and she could not stay with the conversation. I took her to the other room and put her down on the couch.

"Tanks, I owe you one," she slurred and was out.

I covered her with a thick bathrobe. There were very few things in the apartment: a wobbly table, a few broken, duct-taped chairs, a pile of rags by the wall—dirty laundry. I left, closing the door behind me.

What I'd seen and heard was enough to keep me awake. I lay in bed in the dark for a long time, staring at the ceiling.

I remembered our street in Panjakent, a late night, and the silence suddenly exploding with wild screaming, the thunder of shattered glass and the pop of a busted window frame. Kostya Murad—the terror of the street, a seasonal worker—nosedives out of a second-floor window of the geologists' dorm across the street from our apartment building. I, a girl then, am watching this from behind a curtain; the screaming scared me awake when I had just fallen asleep, and now I'm up and by the window, watching this fight.

For a long time, Kostya lies immobile on the ground. Finally, he begins to stir, as if in slow-motion, gets up on his fours, looks around and tries to figure out where he is and how he got there. He feels himself and wipes his face; his hands are covered in blood: he must have cut his face when he split the window with his head. His constant drinking buddy Rauf, nicknamed Lame, appears from the entrance to the dorm dragging his leg (it wasn't set properly after he'd broken it).

It's dark everywhere; not one window lights up in the dorm. Everyone is used to such scuffles… It seems I am the only one spying on the men. The two go to stand under the single streetlight, Kostya crawling on all fours, like an animal, evidently not having it in him to get up. Lame stands above his friend and feels his head. They talk about something, cursing obscenely and loudly and waving their arms towards the dorm. Rauf goes to the water pump, takes off his shirt, soaks it under the faucet, comes back, and carefully dabs his wounded comrade's face. Kostya hasn't yet regained his bearing and keeps blinking as if after a concussion. Finally, the blood has all been washed off. The friends make themselves comfortable under the streetlight.

Rauf rolls up a joint, lights it, inhales once and passes it to his pal. Having smoked, both become still; Lame puts his heavy head on wounded Kostya's shoulder. Now it's Kostya who holds up Rauf, while engaging in a very important task: he violently scratches at his knees as if he'd been bitten by red ants. Finally, that is done, and both men feel a little better. They turn their heavy heads to look at each other and stare as if they'd never seen one another before. What follows, happens at lightning speed: both scream, Lame hits Kostya's face with his fist, Kostya pulls out a knife and sinks it in his friend's side. The street explodes with noise: there's now screaming from all sides, and men are running towards the streetlight. They take the knife away from Kostya and tie him up with a belt. An emergency vehicle and a police cruiser appear on the scene.

The last thing I see is the childlike, smiling face of the murderer: he laughs and mutters to himself as they pack him off in the police car. The emergency van evacuates Lame, who will survive to roam the city for a long time, looking for jobs to do and drugs to score until someone finds him drowned in the frigid February water of an *aryk*.

Mom comes from the other room, puts me back to bed, tucks me in and sits on the edge of my bed, lightly stroking my hair.

"Go to sleep, Verunchik, don't you mind, forget those bad men. They fought because of weed, weed robs people of their minds, makes them slaves."

I remember, I remember many things that night. The memories steal my will to resist them: my past comes to stand before my eyes, presses me down into my mattress, and I cannot move under its weight. Images, words, smells and sounds flash in my mind and retreat into the shadows again, to be replaced by others, and then others still. It is like diving into an ocean, only the world that fills the caverns of my soul is not at all like the splendors of sea life that you see on TV—it is straight and hard, like the iron stake that nailed Nasrulló. It appears he has always remained with me, but to what end? What for? The night is endless when it is filled with thoughts that never reach the morning sun.

· 7 ·

IN THE MORNING, a ringing doorbell woke me. Ready for the next install-
ment of last night's saga, I threw on my robe and rushed to the door.
Imagine my surprise when I saw Mark Grigoriyevich there. It turned out
he was returning from his Australian tour and decided to make a detour
to surprise us in Moscow.

While he showered and made breakfast, I took care of Grandma. She
accepted the usual procedures—pureed vegetables and juice—like a queen
receiving an ambassador from a small nation, her entire countenance
filled with superiority and boredom by this tedious ritual.

After breakfast, Mark Grigoriyevich asked suddenly, "You about to go
to the pharmacy and shopping?"

"As always, Mark Grigoriyevich."

"Could you please keep yourself busy out there for another hour or so,
and come back at noon?" he blushed brightly. "I have a student coming
and don't want to be disturbed."

The pharmacy was next door, all the shops were on the same block;
I didn't feel like hanging out with Petrovna downstairs and decided to
check on apartment 84. Anton was still asleep. Yulka, on the other hand,
had been to the pharmacy and back already, bought haemodesum and
relanium, and—as she assured me—was just about knock on my door. She
welcomed me like an old friend.

"Great to see you! I was sure you would come."

"How so?"

"You're simple. I can feel it. I can smell who's got what going on."

"Right. You just don't want to call a real doctor."

"No, I don't. But it's still true about you."

"Well, you're in luck: the owner came and told me to take a hike while
he gives a lesson to a promising student."

"Ah! You got it, didn't you?"

"What was I supposed to get?"

"You think they'll be playing Mozart there? She comes to fuck—
have you seen them together? They hold hands when they get into
the elevator."

"That's beside the point. Let's go take a look at Anton."

"Of course it's the point. People should fuck more, like rabbits. Without sex, we'd all die of loneliness." She looked into my face plaintively. "Vera, I like your Mark Grigoriyevich, he's alive, and you are alive, I trusted you right away."

"If you trust me, call a doctor. He's sure to go through the same thing as yesterday again."

"Don't I know it! I'll call a doctor, just give him a shot now, he's got no business waking up."

There was no harm in another drip and a little relaxant, so I gave up. With difficulty, we roused Anton, and Yulka took him to the bathroom. He was pale and didn't quite know where he was. He wouldn't have made it back to the bed without her help. He saw me and, with great effort, remembered what had happened the night before.

"You the one who cleaned me up? I thought I was a goner, I had such nightmares," he rolled his eyes.

"Lie down and give me your arm."

He obeyed.

"Hey, lady, the IV is ok, but hold off on the tranquilizers, I don't want to sleep, it's pure torture," he suddenly burst out in tears and burrowed into the pillows.

So I had to placate, soothe, comfort, threaten, and encourage him. In another half an hour, we got it done. Yulka now took my side and seconded everything I said, which irritated Anton. I had to do battle on two fronts, but carefully, since neither one of them responded to straightforward force. Finally, I got them both settled with my negotiations: Yulka stopped talking, and Anton accepted his part as the sorrowful sufferer, which he enjoyed quite a bit, surrendered, and fell asleep under his drip.

I still had an hour before noon. I did not want to go to the pharmacy and to the shops—I did not need anything. Yulka made coffee and started chatting again. I did nothing to encourage or discourage her.

She told me they met at a friends' apartment, a den, basically. Each had a couple of trips to the "clinic" behind them. Both were tired. They gave each other a pledge that they would get clean, get off the drugs. Their fathers supported them financially.

"Mine, did you see, gave me that Volkswagen, just so I would stay a good girl."

But Anton couldn't do it.

"It must be my fault: he fucks better when he's high."

"And when he's not?"

"When he's not, he's lazy. I can't explain it so that you'd get it."

Yulka defended him. She believed what she was saying, but I could sense a lie hidden somewhere. Her father had left the family; he helped her mother and her sometimes, but irregularly, and disappeared for long periods of time.

"He really only started paying attention to me when I was fifteen and I got pregnant the first time. He took me to the doctors, paid them—it woke him up. He was ashamed: I'm a general's daughter and an addict."

She never once called him by name: only "Father," not even "Dad." She didn't go as far as to chalk it all up to his neglect, but it was clear that she blamed him rather than holding herself accountable for anything. Once she assigned the responsibility to him, she liked it; she could feel sorry for herself. After everything she's been through, after burying her mother between two trips to the detox, being all alone in this world, she did not seem to fear anything. She talked about her life easily, as other people chat about everyday things, even laughing while she recalled such terrible things as a normal person couldn't even imagine. Anton picked her up when she was already losing her mind and fussed over her as if she were a purebred puppy. He nursed her back to health and fell in love.

"Would you believe it, what made me like him was that he didn't drag me to bed. That was the first time in my life."

But the vicious cycle kept repeating itself, and they could not break it. Now she needed to talk, to vent. I listened, nodded and asked intentionally naïve questions:

"Being high—is that bliss?"

"Bliss? Oh yeah! When it comes on, it's a warm, pleasant wave that rises from your stomach, up, up, until it envelopes your entire self, and spills into every single cell of your body, floods your head. It lasts for a couple of seconds and then passes, or rather, it transforms into a different state of being: you are suddenly plunged into a joyful, bright world. You feel you can fly. Everything around you is so lovely—the trees, the people. Everything is weightless; the air is crystal clear, and so is your mind. And everything around is yours, and there's nothing you can't do. You see things you would never see otherwise: you see the air moving around you. You feel like you can see the atoms it's made of. And everything is so soft, so intent on pleasing you, like music that you can almost hear, and so fluid, so new. And you are floating in this new universe as if in a huge back-lit aquarium and the world is yours to observe.

"In another hour or two you go down, though. Everything turns inside out and gradually dims. Everything that made you so happy hides, skitters away. All the things and objects become gray, dirty, drab, as if filled with a malicious force. People's faces look foreign and glum. Your body becomes heavy and weighs you down; you feel as if you spent all day laying railroad tracks or loading potato sacks. The fatigue comes. You can see it coming, creeping up, it's a dense grey cloud that wraps around you, seeps into your nostrils, crawls through your mouth to your insides. Your arms hang like ropes, you can't move your feet. Your body doesn't listen to you and doesn't belong to you. All you want to do is hide in a hole in the ground or under the bathroom sink, bury yourself in pillows, towels, or rugs, and be quiet, and be alone. Everyone who happens to be around irritates you; voices seem to punch your eardrums like fists, causing pain and nausea. Other people threaten you; you hate them. The pain rises from your gut to your head; you want to give everything, anything for another dose. And the most terrible thing is that you are fully aware of all this and resist it for a while, but then it breaks you and you get the blues. If you can fight with yourself, if you can hold your ground and suffer for a couple of days, it all passes. But sometimes you feel it's better to shoot up than to die. Those thoughts of death—they're there all the time, like this kettle on the stove, only inside you and all around you. Your heart hops like a cricket in a jar, a hundred miles a minute."

"Tachycardia is always accompanied by fear of death."

"Well, you've seen it in your patients, and I've felt it on my own skin. Everything, you know, loses its meaning. You start bargaining with yourself, like, if you have a fever, you take something for it, aspirin, right? And your meds are right there. You hate yourself; you just sit there and curse, 'You bitch, what do you want, you slutty little bitch,' and then you give up. Right then, you have strength in your legs all of a sudden, and your body is tight, like a ringing string—it knows what's coming. This is very scary. When you give in and go after that dose, you can get hung up, I mean, drop out of reality. When I got my dose up to two cubes, I was truly hung up.

"I remember, I left Anton by himself and went to the boy who used to sell me drugs. It was winter; I wore a nice shearling coat. And then... I lost it, completely. I came back in May. What I did in between, for three months, I couldn't tell you to save my life. The coat, of course, was gone—either stolen or I'd bartered it myself. So I'm wandering around

Moscow in a torn fox-fur hat and someone else's cotton-padded coat. I'm trying to get home to Toshka, and I'm throwing up at every step. Later we found out that I was pregnant and with a ruptured anus on top of that. Sometimes I remember, in flashbacks, what they did to me, but it's better not to remember. Antoshka and his father took care of me, nursed me, kept me in detox; I wouldn't have made it alone."

"Now you want Toshka to lose it like you did?"

"Of course I don't. We have to wait, Vera, wait and see. It's no use to plan."

She was lost and fearless, silly and experienced, gullible and manipulative; she needed someone who would know how to talk to her, how to lead her through therapy. I am not a psychiatrist, and I don't know how to do it right, but I kept talking to her. I told her about my friend Ninka. Yulka only smiled—she knew this story, it was her own. Love? Anton started doing drugs with his wife Svetka; she later got clean and left him, found herself a sugar daddy. Yulka had something similar at the beginning; she and Anton had found each other.

"It's easier together, not as scary, you know?"

What I knew was that they both had to be admitted, and the sooner the better. It was getting close to noon; I had to get back.

"I'll stop by later. If you need me—knock."

"He'll sleep for a while now," Yulka smiled a soft, peaceful smile at me, hugged me and kissed me on the cheek. "You go now, thank you."

Mark Grigoriyevich and his student were having tea; they had finished their lesson. The student's name was Natalia, and she was very young, no more than twenty. They had a strange way of taking their tea: they kept looking at each other with such electricity that my hair started crackling just being in the same kitchen. The both shone like the gold medal that Natalia, "thanks to Mark Grigoriyevich," had won at a prestigious contest in Prague. Tired and happy, he couldn't take his eyes off her; his hands, which had been hidden under the table when I came in, now reached helplessly for her long, musical fingers.

I turned and tip-toed out of the kitchen. I went to Grandma's room and held her hand. I sat at her side and waited for her to open her eyes. My pulse slowed and the blood that had rushed to my face in the kitchen slowly retreated. I felt peaceful and comfortable here. The door to the apartment opened and closed. Grandma opened her eyes and gazed at the ceiling from under lowered brows, as if she could see angels dancing on its white expanse.

"It's Vera, Grandma."

"Vera-Vera," she echoed.

She was in splendid mood. Her feeble hand tensed into a weak fist, capturing my fingers.

. 8 .

MARK GRIGORIYEVICH FLEW out the same evening. He called from the airport, apologized for not spending more time with us and piled on excuses—his master-class, his rehearsals...

The next day, the doorbell rang when I was in the middle of ironing. Grandma was sleeping and I had started on the housekeeping chores. I had not gone back to apartment 84 because I knew that I had exhausted my resources there. Yulka had to find it in herself to make the decision. I did not know her world, but I suspected that one's will is the first thing the drugs take.

When I opened the door, I saw a tall, fit man wearing a jeans jacket and corduroy pants. I noticed his hands: large, knotty, and covered in bulging veins, very strong. He had a short, neatly-trimmed beard. He looked to be well in his fifties, pushing sixty. I had expected to see Yulka and my face must have betrayed my displeasure.

"I'm sorry, Vera, Yulya told me about you. I am Valentin Yegorovich, Anton's father."

"Oh sure, please come in," he'd taken me by surprise: I had no intention of crossing paths with him.

"Vera," he said urgently, "you must come with me now. Please, bring your kit. Anton is much worse."

"Have you called the ambulance?"

"Yes, but I'm afraid they won't make it in time. I want to take him to Botkin Hospital, it's much closer. If you can hold off the crisis, it would be better to take him to his attending. The doctor is waiting, I phoned him."

"What's happening?"

"He can't breathe; he's turning blue. I just stopped by accidentally—the door was wide open and Yulka's gone. Please, hurry."

I followed him as I was—in a t-shirt and my house-skirt.

Anton sat on his bed, leaning against the wall—eyes darting about, cold sweat on his forehead. He extended his arm to me, but then had a fit of coughing and spat out a light-colored frothy glob onto his pillow. He could not speak; he tried to exhale, but it was difficult. His chest sounded like a volcano ready to erupt. His face was pale and bluish. Finally, with enormous effort, he managed to push the air out, but then he began to choke; his face distorted with horror, and his arm that was reaching towards me hung limp like a noodle. I used my stethoscope to check his heart and lungs; I could clearly hear moist crepitation in the lungs. Heart tones were dim, the pulse was frequent and weak.

"What's wrong with him?" Valentin Yegorovich asked as I handed him my stethoscope.

"Sounds like cardiac asthma. Was he on his back this whole time?"

"I don't know. He was sitting up when I found him."

"It often happens at night, when the body is horizontal: it increases the flow of blood to the heart. The psychological stress may have contributed as well."

Hearing the diagnosis, Anton shook with another fit of coughing.

"Open the window—he needs more air. And hold him up, he can't sit upright by himself."

Valentin Yegorovich followed my instructions with military precision; there was not a trace of hesitation in him as he took a firm hold on his son's shoulders. I injected camphor, then, slowly, strophanthin with glucose, and finally, intramuscularly, eufilin. Anton was visibly revived, he felt a little better and began to breathe more evenly. His hand searched his chest as if trying to find the object that obstructed his breathing.

"Can we take him now? I think we'll make it in forty minutes."

"Call the ambulance, now's the time."

"Vera," Valentin Yegorovich spoke sharply, "you must help me. The ambulance will take him to Botkin or the district hospital. He needs *specialized* (he emphasized the word) care. I just don't trust regular doctors."

Anton, the sucker, as if to spite me, was breathing almost normally. The blue tint retreated as the flow of oxygen restored color to his face.

"Vera, listen to him. Dad knows..," he started coughing again, but easier and without hacking up his insides.

"Please, I implore you," his eyes drilled into me as if in a hypnosis session.

"It'll be on your conscience."

The son nodded obediently. We dressed him quickly, holding him up on both sides, and walked him down the stairs. I got into the back seat with him.

Valentin Yegorovich took off with a whine of spinning tires. I opened both back windows: Anton needed fresh air. He fell onto my shoulder and blinked frequently; the seizure had given him a good fright and wore him out. Now he was breathing carefully, listening intently to his body. Automatically, I began to stroke his head to comfort him; the boy pressed against me like a rain-soaked little monkey, shuddering.

Valentin Yegorovich made use of every gap in traffic; other drivers let him pass, but finally, at a traffic light, we ran into a jam.

"How is he?" Valentin Yegorovich asked suddenly, not turning his head.

"He's alright, coming back," I caught his eye in the rear-view mirror: it was focused, scrutinizing.

The cars crawled along. Street vendors walked against the traffic, shoving fake watches or promotional leaflets through open windows; beggars trailed after them. Familiar clothing caught my eye: a padded Tajik robe, belted with a sash, and a skull-cap. An old grey-bearded man with desiccated face led a small girl by the hand. His right hand, folded into a cup, reached towards the car windows. People didn't give him much, but the Tajik bowed and thanked them every time. I knew, of course, that he was not a real Tajik, but a Tajik gypsy—our men would never stoop down to begging. Finally, the old man came to our car. Valentin Yegorovich gave him some small change.

"Thank you, sir."

The gypsy glanced at the back seat. It was Ahror. The traffic light turned green, and the car slowly moved forward. I leaned to the window, rolled the glass all the way down, and stuck my head out, calling,

"Ahror! *Akó* Ahror!"

He did not look back. The noise of the engines drowned my voice.

"Ahror! Ahror!"

The girl turned to look and followed us with an indifferent gaze. She could not hear me either.

"Was it someone you know, by chance?"

Valentin Yegorovich's voice brought me back to reality.

"My eyes played a trick on me... He cannot be here in Moscow, no way."

"We can stop and check on the way back. They usually don't leave their spots."

The car sped on; we did not talk anymore the rest of the way to the clinic. When he drove through the gate, Valentin Yegorovich said to his son, "They are giving you quite an honor: Alexander Danilovich himself has come out."

The doctor, an easy-mannered bear of a man with a smiling face, opened the car door, pulled out Anton and patted him on the shoulder.

"Welcome back, buddy. Come on, you can make it on your own," he prodded, seeing Anton's legs folding limply under him. Anton responded to his voice, straightened up and made an attempt at looking tough. I told Alexander Danilovich what I had injected.

"Excellent, excellent! Surgical training, huh?" nothing, it seemed, could cloud his jolly disposition.

"Nursing, but I used to work in a hospital."

"Aha," he scratched his nose meaningfully. "Feel free to call, as always," he nodded to Valentin Yegorovich by way of sending him off and then whispered to my ear: "Thank you, you handled everything like a true professional. We'll go to work on him right away."

Then he re-assumed his bravura and walked the patient into his realm.

We rode back more slowly. I don't know why, but I suddenly started talking about Panjakent and about Ahror. The fear that we wouldn't get Anton to the clinic in time was gone, the doctor's praise had given me a shot of confidence, Valentin Yegorovich felt trustworthy, and I kept talking and talking, unable to stop; my outpouring must have seemed a touch neurotic.

When we reached the intersection where we'd gotten caught in the jam, Valentin Yegorovich pulled over, and threw his raincoat over my shoulders. We walked over the entire block, looking into courtyards and alleys, but the Tajik and his girl were nowhere to be seen.

"He looked like him, he looked just like him, but I must have made a mistake," I said for the hundredth time.

And still I was convinced that it was Ahror I had seen. Sure, the man was bearded and much thinner, but his face, his eyes, his shape were all Ahror's. Except that there was absolutely no way that Ahror had made it to Moscow. The war in Tajikistan had passed by the Panjakent valley and Ahror was not the kind of person to uproot and take to the road.

Valentin Yegorovich walked me to my apartment.

"I'll go clean up now," he nodded at number 84. "Thank you, Vera."

"Thank God that it turned out ok; we were lucky he didn't get lung oedema."

"You're just not used to it; you can't kill those bastards with an axe," he looked up at me. "But I still intend to thank you. Tonight I am taking you out to a restaurant, and I will not take no for an answer. When should I pick you up?"

To this day I don't know why I said:

"At nine."

· 9 ·

WHY DID I THINK I saw Ahror? The look in his eyes? The old man that fed linen hay to the line at the factory in Zhukovo had eyes like that. He fed it, the machine ate it; he bent again, picked up a new roll, unfolded it, and threw it onto the conveyer belt to be chewed up like dry feed. The old man worked as he'd been taught when he was little: with respect for his task, neatly raking up loose hay from the floor, but without taking any pleasure from his work. The Gypsy could not have been Ahror; Ahror is shorter, and, I think, his arms were not as long, and his fingers were different... But I haven't seen Ahror for so many years, who knows what he looks like now, and whether he is alive at all. Why did fate chose to bring back my childhood? Should I blame all the sleepless nights by Grandma's side when I indulged in reminiscing? His daughter from his second marriage could not be as young as that girl; she must be an adult now, with her own kids, Ahror's grandkids. Or was it the robe and the skull-cap? I haven't seen them for so many years, and would rather not see them ever again, and still, still I stuck my head out the window and called after the old man's back!

What did I blabber on about the expedition and the museum? In Soviet days Valentin Yegorovich had been to Tajikistan, but never to Panjakent: he photographed various construction projects for a newspaper.

And what does he do now? He didn't say. Why did I agree to go out to a restaurant with him? Because I'd never been to a restaurant—only to a café that one time with Viktor? He has a nice foreign car, fast and comfortable. So he must have a job. How, then, did he manage to stop by in the middle of the day to check on his son? And where was Yulka? Why did she leave Anton alone? Why does Yulka call him "Skull"? What should I wear to the restaurant? Ilsa's embroidered blouse? Mark Grigoriyevich oohed and aahed when he saw it on me.

At least Grandma didn't demand my attention: she sensed that I was too preoccupied with something else and retreated inside herself.

I did have a leather jacket I bought at the Vietnamese Market at Savyolovsk, a warm and thick jacket to wear in bad weather, but of course I had to forget it and instead bundle up in his oversized coat when we were searching for Ahror.

Grandma made groaning sounds and produced a hard, dry pile of feces, like donkey droppings. I washed her, and she immediately fell asleep. That's why she seemed so inward: she must have been uncomfortable since morning, poor thing.

I have to put the fish from the sink back into the fridge. I won't be eating in, and I have no energy to cook it now.

He said one of the things he remembered about Central Asia were the donkeys. I did not tell him about the asinine torments I spied on the day I ran away from Ahror.

The old man in the worn robe—was it Ahror? No, of course it wasn't.

What should I talk about at the restaurant? Does he want me to keep an eye on Yulka while Anton is in hospital?

At nine, he was at the door, wearing the same corduroy trousers and jean jacket, only having changed into a lighter-colored shirt.

"Vera, is this from Central Asia?" he felt the hem. "Pure linen, it looks great on you."

My shyness delighted him, and he smiled kindly. We found something to talk about.

The rest was like a page out of my long-loved *Arabian Nights*. That, accidentally, was the name of the restaurant, which looked like a castle built of shimmering cornelian: everything inside dazzled and reflected in countless mirrors. There was a fountain in the center and tiny backlit fountains in spots where you least expected to find them. The doors to the main hall were studded with silver nails, my feet sank into lush carpets, and the tables appeared to have been carved out of precious sandalwood. Goldfish swam contemplatively in a shallow pool fed by the fountains; a pair of pet ducks, beaded with glittering drops of moisture, preened next to a hut built for them on a small raft. The only thing missing was the peacocks to strut around on the mosaic marble floors. A fire roared in the hearth, fed by large logs, but I hardly felt its heat when I walked past: the heat was already inside me, it ran in my veins, and it took all I had not to reveal my excitement.

We sat down on soft sofas. As if summoned by a magic wand, Oriental beauties appeared—their pale faces like breathing moons—and brought in foods on silver platters and drinks in sweating decanters. Valentin Yegorovich filled our glasses with thick, dark wine.

"Let's not think about sad things. Let us feast!"

And feast we did, and laugh—he as much as I—and reminisce about things, interrupting each other. He started an Arabian Nights game: we were to speak ornately, as in the Orient. Words suddenly surfaced from the depth of my memory; Valentin Yegorovich had also loved the tales since he was a boy.

He was out to make an impression—and he did. I had no idea I could be so carefree. I drank freely and easily, the way I had never drunk before. They had real *plov*: with cumin, tangy barberries, and large heads of garlic topping the pile of rice like golden church domes. The rice was not too soft, and the juicy meat cooked to perfection. Valentin Yegorovich ate with gusto, biting off mouthfuls of hot peppers and grinning at me happily as I kept up. We discussed the *plov*, and gave the chef a heart-felt A. He then literally forced me to eat a lamb kabob which he had dipped in pomegranate juice—and it was so good! Not even good—wonderful! Afterwards, we had cantaloupe so aromatic it could beat any incense, sultana, and lady's fingers grapes, sweet as sugar. It felt good to dip my fingers into a bowl of cool water strewn with rose petals and wash off the grape juice. Valentin Yegorovich, like a pasha rewarding a faithful subject, kept ordering new dishes, and we were served crumbly sorbet, pistachio halvah, thick and soft like butter, and savory dogwood jam which had to be washed down with dark thyme-infused tea, slightly bitter, like the wild blackthorn berries that we used to devour on the way home from school when we were kids. It was a magical night.

We walked back. Valentin Yegorovich slipped his hand into the crook of my arm, and told me how, when he was a newspaper photographer, he did a series about the settlement in Pitsunda.

"Yes, I've heard of that. Aunt Leyda told me that her ancestors came to Tver region from the Black Sea shores."

"There they lived, blonde among the black-haired Abkhazians and Georgians, speaking their strange language."

For some reason, we both found this observation very funny. Anton and Yulka could not be further from our minds. Throughout the night, he was in character: puffing his cheeks like a ferocious shah when he summoned the waitress and speaking in a solicitous falsetto when he begged me try yet another dish, like a court flatterer. When we reached our apartment building, he unsealed the lock on the outside door with the magical, "Open, Sesame!" and then suddenly put his face close to mine, so that I looked straight into his crazy eyes, and whispered:

"I won't let you go before you let me know you."

"Your wish is my command," I exhaled my answer.

His shoulder was like Mustang's neck: it exuded the same intoxicating smell. We rode the elevator to the ninth floor, the top of the building; the machine crawled slowly, creaking and shaking. I had lost all ability to reason, and he kept whispering, "Let me know you, let me know your want and your secret thoughts. Perhaps you have a dream I could help you make true? Ask me, vizier's daughter, ask me, maiden, you, who are so innocent yet so clever and wise, so insightful and with such excellent mind, you, who could become the balm of my heart, ask me whatever you want. And if you ask me for that which your heart desires, I shall grant it to you."

My knees buckled under me, but I willed myself to walk on; he held me by my elbow and led me on, ahead, all radiant with a secret delight, saying all the right words at the precisely perfect moments, so tender and touching.

"I swear to Allah, I shall be among those who perish lest I find aid and advice!"

I had said these words a thousand and one years ago in a school play, and now I knew why I had remembered them.

"Let it be as you say, oh, the princess of beauties!"

He opened the door to his apartment. We crossed the threshold in each other's arms. Night had fallen and the daytime ended with it.

. 10 .

WE RUSHED TOWARDS each other like two mighty rivers falling from unimaginable heights; like two armies, worn out from the long wait for a battle, simultaneously hearing the call to attack. Like two streams, full and ferocious, we melded together and skipped over hidden rocks, beating with the inextinguishable energy that had lain shackled for the thousand years of our slumber under the glacier; wild and berserk we clashed, with no shame or fear of death, like the mythical warriors battling demons in the name of Allah, the only, the conquering. Ecstasy ruled our battlefield and the ground shook under our entwined feet, as if armored elephants took flight upon it like fearful gazelles. The air filled with our coarse cries, our voices made rough with the desire to conquer, to savor the victory, to subdue. One army came over another, a nation flooded a tribe, and our souls caught a glimpse of heaven. The thrill of combat blinded us to its barbaric ugliness; we had eyes for each other's glowing eyes alone, and our hands took flight like wings, and all was mixed: the charged air, our sweat and our breath. And forward stepped the brave, and he was hard and unshakable like a king's wand cast of tempered iron. And the brave attacked, and threw himself onto the hard shield, and then again, crushing its bolts with his sword that had known no loss. And the enemy retreated, luring the hero into a trap as he lunged, like a chained lion, again, and again, and again. And the battle went on, and more than once did the sides trade places and the attacker became the one defending himself, helplessly throwing up his hands and letting his armor be hammered and drummed with the maddened fists of the one who just a minute ago had pretended to cower. Soon the parts became a single being and birthed a monster with two heads, four legs, and four arms. In its ancient battle with itself, the beast aimed not to maim but to partake of both its strength and its weakness, melded like copper with tin, to reach the depths where time stands still, and there are no more corners, or up, or down. The air filled itself with spice and acid, with our sharp and marvelously shameful smells, with tender, and sad, and triumphant scents, sweet and salty, and lay heavy upon us, pressing down like a love-soaked blanket, and so it was until night turned to face the day and the first light dawned through the window.

The light drained the darkness, put the walls and bookshelves back into their places, found the writing desk and the armchair in front of it, and the antique engraved map with a funny portrait of the Northern Wind as a furiously puffing putty face. The light filled the space with all the hushed objects that had served their master so faithfully. And that's when the drums beat the victory and the warriors parted. The two reveling streams finally merged and spilled out from the narrow gorge onto a vast plain where they could slow their flow and even their breath. They had known each other in this wild race; they had felt each other inside and out and drawn forth many secrets. They'd played and laughed their hearts out, they had submitted and insisted, they had touched each other innocently and violently, shamelessly and timidly and now, sated and drained, happy and exhausted they continued their journey together as a full and quiet river.

Valentin Yegorovich soon fell asleep. He slept as if he were swimming—with his arms thrown wide in a breaststroke and breathing heavily. A long-time smoker, he had chronic bronchitis. Quietly, so as not to wake him, I got up and went to the window. On the other side I could see the racetrack. I could not see it out of my second-floor apartment: the buildings on the other side of the street blocked it from view. Here, so high up, I could see pieces of it through the breaks in the treetops. The lights were still on, and the sand of the track appeared to be orange, as if someone had just dredged it up from a river bottom, brought it to the city this very night and spread it under the horses' feet. Two drivers came out to the track in their sulkies. They moved slowly along, side-by-side, their reins hanging loose off the horses' croups, talking to each other... For some reason, suddenly I really wanted to know what they were talking about. Finally they passed out of sight behind the stands, and only the lights remained until an invisible hand turned them off, all at once. A pink stripe appeared above the mass of the city buildings as if above the half-imagined wall of an ancient fortress. The sky turned blue; a few scattered clouds hung wide and still.

A sudden flash of light hit my eyes and reflected in the window, startling me. Valentin Yegorovich stood by the bed with a camera in his hands.

"I didn't mean to startle you. You were so beautifully posed against the window."

"I'm cold."

"Come warm up."

I went to him. The cold eye of the camera's lens pushed under my breast like a stethoscope's chestpiece.

"You poor, pretty girl. You gave me bliss," he whispered.

It was such a grandiloquent thing to say—he was still playing his Arabian Nights game, but I was grateful for it: I, who was unworthy of ever mixing my breath with his, had been granted royal favors.

I climbed back into the bed, pressed against him like a spoon to another spoon in the dark of a sideboard drawer, and pretended to fall asleep. Last night I had told him everything: about Panjakent, Gennady, Pavlik. He kept a tactful silence and just stroked my hair.

. 11 .

HE LIVED A RESERVED LIFE and didn't have many friends, only acquaintances. These were plenty: his land line and cell phone often rang at the same time. He would pick up both, politely ask one person to call him back later and go on talking to whomever he considered more important. He was always calm and business like, sometimes leaving to another room or asking me, with his eyes, to step out. I wasn't privy to his affairs. I surmised that he had a business, and possibly more than one. It appeared that he functioned as a middle-man who put people together, smoothed over sharp corners, and made things happen. Once I accidentally overheard him making a deal about a shipment of tractors to Krasnodar, and another time he was talking about some quotas and licenses. He made good money, enough not to count it, and spent it generously. He took me to restaurants twice, and would have done it more if it weren't for my Grandma. She, as if sensing my betrayal, caused all kinds of trouble, so much so that at one point I became convinced that was it and waited for the end, keeping night watch at her bed. But she pulled through.

Valentin Yegorovich did not reproach me once about her, and never suggested that I abandon old Lisichanskaya. On the contrary, he always listened attentively when I talked about her health, inquired after her, and several times, when I asked him, bought drugs for her. He respected my work.

He had no interest in housework, so I added his apartment to my duties. Somehow, without wanting to, I had turned into the kind of parasite fish that sticks to the big shark's belly. He offered to pay me for cleaning his place, and, of course, I refused. Then, at the end of the month, very straightforwardly, he handed me an envelope.

"Spend it on candy. I won't take no for an answer."

There were nine thousand rubles in that envelope. I thought about it a little, and kept the money, put it in a bank. He certainly knew how to exercise his will. We went on like that, sort of together, but more apart. I got used to it, and did not make any plans. We saw each other almost every day: I stopped by his apartment, but he never came to the Lisichanskys' again. I'd call first, and go upstairs; if he wasn't there, I would clean while he was gone. He had prohibited me from cooking—he enjoyed doing it himself, and he actually taught me quite a bit: not to salt the meat while it's frying because it'll bleed too much; to roast steaks on high heat, but quickly, so they stay "rare." Soon I began to add raw mushrooms and cauliflower to my salads, got over my fear of shrimp and developed a taste for mussels. He could talk about food forever—but he never told me much about himself. After he evaded a couple of direct questions, I stopped asking. Instead, I spent a lot of time trying to imagine his life; it became my new favorite pastime during my night watches and I read much less.

After that first incredible night that robbed me of all reason, our passion was replaced with tenderness. Several times he mounted new attacks, but was defeated every time. Unlike Gennady, who was enraged and ashamed of his insolvency, Valentin Yegorovich thoroughly impressed me with his good humor. He laughed at himself, and was always so tactful, rejecting any hint of my guilt, not drawing any attention to his problem but deemphasizing it. I found my own rhythm and got used to it; the doubts that tormented me when I was alone disappeared as soon as we were together. We'd lie on his wide bed and he stroked me like a father comforting a wayward daughter. We touched each other lightly and carefully, and, it seemed, without a shred of disappointment. This was the deepest level of trust, and it was enough—at least as far as I was concerned. He did feel pity for me, but never uttered the word, knowing that it would wound me. When I was with him, the world disappeared. I could close my eyes and float in wonderful calm, caressed as if by a warm nocturnal breeze after an exhausting hot day, like when I was a child and would fall asleep naked with the unnecessary sheet wrapped around my ankles.

Sometimes Valentin Yegorovich also whispered kind words into my ear and I would fall into a short, restoring nap, to be awakened again by his voice, "Vera, wake up, Grandma is waiting."

Oh, Grandma! I so didn't want to leave—be it during the day or in the middle of the night. But I had to get up, give him a peck on the cheek, and ride the elevator down to my real life. I don't mean that I cared for my patient less; quite the opposite—I loved her even more now and told her stories about my pasha. Whatever did he see in me? Why doesn't he end it? I wished I hadn't told him all about Pavlik and Gennady! Did he feel sorry for me? It seemed there was nothing I could give him, and yet, he must have needed me for something, if only as a distraction from his depressing thoughts.

And thoughts he had. Without warning, he could retreat into himself; he got this heavy look in his eyes and responded to my touch with effort, as if overcoming some internal obstacle. He was used to living alone, having left his wife twelve years earlier, when Anton was still small. He still helped them; he had bought the apartment for Anton, and was now fighting his addiction. But he did it as if he were just buying another pair of jeans: it was just something that needed to happen. I could sense that his reserve and serenity were both superficial, a mask. In bed, he allowed himself to step out of his usual role and did not shy from his feelings, but when that was over he always went back to his icy competence, occasionally broken with an impromptu joke. He lived for himself and with himself; sometimes there was something inside that made him talk to me as if I were just another stranger in the street—precisely, politely, without emotion.

When his eyes grew heavy, he resembled an animal: he was as lonesome and taciturn as a moose in the woods. It was easier for him to travel like this, blending in with the leaves, listening attentively to the world around him, and these moments made me feel achingly sad for him. I tried to melt the ice that shackled him inside, but my hand, so well-versed in reading incoming signals, often hit impenetrable armor, and I had to retreat.

If I did succeed at breaking his trance, he would take my hands into his, and say softly, "Go."

And I would go. He'd kiss me on the forehead wearily, to say goodbye.

He never neglected his obligations: he visited Anton regularly at the clinic and met with Alexander Danilovich.

What did we talk about when we were together? What do people talk about when they are close? Nothing special. About another book I had read to Grandma—he had read many of the same books when he was a child. About the weather. It amused him that even here, in Moscow, I am always looking at the sky.

"Those clouds—it will snow."

"God, Vera, this is so great! No one here cares any more. I thought Muscovites had forgotten the sky even exists!"

"It's just a habit."

"That's what's great about it!"

He teased me for this ruralism, but I liked it. I could feel that he was at ease with me.

"Live and learn. I made a living out of noticing things, but you just taught me to look at the sky."

He did enjoy noticing things; it was part of his vocation. He loved talking about photography. At some point he had grown disappointed in it—the reporting routine grew old, he said. From the heat with which he criticized younger photographers, though, I deduced that there may have been another, secret reason, that he did not want to talk about. He had a studio set up in one of his rooms. He took pictures very rarely now, only for his own pleasure, and only with a wide-angle lens and black-and-white film; he didn't care for digital photography at all.

"I'm not interested in retouching and drawing on the computer. I want to turn a living thing into a painting, to catch it and not let go."

I became his audience when he talked about photography: how to construct a shot, how hard it is not to rush but to wait for that one shot that is so clear in your head—to wait for days, months. Sometimes he'd forget and go on about technical nuances that were important to him; I couldn't follow everything, but he needed to think out loud. He showed me a series of pictures called "Birds": pigeons, sparrows, black-birds, crows, seagulls—all caught in fierce urban scenes, being greedy, shameless, idly curious, narcissistic bullies.

"You've given the birds human characteristics."

"Is it obvious?"

"Of course."

"Then it worked."

He never boasted about his own accomplishments, but praised me constantly: I was insightful, and smart, and intuited things, and… I just melted, surrendered, and closed my eyes. His magical hands picked up where the words left off. It was so easy and sweet to put myself at my conqueror's mercy, to step out of time and space, and soar over the abyss, like the catfish in the moon-path on Babkin Dip on a quiet, still night. It was pure bliss, and I didn't ask for anything more than what had been given me. With him, I could forget about everything; it felt good, natural and not shameful, like in heaven.

. **12** .

WINTER, SPRING AND SUMMER passed in this manner. It seemed I would not have been able to live a day without his attention, or simply his voice. Every morning, after I got up and checked on my Grandma, I called Valentin Yegorovich. It became a habit; it was important for me to start my day with his greeting.

"Did you sleep well, Verunchik?"

"I did, and you?"

"Pretty well." "

"When are you coming over?"

"I'll take care of Grandma, and be there right away."

"Very well, I'm home until two."

If he left early, I went to his place anyway, having called ahead even though I had my own keys. He had once asked me to do it this way, and I dutifully observed his rule. I cleaned his apartment, did his laundry, and took the dry clothes downstairs, to be ironed together with Grandma's sheets. If we didn't see each other during the day, we always made sure to do so at night. Occasionally, he had days that were booked all the way through, and he always gave me advanced notice about those, with apologies.

Sometimes when I came over he would be sitting at his desk, reading some papers. Then I would take a seat in an armchair under a yellow floor-lamp, with a book, and glance furtively at his strong, straight back. I liked his self-control. I knew that he knew I was looking at him, but he wouldn't turn and look back at me. He once confessed that feeling my eyes on his back was torture for him. Every time I remembered this silly confession, an idiotic happy grin would bloom on my face. I looked at myself in the mirror and wanted to cry.

Anton got locked up in the clinic for a good long time; Valentin Yegorovich made regular payments to cover his treatment. The doctor was pleased with his patient's progress, and it seemed even the father came to believe that full recovery was possible. I deduced as much from a few things he said.

"You wouldn't recognize the boy. He is calm, but not depressed, reads plenty. He might even go back to college."

Anton was enrolled at the Economics department at MGU,[5] but for the last three years he'd been taking one leave after another.

Yulka lived in Anton's apartment, but we rarely saw each other; she told me she was working at a marketing agency. One day we ran into each other on the landing in front of the elevator: I was washing the floor. She looked a little slow to me.

"Yulka, what are you doing?"

"What?"

"Yulka! Are you up to your old stuff? I'll tell Valentin Yegorovich everything!"

She forced a lop-sided smile.

"You out of your wits, finally? I'm just tired—we've been shooting all day."

"Seen Anton recently?"

"Two days ago. He asked about you, by the way."

"When are they discharging him?"

"Ask Skull, he's the one who keeps him there. We're just waiting."

And she walked away to her apartment, clicking her heels, red-headed bitch. She did visit Anton regularly, two or three times a week. Valentin Yegorovich went once a week, so the boy didn't feel completely abandoned in his imprisonment. He wanted to prepare for his freedom and made a lot of effort.

Mark Grigoriyevich now came to see his Natalia for three or four days twice a month. This broke his touring schedule, and he quarreled with both his impresario and his wife. When he saw me ironing men's shirts one day, he asked who they belonged to. I gave him a straight answer; I had nothing to be ashamed of. This had an unexpected effect: Mark Grigoriyevich began to pester me with stories about his Natalia. The girl insisted they get married, but Mark Grigoriyevich could not leave his wife. The wife was ill.

"And she's been with me for twenty-seven years, she can't come back to Russia and I don't have a right to just leave her there in Italy, to fend for herself. Vera, what should I do?"

"Break up with Natalia."

"That's impossible."

He would jump up, dash around the kitchen, then throw himself back onto the chair and remain there in mournful silence. I didn't share much about my relationship with Valentin Yegorovich, and nipped in the bud his attempts to find out more. We focused on suffering through the Natalia situation. Natalia suffered in Moscow, his wife suffered in Milan, and Mark Grigoriyevich suffered in both places.

Finally, the ticking bomb exploded: Natalia gave him an ultimatum. Mark Grigoriyevich found the will to refuse it.

He came home sick as a dog, fell onto the bed without taking his clothes off, and cried until late at night, when I finally convinced him to undress, take a bath, and go to sleep. I sat by him the entire evening—he asked me not to leave him. He lay, face in the pillow, hiding his tears; now and then he would calm down a little, and then he'd start sobbing again. He was mourning the life he would never have again.

In the morning, on his way back to Italy, he squeezed my shoulder warmly and kissed me on the cheek.

"Vera, Vera…"

Then he turned and left, and did not come back to Moscow until the end of the summer.

I told Valentin Yegorovich about his tragedy, and the man's answer stunned me:

"What a hysterical wimp! So he cried a little and then forgot all about it. He avoided taking responsibility."

He said it angrily, sharply, not looking straight at me. I did not know what he meant by "taking responsibility" and became scared: I took the sentiment personally. At night, I was filled with doubts, and he wasn't there to dispel them. I slept poorly.

· 13 ·

I HAVE HAD many chances to observe that our judgments of other people are very superficial. We snatch up one trait, convince ourselves that it's the center of another's being, and rest in conviction that we've got the person figured out. The speed of modern interactions does not leave us room to consider a person deeply; first impressions suffice, and perhaps it's to the best, or else we'd all drive each other crazy. When you love someone, you forgive them their shortcomings and overlook anything that you don't need. The scary part starts when you begin to second-guess yourself.

One morning, having tidied up Valentin Yegorovich's apartment, I set out for the store and the pharmacy. The door to the concierge's tiny room was ajar, and I poked my head in to say hello to Polina Petrovna. I found the old lady lying on her daybed, staring at the wall.

"Polina Petrovna, are you not feeling well?"

"Vera, is that you?"

Her little eyes slowly found mine. Her lips, pressed into a thread-thin line, forced out the words, "Oksana died."

Oksana was her prostitute daughter. I entered and sat at the edge of the daybed. Not looking at me, she started to talk, as if to herself.

"Where do I go now? I should go home. But here I'm with people, and who needs me there? Dad always said, 'Watch, remember, report.' So I watched. There's no one to report to, but I know it all, the whole building, everyone. I don't even want to, and I watch anyway, I watch and remember, just in case. Dad served at Kanalstroy[6] out around Dmitrov. I was born in a camp, in North Labor Station, in the guards' shed. Later, they gave Dad a cottage when he got his major's star... Grandpa swept the yard for a Duchess, and Dad made his way to an NKVD major—that was as good as an army colonel. Now I have this apartment all to myself, exactly when I don't need it. Time to go."

"You have a grandson. Why don't you let him live with you if you don't want to leave?"

"He's got a place, his wife is rich. Two whole rooms. It's time I went—I don't have any strength, I barely walk. You think I'd trust you to keep the stairs clean if I could manage myself? I checked on you first—you wash well, you respect work. Take my place here, I'll leave in peace—I'll have left the building in good hands."

"Thank you, Polina Petrovna, but I'm not cut out for this kind of work."

"You want more money? Or you think Kolchin will marry you? Trust me: it's better alone, without passions. I know it from experience. I told Oksana as much, but she didn't listen to me, and was burned up by her passions."

"What do you know about Valentin Yegorovich? Tell me!"

"No, Vera, I don't sell information. I have my honor, and I know my place, I'm just too worn out. It's the end. And you don't have to believe me. One person sees one thing, another—another, and I just observe. You go on where you were going, I'll make up my mind. I've always made my decisions alone, ever since they put Dad up to the wall. Only he was no Enemy of the People. He *was* the people."

She didn't need me. Even with nothing to lose, she did not take off her mask, only allowed me to glimpse her real face. She has been frozen still with loneliness, and no desire for human warmth burned in her. I left. The old woman's words turned in my mind. She knew something about Valentin Yegorovich that she did not think I needed to know. She knew, but she didn't tell: empty gossip was one thing, and important information was quite another.

I felt sorry for her that day, but my pity was probably wasted: the hag recovered from her grief, buried her wayward daughter and went nowhere. She creaked and moaned, but she did her job. She rented out the apartment so it wouldn't just sit there vacant. Eventually, I did learnt what it was that she hinted at, but I still have no idea how she could have found out.

· 14 ·

AUGUST NINETEENTH. I fixed this day in my memory. I spent a lot of time on Grandma, so I called him later than usual, close to noon. Valentin Yegorovich didn't answer, and I presumed he had left for the day. Grandma finally fell asleep—we had a very busy night. I rushed upstairs thinking I'd give his place a quick tidying-up. As always, I opened the door with my key. I heard loud music coming from his room. Valentin Yegorovich liked British rock—"in honor of my youth," he said. Did this mean he was at home? I dashed to his room—for some reason the idea of him having a heart attack lodged in my mind, although he had no complaints about his heart. I threw the door open. They were in bed—he and Yulka—and at first they didn't even notice me. The speakers blared full blast, and I knew it must have been at Yulka's request. She didn't go as far as the bathroom without her ear-phones.

The rush of air from the opened door reached them, or perhaps he felt my presence with his back, and he turned sharply towards me. After him, Yulka saw me too. Valentin Yegorovich rolled away, bounced to his feet like a rubber ball, and stepped towards me. He was naked, angry, and foreign; he stood there silently, glaring at me. I looked away. My heart sank and a wave of old, stagnant terror flooded my body. He reminded me of Gennady in Kharabali: the same insanity and merciless will were in his eyes. Another pair of eyes, Yulka's, carefully took in the battle scene. But there was no battle.

Valentin Yegorovich suddenly slumped his shoulders and noisily exhaled the air he had drawn in to blow me wrathfully away, like the Northern Wind on his favorite map.

"You shouldn't have come, Vera."

His eyes bored into me. I froze up and couldn't make a move.

"You wouldn't understand. Go."

He said it sharply and bitterly. His words hit my face as if he'd slapped me. I looked away. Yulka stared at me indifferently, and her pupils were tiny as pinheads. She had told me she liked to be high when she fucked. This final realization was the last straw.

Valentin Yegorovich stood his ground, not moving, but banishing me forever with his eyes. I turned and left.

It took me a long time to recover. I thought about myself and about what he did. Should I blame myself, like I did with Gennady? I realized that they must have been doing this for a while. Did both Yulka and his son live on his support? Or was Yulka manipulating him, the rich daddy? There was no job at any marketing agency, and there could never be. There were drugs that had mangled their humanity and replaced it with lies and indifference. He must have thought he was just helping out, at first. Must have? Did he decide to help me, too? Or did he get sucked in, as if into a bog? Was he now sinking, deeper and deeper, so proud and self-sufficient? He who was hard as the earth's immutable core?

A month later, I called him. He answered:

"How's life, Verunchik?"

"And you?"

"Anton got discharged and blew the gasket right away. He'd been lying all this time. He bided his time, in anticipation—and he finally got it."

"Do you want me to stop by?"

"I'm sorry, I gotta go."

That was his way of apologizing. He had no need for me, the cursed fish. No one needed me, except my Grandma. Did she, really? Maybe I had imagined it all, maybe I had deluded myself, and in fact I don't feel anything special, and I don't know anything? I fell onto my knees in front of her bed, pressed my forehead into Grandma's linked hands. It was as if a rock hit a rock. No sparks flew up. She didn't feel a thing.

Valentin Yegorovich spoke of responsibility. What did he mean? His pity for me? It can't be true! And yet he felt compelled to apologize. He was leaving, sinking to the bottom, to the murk and the silence. I did not think I could survive this loss.

And yet I did. When I could no longer feel my feet and back, when I began to think I would never be anything but an object bent like a scythe, my warmed-up forehead sensed the life-saving call of my Grandma's inert hands. The signals persisted, grew stronger, and pricked at me like sharp sloe thorns. They pricked just as they did when we were children, and Ninka and I fought our way through orchards to that half-dead horse, an old nag covered in flies.

I raised my head from her hands, stood up, went to the bathroom and got under a hot shower. I felt myself warm under the tight jets; the water ran down my hair and face, mixed with hot tears and flowed away through the drain's black hole. Valentin Yegorovich told me of the ancient goddess Aphrodite who emerged a virgin from each fresh ablution in the sea. I understood now the meaning of that old tale.

The half-dead Grandma Lisichanskaya, mute and paralyzed, gave me more warmth than the scalding water of the shower. I stood under the spout and I didn't feel the heat: the fire was once again inside me.

· 15 ·

PETROVNA FILLED ME IN: Anton and his junkie-buddy attacked a taxi driver one night. They tried to strangle him, but they picked the wrong victim. The man was strong, got away from them, and then beat them up in return. He handed them to the police, himself.

Valentin Yegorovich paid people off. They did an expert assessment on Anton, deemed him mentally incompetent, and locked him in the loony bin for an indeterminate time.

"He goes to see him, visits. I asked him, and he said the boy is getting better."

I listened and prayed she wouldn't let anything else slip, but Petrovna had iron discipline, and said no more. Valentin Yegorovich continued to live alone. I saw him a couple times, through my window. He climbed into his car, still trim and strong. I wondered if he could feel my eyes on his back.

I doubt it.

Grandma Lisichanskaya passed in her sleep on November 12. It happened in the middle of the night; I was asleep and couldn't help her. I didn't grieve for my dear Pavlik or fro my Mom as much as I cried after her passing. Tears poured from my eyes, and I had no will or desire to hold them back.

A day later, Mark Grigoriyevich arrived. He hugged me, this dear, lost soul, and did not let go for a long time.

After the wake, he said, "Pack up, Vera, you'll come to Italy with me. My friends are looking for a nanny for an eight-year-old girl. The Dad is Italian, and the Mom is Russian. The girl is starting to forget the language."

I told him that first I had to go to Volochok to see my granddaughter Dasha. She was born two months earlier, and I hadn't yet had a chance to see her. Svetka and Valerka asked me to baby sit. Viktor Bzhania offered to look for another patient: Moscow had a huge demand for live-in nurses.

For the last time, I slept in my bed on Begovaya. Mark Grigoriyevich slept in the other room. The Grandma's nieces would inherit the apartment.

I didn't close my eyes that night.

It was after the break-up with Valentin Yegorovich that I began to reminisce: about Panjakent, Dushanbe, the journey to Kharabali, Volochok, Gennady, my Pavlik's death, Leyda and Yuku. As long as I did, at my sleeping Grandma's bedside, time stood still. I lived in the past, and relived it all, over and over, as if I had swallowed a mouthful of *kuknar* from Nasrulló's cup again. My self left my body and stood to the side, filled with pain and joy more intensely than in real life. Yet I lost neither will nor reason, and in that was my salvation, in the power of life itself. "Learn only to rejoice!" my Yuku used to say.

That last night on Begovaya street I reminisced again, and perhaps I did doze off after all, because I saw them all—everyone I had loved and forgiven. We stood together on the fortress hill in Panjakent, the sun was rising, and horses and donkeys grazed around us.

Father-God, help them and do with me what you will. Amen of the Holy Spirit!

NOTES

PART ONE

1. The full version reads: "The house makes noise, but the owners are mute. Thieves came and stole the owners, and the house left through the windows." It is a word game, a riddle. The answer: fishing with a net.

2. A famous girl-hero of World War II. A *partizan* caught by the Germans, she refused to give up any information, famously yelling just before her hanging, "There are two hundred million of us! You can't hang us all!"

3. *plov* (pilaf) – a traditional Central Asian dish, made with lamb meat and fat, carrots, onions, spices and rice.

4. A Russian ball and stick game, similar to rounders.

5. A game that is something like a cross between dodgeball and "Red Light Green Light."

6. Shahristan is a district in Daykundi Province, Afghanistan.

7. "Aunt" is both a term of kin and a term of address to an older person, like "Mrs." Or "Mr."

8. The car described here is likely to be GAZ-AA, a 1.5 ton truck manufactured from 1932 to 1936 on the basis of the Ford AA model.

9. *arýk* – a (usually) small irrigation canal in Central Asia.

10. The Russian word Vera uses refers to epididymides and seems based on the persistent superstition that sitting on a cold surface can lead to sterility.

11. A female donkey. A male is referred to as a "jack."

12. This city is now called Qurghonteppa.

13. *shashlýk* – a traditional Central Asian dish of skewered meat grilled over an open fire, usually made with lamb.

14. Chust – a city in the Namagan province of Uzbekistan, famous for its crafts, especially highly tempered, sharp, but brittle knives.

15. A technical college (abbreviated PTU) admits students who have completed 9 grades of secondary education. The PTU curriculum completes requirements for high-school graduation and extends another year or two for vocational schooling.

16. *dehkani*, pl., from the Persian *dehg*, land owner – the Central Asian term for independent small farmers.

17. The narrator is romanticizing – white markings have nothing to do with a horse's pedigree.

18. "The Giant Roach" (1921) is a children's fairy-tale in verse by Korney Chukovsky (1882-1969). It occupies the same cultural niche as Dr. Seuss's books do for Anglophone readers.

19. *Inshallah*, transliterated from Arabic, "God willing." Mukhiba appears to be agreeing with her husband's wish that she keep sleeping until she passes.

20. The author may be hinting at the common belief that a howling dog portends someone's imminent death.

21. In the Soviet educational system, one had to pass entrance exams to be admitted to a college or a university. Considering that Vera dropped out of school, this would be no easy task, even though a college is an institution that admits students after the 8th or 9th grade and teaches a high-school curriculum in addition to vocational classes. (See also note 15.)

PART TWO

1. A novel by Jack London, first published in 1912. Many of London's works were translated by the Soviets and were extremely popular.

2. Chapter 1 of *Smoke Bellew*.

3. This is a reference to Hans Christian Andersen's fairy-tale "The Snow Queen" in which the evil Snow Queen breaks her mirror of ice, shards flying all over the world. Those into whose bodies these shards lodge become cold, selfish people, servants of the Snow Queen.

4. *The Heir from Calcutta* (Наследник из Калькутты)–a historical adventure novel by the Russian writer Robert Shtilmark. Shtilmark wrote it in a labor camp, trad-

ing new installments of his pirate saga for release from labor duties.

5.   The Doukhobor ("spirit wrestlers") are a religious sect with origins in the 18th century. They rejected secular government, Russian Orthodox priests, icons, all church ritual, the Bible as the supreme source of divine revelation, and the divinity of Jesus. Their pacifism and anti-government stance led most to leave the Russian Empire for Canada at the close of the 19th century, with financial assistance from Leo Tolstoy.

6.   Oswiencim (Polish) – the Slavic name for Auschwitz.

7.   *mumijé* – a thick, sticky tar-like substance, petrified bat guano mixed with dust; it has been shown to have antiseptic and stimulant effects and promote the healing of wounds.

8.   The ninth day after a person's death, according to popular belief, is when the soul of the departed ascends to heaven. A wake is usually held by the family on this day.

PART THREE

1.   Zaporozhets – the smallest and humblest of Soviet cars, copied off an early Fiat.

2.   *kutyá* – an ancient ritual dish shared by many Slavic nations; the basic recipe mixes boiled wheat with honey, but it can also include poppy seed, raisins, and nuts. The narrator, of course, is blind to her own customs – kutya is not an exclusively funeral dish; in fact, in many parts of Ukraine and Russia it is only made for Christmas.

3.   Russia has mandatory two-year military service for men who are not attending an institution of higher learning.

4.   *lagmán* – a Central Asian home-made noodles with various sauces.

5.   The Reader (Чтец) in the Russian Orthodox Church is responsible for reading certain portions of the Holy Scripture during the services. Normally readers undergo a special tonsuring service, but in contemporary practice a layman may receive a priest's blessing to read.

6. The practice of "registering" (прописка, *propiska*) is a long-living Soviet institution that involves assigning every citizen to a specific place of residence at any point in time. This becomes problematic when, for example, one cannot get a job in Moscow without being "registered" there, and, simultaneously, cannot get "registered" without being employed.

7. In most cities, one can recycle glass bottles and jars for small change.

8. A thin coat of whitewash on the trunk repels rodents and protects young trees from disease.

9. Isabella – a sort of grape grown in Moldova and Transcarpathia and the eponymous cheap red wine.

10. Alexander I (1777-1825) ruled Russia from 1801 to 1825.

11. Pitsunda   a resort town in the Gagra district of Abkhazia. Abkhazia, a northern separatist region in Georgia, has been recognized as an independent state by Russia and Nicaragua.

12. In ancient geography, Colchis was a Georgian state; it is referenced in the myths of Jason and the Argonauts.

13. *kirk* – Estonian for Church; in Russian, Aleshkovsky uses the word "kirkha," which is a transliterative Germanism (from *kirche*) that indicates a Lutheran denomination.

14. The Soviet Union (and, by legacy, post-Soviet states) provided financial aid to families with multiple children. In the Soviet era, families had to have five or more children to qualify, but in the light of Russia's demographic crisis this number has been lowered to three.

15. This is a reference to the practice of treating alcoholism with "coding." One common practice involves injecting a drug capsule under the patient's skin to produce nausea, etc. if the subject imbibes alcohol. This process is also referred to as "stitching" in Russian. The patient cannot drink while the drugs are present in his body; thus, people must "come unstitched" (remove the capsule) before going on a drinking binge.

16. "Moskvich" means "Muscovite" and is a four-door automobile produced at a factory near Moscow. It is one of those archaic-looking pieces of Soviet machinery that never break down because they only have a dozen moving parts.

17. The Siege of Leningrad is such an important event in the history of the Great Patriotic War (1941-1945) and the Soviet psyche that it is often referred to simply as "the siege."

18. This refers to *The Wonderful Adventures of Nils* (1906) by the Swedish writer Selma Lagerlöf, a children's literature classic.

19. Varyag – a Russian cruiser in the Japanese war that engaged enemy forces against lethal odds. Varyag, in Russian consciousness, is synonymous with laudable, albeit perhaps ill-timed, heroism.

20. The Soviet institution of registering people according to their place of residence. Post-Soviet law hasn't entirely done away with it. (See note 6.)

21. Made from wood-processing waste.

22. *gogl-mogl* – a soft food made from raw eggs yolks beaten with sugar, and any number of flavorings; it is highly nutritious.

23. *mors* – a home-made fruit drink; essentially, fruit or berry juice, diluted with water and sweetened.

24. Taishet – a town in Irkutsk oblast. The BAM railroad begins here and the town was an administrative center for the gulags. According to gulag lore, there is a prisoner under every sleeper of the BAM. Rechlag was a system of strict-regime camps.

25. *pood* – an ancient Russian measure of weight, about 36 lbs.

26. *válenki* – thick felt boots without laces or zippers, traditional Russian winter footwear.

27. Vera is referring to the May holidays, the 1st, Day of the International Solidarity of the Working Class, and the 9th, Victory Day. Since May in European parts of USSR is high planting season, this is usually when people use their holiday leave to plant potatoes, the most labor intensive of suburban crops.

28. Of course, Lutheran Christians, like Yuku, celebrate Christmas Eve according to the Gregorian calendar, on Dec. 24th. The Russian Orthodox Church, however, and a number of other Eastern European Churches, celebrate Christmas Eve according to the Julian tradition, on January 6th. This tradition was commonly known among the Russian population of the Soviet Union, and Vera, whose grasp of religious holidays is tentative, assumes that's when Christmas is for Yuku, too.

29. The corner to the right of the entrance has a special traditional significance. It is also the corner where the family's icons were displayed, and thus it was called "the red corner," "red" being used in its archaic meaning of "beautiful." (See also note 3 of Part Four.)

PART FOUR

1. *mantakásh* – a flat-shaped Armenian bread that is same consistency as a baguette, i.e. soft inside, unlike *lavosh*.

2. Borodino bread – a specific recipe of extremely dense rye bread; its color resembles pumpernickel but it is much heavier due to the bran added to it. It has a distinctive odor, from cardamom seeds.

3. In Soviet times, the Red Corner was a meeting room for conducting Party events. It was equipped with the red flag and a portrait of Lenin or another leader, and yes, the name was appropriated from the reference to the icons' place in the home. (See also note 29 of Part Three.)

4. Ten years old at the time of the Nazi invasion of the USSR, Ukrainian Valentin Kotik fought for three years in the partizan resistance, before being mortally wounded in a battle. He was posthumously decreed a Hero of the Soviet Union and held up as an example of vigilance and strength for Soviet schoolchildren.

5. MGU – Moscow State University, Russia's most prestigious university.

6. *Kanalstroy* – Short for "canal building." An abbreviation for a labor-camp system.

Other Fiction Titles from Russian Life Books

Life Stories: 19 Stories by Leading Russian Writers

A collection of original works by 19 leading Russian writers presents life-affirming stories of love, family, hope, rebirth, mystery and imagination. Authors include: Vladimir Voynovich, Andrey Gelasimov, Boris Grebenshchikov, Yevgeny Grishkovets, Victor Yerofeyev, Alexander Kabakov, Eduard Limonov, Dmitry Lipskerov, Sergey Lukyanenko, Vladimir Makanin, Marina Moskvina, Victor Pelevin, Lyudmila Petrushevskaya, Zakhar Prilepin, Dina Rubina, Dunya Smirnova, Vladimir Sorokin, Alexander Khurgin and Leonid Yuzefovich. Translators: Alexei Bayer, Michele Berdy, Liv Bliss, Lise Brody, Nora Favorov, Anne O. Fisher, Deborah Hoffman, Marcia Karp, Michael Katz, Peter Morley, Susanna Nazarova, Anna Razumnaya-Seluyanova, Paul E. Richardson, Marian Schwartz, Bela Shayevich and Nina Shevchuk-Murray.

(336 pages, paperback • $25 • ISBN 978-1-88010058-5)

The Little Golden Calf

by Ilya Ilf and Evgeny Petrov, translated by Anne O. Fisher

This new edition of *The Little Golden Calf*, one of the greatest Russian satires ever, is the first new translation of this classic novel in nearly fifty years. It is also the first unabridged, uncensored English translation, is 100% true to the original 1931 serial publication, is copiously annotated, and includes an introduction by Alexandra Ilf, the daughter of Ilya Ilf.

(448 pages, paperback • $20 • ISBN 978-1-88010061-5)

Peter Aleshkovsky was born in 1957 and graduated some two decades later from Moscow State University. He worked for several years as an archaeologist in Central Asia and as a historical preservationist in the Russian North before turning full-time to literature in the mid-1990s.

He attained literary success with his collection of stories *Stargorod*, followed by his novels *Seagull*, *Skunk: A Life* (translated into English by Glas), *Vladimir Chigrintsev* and, most recently, *The Institute of Dreams*.

Aleshkovsky's style is decidedly in the realistic tradition, but that does not stop him from investigating the mystical and miraculous in everyday life. His works are richly descriptive and evocative of the uniquely Russian worldview, while at the same time tapping into universal human emotions and experiences. He has three times been short-listed for the Russian Booker Prize, most recently for his novel *Fish*.

Born and raised in the western Ukrainian city of L'viv, translator Nina Shevchuk-Murray holds degrees in English linguistics and Creative Writing. She translates both poetry and prose from the Russian and Ukrainian languages. Her translations and original poetry have been published in a number of literary magazines, including *Chtenia: Readings from Russia*. With Ladette Randolph, she co-edited the anthology of Nebraska non-fiction, *The Big Empty* (University of Nebraska Press, 2007).